Reps Over Brains

Reps Over Brains

Why Consistency Beats Genius (and How to Get It)

Victor Serrano

Mindful Pages

Published in 2026

ISBN: 9789376551804 (PB)
ISBN: 9789376551736 (eBook)

Published by

Mindful Pages
Imprint of Alpha Editions LLC
312 W. 2nd St #1834
Casper, WY 82601, USA

This book was developed using advanced writing tools to support the drafting and ideation process. All content has been thoughtfully curated, refined, and reviewed to ensure quality and relevance.

Content

Introduction

In the velodrome at the Manchester National Cycling Centre on a damp morning in March 2003, the air carried that particular cocktail of hot rubber and disinfectant, sharp as a freshly struck match. A rider rolled onto the boards and began the work that nobody pays to watch: the same line, the same cadence, the same controlled discomfort. The chain made a dry, sandpapery whisper as it ran; each lap returned like a metronome's tick, dull and faithful. Dave Brailsford stood trackside with a notebook, not shouting, not performing certainty, simply observing what repeated when nobody was impressed. The chain did not care. It did not know who had potential. It only answered to torque applied again and again, cleanly, on schedule. The rider looked ordinary in the way that matters to scouts and commentators. The outcome, years later, would not.

It is tempting to believe that progress has a personality: brilliance, charisma, the sharp elbow in the meeting, the spark that makes other people lean forward. Many of us were trained to treat life as a talent show. The trouble is that talent shows end quickly; the real world is a longer season with fewer spotlights and more Tuesdays. The people who quietly win over decades often do not look like winners early on. They look like grown-ups. They look like someone who turns up.

The appeal of genius is obvious. Genius promises speed. It also promises a kind of innocence: if success is a matter of giftedness, then failure can be explained as an unfortunate but natural distribution of gifts. Consistency is a harsher story. Consistency suggests that outcomes are dragged into existence by repetition, that excellence is less a lightning strike than a weather pattern, and that the unglamorous part is not an inconvenience but the whole mechanism. This is why consistency feels morally heavier than talent. It is also why it is available.

Consider how reputations form in ordinary workplaces. The charismatic person has a brilliant quarter, then disappears into distraction, conflict, or the fatigue of their own intensity. The dependable person is rarely the most thrilling hire, rarely the one people point at and say, "That's the future." And yet, over a year, they are the one clients request by name. Over three years, they have the deep account relationships because they are there when the mood has gone. Over ten years, they become the reference point: the person a team trusts with the difficult handover, the delicate negotiation, the work that is too important for drama. Trust, here, is not a feeling; it is a measurable accumulation of kept promises, returned calls, deadlines met, error rates reduced, follow-ups completed. Reliability has a quiet arithmetic.

Sport offers a cleaner view because it is less polite about outcomes. When British Cycling rose from decades of mediocrity to sustained dominance, it was tempting to narrate the story as a sudden discovery of exceptional athletes. The more useful explanation is less cinematic. Brailsford's now-famous emphasis on marginal gains—small improvements stacked relentlessly—was not a slogan so much as a method of living inside boredom without being devoured by it. The results are checkable in any official record: at the Beijing Olympics in August 2008, Great Britain's track cyclists won the majority of the available gold medals, a performance that shifted expectations, not merely results (International Olympic Committee official results, 2008). Four years later, in London in July 2012, they repeated a version of that dominance under even brighter pressure (International Olympic Committee official results, 2012). The point is not that a national programme can be copied in a living room. The point is that excellence, at scale, was treated as a sequence of small, repeatable actions that could survive mood swings, media noise, and the ordinary mess of life. It sounded, from close up, like that chain: the metronome of repetition.

This book's argument is simple enough to offend the part of the mind that likes elegance: consistency beats talent because it keeps producing work after the novelty of talent wears off. The implication is uncomfortable because it refuses the romance of exceptionality. And yet it is oddly liberating, because it relocates power from innate attributes to repeated choices that can be designed. "Design" matters. Consistency is not a personality trait handed out at birth; it is an engineered set of defaults. It is the deliberate reduction of the distance between intention and action.

The modern world flatters intensity. It rewards the dramatic sprint: the crash diet, the heroic all-nighter, the sales blitz fuelled by caffeine and panic, the sudden reinvention announced in a flurry of posts and plans. Intensity creates a story that can be told; consistency creates a record. Records are quieter. They are also more predictive. A person who studies for twenty minutes most days for six months becomes competent in a way that a person who studies ten hours once a fortnight rarely does. A person who sends one high-quality outreach message daily for a year builds a pipeline that is less sensitive to luck. A person who practises a craft for half an hour on weekdays ends up with an unfair advantage over a decade, not because they are working harder in any heroic sense, but because they are accumulating a private inventory of solved problems. Reps are unglamorous. They are also decisive.

There is a psychological trap in early talent. If a student is praised for being bright rather than for learning how to study, they can reach adulthood without ever building a relationship with repetition. They discover, painfully late, that there are domains where cleverness is merely the entry ticket and the actual currency is practice. The first serious exam that cannot be improvised becomes a crisis of identity. The first job that requires sustained output rather than occasional brilliance feels like a personal betrayal. The first creative project that demands draft after draft exposes a hidden dependency: not on skill, but on novelty. What looked like confidence was often simply the absence of resistance. When resistance arrives, the talented person sometimes has no method except force. Force works briefly. Then it breaks.

A subtler version of the same trap appears in sales, in leadership, in health. The charismatic salesperson can ride charm for a while until they meet buyers who do not buy charm. The leader with a magnetic presence can carry a team through a crisis until the crisis ends and the slow work of execution begins. The naturally athletic person can coast until age, injury, or a change in schedule removes the effortless advantage. At that point, the question becomes brutally plain: can the person do the work when it is dull? The metronome does not stop. It simply keeps time, and it exposes what is missing.

Consistency is often misdescribed as a kind of grit, as though it were mostly about refusing to quit. That is a partial truth and, for many people, the least helpful one. Endurance matters, but endurance without design becomes a moral theatre: a person pushing themselves in the same way, failing in the same way, and calling it character. A more accurate view treats consistency as the outcome of systems that reduce decision-making, shrink the starting cost of action, and protect identity during disruption. It is less about feeling determined and more about making it difficult not to begin.

This is why habits matter—not as self-improvement decoration, but as infrastructure. Habits are not noble; they are efficient. They allow the brain to spend less energy deciding, which is why they are so stubborn when they are unhelpful and so powerful when they are useful. A person who reaches for a phone without thinking is not weak; they are automated. The same automation can be shaped towards repetition that builds skill, health, or professional momentum. The mechanism is not mystical. Cue, routine, reward: not as jargon, but as a practical loop that can be observed in a kitchen, an office, a train carriage. The implication is sharp: a life is partly a set of loops. Change the loops and the life changes, not by inspiration, but by accumulation.

Environment is the quiet partner in this story. People like to imagine their decisions occur in a vacuum, as though "choice" were an abstract act performed by a free-floating will. In reality, choice is often a negotiation with objects, timing, and other humans. The kitchen counter, the notifications, the commute, the social group that normalises or mocks discipline—these are not background details. They are triggers. They decide what gets repeated. The outcome is measurable in visible behaviour: the number of days one opens a textbook, the number of calls made, the number of workouts begun, the number of pages written. A person can be sincere and still lose to a badly designed environment. A person can be tired and still win if the environment makes the next good action the easiest one.

Reward is the other neglected lever. The brain remembers what felt good or relieved discomfort. This is not sentimentality; it is learning biology. Small wins matter because they create a memory of return.

A person who finishes a short session and experiences a tiny sense of completion is more likely to repeat than a person who finishes exhausted and resentful. The implication is not that everything must be pleasant, but that disciplined behaviour becomes easier when it is paired with a reward that is immediate enough for the brain to notice. The most dangerous rewards are often the ones that arrive instantly and cost later. The most sustainable ones are small, honest, and frequent: a tick on a log, a brief ritual, the calm knowledge of having kept a promise.

Willpower, in this context, is over-celebrated and under-understood. It exists, and it helps, but it is not a foundation. Willpower is sensitive to sleep, stress, hunger, conflict, and decision overload—conditions that are not rare but ordinary. Treating willpower as the main strategy guarantees that consistency will be fragile. This is not a moral judgement; it is a design problem. If discipline requires daily heroism, it will not survive a normal week. Still, there are seasons when structure collapses—bereavement, illness, sudden work crises—and pretending otherwise turns discipline into a performance. The honest aim is not invulnerability. It is recovery.

The most revealing stories of consistency are therefore not about people who never miss. They are about people who miss and return without theatrics. Think of the writer who produces work across years not because every day contains inspiration, but because the day contains a small, non-negotiable start. Think of the student who keeps learning during a busy term because the study session has been shrunk to something that fits rather than something that impresses. Think of the salesperson who keeps prospecting through rejection because the unit of work is not "close a deal" but "make contact", a leading indicator that can be counted without begging luck for permission. The metric changes the emotion. The repetition changes the identity.

There is, however, a credible limitation to the cult of repetition. Not every domain rewards consistency in the same way, and pretending otherwise becomes ideology. In some arenas, the winner takes all, and a single invention, discovery, or performance can eclipse a decade of steadiness. The Manhattan Project in Los Alamos in 1943–45 did not succeed because the scientists were merely steady; it required rare intellectual leaps under extraordinary conditions, with resources and secrecy on a scale that most human lives will never touch (U.S. Department of Energy historical records, published 2015). In certain artistic moments, a new form appears, and the person who sees it first changes the field. Acknowledging this does not weaken the argument; it refines it. Breakthroughs matter, but they are often purchased with repetition anyway: the inventor who can see the new possibility has usually built a dense internal library of prior attempts, failures, and partial solutions. Even then, breakthroughs are noisy, unpredictable, and hard to schedule. Consistency is quieter and more controllable. It governs the parts of life where most people actually live: health, craft, sales, study, relationships, the slow maintenance of competence.

The deeper claim, then, is about risk. Relying on talent is a high-variance strategy. When it works, it can work spectacularly. When it fails, it tends to fail suddenly and publicly because the person has built little scaffolding to catch them. Consistency is a lower-variance strategy. It produces a steadier distribution of outcomes and, over time, a higher floor. That floor matters more than it is fashionable to admit. A high floor makes a person employable, dependable, calm under pressure. It makes them someone others can build around. In practical terms, it means fewer catastrophic weeks. It means fewer panicked resets. It means the capacity to improve while life continues to happen.

This is why the book's focus is not on grand plans but on small disciplines that can be made reliable. A minimum viable habit is not a cute trick; it is a refusal to be held hostage by one's own standards. It is the smallest honest unit of repetition that keeps the identity intact: the person who shows up. That identity is not a slogan. It is a record: the number of days one begins. From there, friction becomes the enemy worth studying, not the self. Friction is not merely inconvenience; it is the hidden cost that stops action at the starting line. It lives in cluttered rooms, missing tools, vague next steps, perfectionist fantasies, and the simple fact that a mind under stress chooses the familiar, not the wise. A friction audit turns self-reproach into a map. Maps can be edited.

Habits rarely succeed as isolated acts. The day is a chain of cues already; the question is whether the chain leads anywhere. When one behaviour reliably triggers the next, discipline begins to feel less like pushing a boulder and more like sliding into a groove. This is what makes stacking powerful when done with restraint: sequences reduce the number of decisions required. They also expose overload quickly. A routine that looks admirable on paper can collapse under a child's illness, a delayed train, a late client call. The mature response is not to scold the self but to shorten the chain until it can survive. The metronome must be protected, not worshipped.

Streaks sit awkwardly in modern self-improvement because they can become a form of superstition, a brittle badge that turns one missed day into a moral failure. Used well, a streak is not a badge but a prompt: it makes repetition visible. The healthier innovation is the shield, the deliberate rule that allows a person to keep the identity of showing up through disruption. When travel, illness, or workload spikes arrive—as they always do—the shield preserves continuity by shrinking the unit of work without pretending nothing has changed. It is the difference between a person who "fell off the wagon" and a person who adapted their wagon to the terrain.

Accountability, too, has been polluted by public shaming and performative tracking. The useful version is quieter and more technical: a feedback loop that reviews behaviour, not intentions. It creates a small consequence for drifting and a small reward for returning. It does not require an audience; it requires a rhythm. The same is true of planning. Calendars are often treated as prisons or fantasies, either suffocating or ignored. The more interesting view treats cadence as a design choice: daily repetitions where they matter, weekly patterns where they sustain, monthly reviews where they correct drift, and longer seasonal focuses where identity evolves. A year is not a single sprint. It is a set of repeating weeks. The work is to design weeks one can live.

The most neglected obstacle in all of this is boredom. People talk about motivation as though it were a personality trait or a mysterious fuel. In practice, the great enemy of repetition is not pain but monotony, the sense that nothing is happening because nothing dramatic is happening. Progress, in most domains, is a slow bending of the curve. The body changes quietly; the mind grows by unglamorous familiarity; sales pipelines thicken by repeated contact. Boredom is not evidence of failure. It is evidence of normality. The mature question is not how to avoid boredom, but how to behave when it arrives: how to add small variations without losing the core rep, how to turn repetition into a game without turning it into a distraction, how to separate feelings from action without becoming a robot.

And then comes relapse, the unavoidable proof that a system meets reality. People often treat relapse as a moral confession. The more accurate view treats it as data: something in the design did not survive the conditions. A reset, prepared in advance, is not a melodrama but a protocol. It asks what happened, shrinks the restart to a minimum viable step, and returns to repetition before the mind has time to build a case for giving up entirely. Confidence, in this view, is not a mood. Talent is noisy. Confidence is a history of kept commitments, even small ones. It is rebuilt the same way it is built: with reps.

All of this leads to a tension worth naming. There are two ways to live when one wants more from life than one is currently getting. One way is to chase exceptional moments: the inspired week, the dramatic reinvention, the heroic effort that proves something about the self. The other is to chase an exceptional record: a year in which a person becomes slightly more dependable than they were, slightly more capable, slightly harder to knock off course. The first way feels exciting. The second way feels almost insultingly plain. And yet the second way produces the kind of outcomes that look, from a distance, like genius.

A decision hides inside that tension. The mind can continue to audition for a life—waiting for the day when motivation returns, when circumstances align, when the right version of the self shows up—or it can treat the next year as an experiment in reliability. The diagnostic question is not inspirational. It is practical: when life becomes inconvenient, what remains? The answer is rarely a plan. It is usually a system. The metronome will keep time either way. The difference is whether its steady tick becomes the background noise of drift, or the sound of a life being built on purpose.

Chapter 1
Why Consistency Beats Talent

On a Tuesday in late November, when the office air is thin with reheated coffee and the week still has too many days left in it, brilliance is an awkward currency. It buys a moment—an impressive meeting, a clever line, a dazzling pitch that makes heads nod and pens hover. Then the room empties. The calendar remains. The pipeline does not care what anyone felt in that meeting; it cares what happens next, and then next, and then next. This is the quiet theatre where the dependable person wins, not by doing something extraordinary once, but by doing something ordinary so many times that it becomes extraordinary in aggregate. The work keeps its own books.

Picture two salespeople starting on the same day, with the same territory, the same product, and the same manager who believes charisma is destiny. The first is a natural performer: quick laugh, quick mind, quick rapport. They have a gift for the room, for the improvisation that makes a prospect feel seen. They can rescue a sinking call with a joke, talk their way into a meeting that should not have been granted, leave the building to the warm glow of their own momentum. The second is less compelling on first impression. Their calls are calm. Their emails are plain. Their presence does not bend the atmosphere. They log everything. They follow up. They keep a list so boring it could be used as a sedative.

In month one, the charismatic one looks like the obvious star. They pull a couple of wins that feel like proof. The manager smiles in that particular way managers smile when they believe they have recruited "talent". The methodical one looks slow, even slightly timid, because their wins arrive quietly and their work leaves few anecdotes. Then the months stack. The charismatic one has a brilliant fortnight and a dreadful one. They chase big deals and ignore small accounts until those accounts become someone else's loyalty. They have bursts of outreach and then periods of silence, because their energy runs on feeling impressive. The methodical one sends outreach whether they feel impressive or not. They talk to the same number of new people each week. They do not confuse mood with outcome. They begin to accumulate what sales actually is: a durable relationship with repetition.

The first lesson of this chapter is that consistency is not mere persistence. It is not the grim refusal to stop, teeth clenched, joy evacuated. It is a pattern of behaviour that is predictable enough to be trusted by time. Predictable does not sound romantic, which is precisely the point. Consistency means the work happens with such regularity that it becomes difficult to imagine a version of your life in which it does not. It is the difference between a person who "gets round to it" and a person for whom the thing is simply part of the week. In that difference lies a kind of power that talent, on its own, cannot reliably purchase.

Talent is real. It is not a myth invented by lazy people. Some minds see patterns quicker. Some bodies adapt faster. Some personalities attract trust with less effort. Some voices carry. Some people begin closer to the finish line. But talent has a flaw that rarely appears in celebration speeches: it is often a loan that comes due. Early ease can teach the wrong lessons. It can make skipping practice feel harmless. It can make failure feel like a personal insult rather than an expected part of learning. It can produce a brittle confidence that survives only in environments where the person is already good. When that environment changes—harder work, smarter peers, higher stakes—the talented person can be shocked, not by the difficulty, but by their own lack of method.

A gifted student offers the cleanest illustration because school is one of the few places where early advantage can carry you without much strategy. There is always someone who reads quickly, remembers easily, writes essays that feel effortless, and gets praised for being "naturally bright". Teachers mean well; they reward what they can see. The problem is that what they reward becomes an identity. The student learns that their value lives in being clever, not in learning how to learn. They sail through early years with minimal study, because they can. They begin to experience practice as beneath them. Revision feels like something for other people, the plodders. Their confidence is real, and it is also fragile, because it has never been stress-tested by disciplined repetition.

Then comes the level where intelligence is no longer enough: a demanding subject, a competitive course, a first job where the work does not grade itself. The gifted student meets material that cannot be winged. For the first time they sit at a desk and discover something terrifyingly ordinary: they do not know how to study. They do not know how to break work down, how to schedule it, how to begin when their mind would prefer to escape. They have spent years practising the performance of competence, but not the process of building it. The fall is not intellectual; it is procedural. Their problem is not that they are not smart. Their problem is that they cannot reliably produce effort. In a world that rewards output, that is a serious disadvantage.

This chapter is an attempt to loosen the reader's attachment to cleverness—not because cleverness is bad, but because it is an unstable foundation for a life. Cleverness is often a story people tell themselves about why they deserve success. Consistency is a method for earning it in public, through evidence. The modern culture that celebrates "hacks" and "secrets" makes this harder. We are surrounded by the fantasy of shortcuts: the perfect routine, the killer app, the one trick that will remove the need for monotony. Underneath that fantasy is a refusal to accept the basic price of competence: repetition. A person who learns to pay that price without drama acquires an advantage that is almost unfair, because so many people refuse it on principle.

The advantage becomes clearer when we consider time, not as an abstract concept, but as a ledger. Over a day, there is little visible difference between the person who practises their craft for twenty minutes and the person who does not. Over a week, there is still little. Over a year, the difference begins to take shape: fewer blank pages, more solved problems, more calls made, more workouts completed, more vocabulary learned, more situations experienced. Over five years, it becomes unmistakable. Over ten, it becomes the sort of gap people explain away with myths about genius. They see the outcome and assume the cause must have been exceptional talent, because the true cause—unshowy repetition—seems too plain to be responsible for such a striking result.

This is where compounding enters, not as a financial metaphor dragged awkwardly into human life, but as a description of how skills and habits accumulate. Money compounds because returns generate more returns. Habits compound because each repetition does two things at once: it produces a small output today and it slightly improves the probability of producing the next output tomorrow. Repetition is both work and training for work. It does not merely create results; it creates a person more likely to create results. That second effect is why consistency has a structural advantage over talent. Talent may produce a higher peak on a good day. Consistency improves the average day.

A small numerical example makes the point without turning life into maths. Imagine two writers. One writes only when inspired, and on those days produces a brilliant 1,500 words. They manage this perhaps twice a week, because they are waiting for the feeling that they associate with "real writing". The other writes 300 words every weekday, even when the sentences are plain. In a single week, the inspired writer may outproduce the consistent one. In a month, it becomes less clear. In six months, the consistent writer has a body of work large enough to revise, sharpen, combine, and publish. The inspired writer has a pile of isolated bursts, each impressive, none part of a reliable machine. They may have more genius on the page. They have less book.

Or consider fitness. A person who does punishing workouts sporadically feels virtuous and destroyed. They spend the next day recovering and the next convincing themselves they need a "proper" session or nothing. A person who moves modestly and regularly accrues something less dramatic but more valuable: a body that treats movement as normal, not as an emergency. Here, too, the compounding effect is not only on the body but on the mind. Regular sessions reduce the psychological cost of starting. They remove the need for motivational fireworks. They create a baseline of identity: someone who moves.

The same logic applies to sales prospecting. One dramatic day of outreach can be exhilarating. It can also produce the wrong lesson, because it encourages the belief that effort should feel intense to count. Meanwhile the quiet discipline of a daily contact—one thoughtful email, one call, one follow-up—creates a pipeline that does not depend on last-minute panic. Over time, the person with the daily habit has more data, more feedback, more refinements of approach. Their rejection becomes informative rather than personal, because it occurs in a stream. They are less likely to catastrophise a bad day because the system continues tomorrow. Consistency is not only an output strategy; it is an emotional regulation strategy disguised as work.

Still, consistency has its own danger: it can harden into mindless repetition. The chapter will not treat repetition as inherently noble. Reps that reinforce a mistake compound the mistake. A person can become consistently mediocre by practising the wrong thing faithfully. This is why consistency must be paired with learning, with feedback, with the willingness to adjust. The aim is not to become a machine. It is to become a person who can generate progress without relying on the mood to do so. The distinction matters. A consistent system that never learns is a treadmill. A consistent system that learns is a path.

The question, then, is what "reliable execution" actually looks like in a real life where the mind wobbles and the calendar is crowded. The phrase can sound corporate, but the experience is intimate. Reliable execution is the ability to produce the next rep without needing to negotiate with yourself for an hour. It is the skill of beginning. It is also the skill of continuing when the work is not flattering. The glamorous version of discipline is intensity: the big session, the heroic effort, the "all in" week. The useful version is smaller and steadier. Smaller than you think, because the brain resists grand commitments. Easier than you think, because effort that requires constant courage will not last. More often than you think, because frequency does the silent work of identity.

These principles do not ask anyone to lower ambition; they ask ambition to grow up. They shift the unit of improvement from the dramatic milestone to the repeatable rep. They replace the fantasy of a future self—disciplined, motivated, endlessly energetic—with the design of a present self who can act under ordinary conditions. This is a subtle but profound reorientation. It treats time as an ally rather than a threat. It treats boredom as a cost of admission rather than a sign that something is wrong. It treats the self not as a fixed personality but as a creature of repetition.

Modern life makes this reorientation urgent. Many people now work in environments where attention is constantly auctioned, where notifications interrupt thought, where novelty is engineered to be irresistible, and where performance is displayed and compared in public. In such an environment, talent can become a distraction: it is easy to confuse being impressive with getting better. Consistency, by contrast, is often private. It does not produce immediate applause. It produces capability. Capability, over time, becomes autonomy: the ability to choose harder projects, to handle pressure, to learn new things without panic, to keep one's promises to oneself. Autonomy is not a buzzword. It is the dignity of not being ruled by impulse.

A motif runs through the whole argument: the metronome. Not because life should be reduced to mechanical ticking, but because progress often demands a steady beat that continues regardless of mood. The metronome is what makes a musician's practice useful. It is what turns a runner's training into adaptation rather than random exertion. It is what turns a salesperson's outreach into a pipeline rather than a desperate gamble. It is what turns study into knowledge rather than occasional comprehension. The metronome is not the goal; it is the condition for the goal. When it disappears, everything becomes improvisation. Improvisation is thrilling. It is also unreliable.

This chapter begins where most people hesitate: with the definition of the advantage itself. If consistency is so powerful, why do so few people embrace it? Part of the answer is cultural. We praise talent because it appears effortless, and effortlessness is associated with superiority. We also underestimate time. We are impatient creatures in a world that trains impatience. We want change that can be felt, not merely measured. Yet the most consequential improvements are often the ones that feel small in the moment and then become impossible to ignore later. That is compounding, not as a metaphor, but as an experience: a gradual shift that, once it passes a threshold, looks like transformation.

From there the chapter presses on the limits of raw talent, not with scolding but with honest anatomy. It examines how early ease can sabotage later competence, how the desire to be seen as gifted can prevent someone from doing the beginner's work required to get good, and how fragile confidence can masquerade as high standards. It lingers on the student who never learned to study because that story appears in different costumes everywhere: the entrepreneur who never learned to sell because early customers arrived through luck, the athlete who never learned to train because youth carried them, the manager who never learned to plan because their charm temporarily compensated. Each story contains the same hinge: what happens when the environment stops rewarding improvisation.

Then comes the most quietly radical shift in the reader's mindset: seeing each repetition as an investment rather than a single event. A single rep rarely changes a life. It changes the next rep. That is the point. When a person begins to think this way, the question "Do I feel like it?" becomes less interesting than "What does this rep buy me?" It buys a little competence. It buys a little identity. It buys a little evidence. It buys a slightly easier start tomorrow. Over time, that becomes a private fortune.

The chapter's final movement establishes the principles of reliable execution that will govern everything else that follows in the manuscript's logic, though they are presented here as lived realities rather than slogans. The work will be framed not as a moral campaign but as an engineering project: making the desired behaviour small enough to start, easy enough to repeat, and frequent enough to compound. The tools that appear later—methods for reducing friction, designing minimum viable habits, protecting streaks through disruption—rest on this foundation. The foundation is not discipline as punishment. It is discipline as design.

The emotional payoff is not merely a sense of control. It is a kind of self-respect that does not depend on performance in public. The person who becomes consistent stops needing to be a genius. They stop needing to be in the right mood. They stop needing to be rescued by inspiration. They can still be inspired; they simply no longer depend on it. This is not a small shift. It changes how a person reads their own life. It changes what they fear. It changes how they respond to an unproductive day, a rejection, a missed week. It replaces drama with data.

By the end of the chapter's opening argument, the reader should feel an itch of recognition: the suspicion that what they have called "motivation problems" have often been design problems, and that what they have called "not talented enough" has often been "not repeated enough". That suspicion is productive. It places the next decision where it belongs—not in fantasy, but in the next rep, the next small action that can be repeated without ceremony. The page turns easily when the stakes are no longer about becoming extraordinary in one leap, but about becoming unignorable by being present, again and again, on days when nobody is watching.

Defining Consistency Advantage

In August 2008 at the Laoshan Velodrome in Beijing, British Cycling turned repetition into a public spectacle. The air inside the arena carried the peculiar tang of warmed resin and metal; the track itself looked almost unreal under the lights, a polished ellipse designed to expose every wobble. When Chris Hoy and his teammates collected medals with the calm regularity of a factory line, the television story was irresistible: a nation had produced exceptional riders. The less glamorous truth sat behind the scenes in training logs, equipment tweaks, recovery routines, and practice sessions that looked identical from one day to the next. The results are easy to verify—Britain topped the track cycling medals in Beijing (International Olympic Committee official results, 2008)—but the mechanism is harder to celebrate because it refuses the drama of sudden transformation. It is the same mechanism that quietly governs careers, learning, health, and craft: the steady accumulation of small, repeated actions until the ledger becomes lopsided.

Consistency advantage is not a slogan about trying harder. It is an edge created by repeatability. A person can be inconsistent and intense, producing occasional brilliance that dazzles colleagues and then evaporates. Another person can be consistent and moderate, producing work that is rarely dazzling yet reliably present. Over time, reliability becomes a competitive property. It attracts trust, reduces uncertainty, and makes improvement inevitable rather than optional. This is not poetry. It is arithmetic.

Talent makes a strong first impression. Consistency makes a strong last one.

Consider a scene that plays out in offices so often it is almost invisible. Two salespeople join the same team. The first has what managers like to call "presence". They can warm up a cold room in ten minutes. They are quick with stories, quick with charm, quick with the kind of confidence that makes clients feel safe. Their meetings are memorable. The second is less captivating. Their voice is steady rather than sparkling. They are not boring, but they do not create a little theatre around themselves. They follow a process, and the process looks plain: daily outreach, tidy notes, scheduled follow-ups, a refusal to let small commitments slide because they "don't matter".

In the first quarter, the charismatic one usually wins the narrative. They land a couple of impressive deals and get talked about. Their wins arrive in bursts—three strong weeks, then a lull—because their activity is shaped by mood, opportunity, and the appetite for big moments. The dependable one rarely wins the narrative because their work does not create dramatic spikes. They send a similar number of emails each day. They make a similar number of calls each week. They hold themselves to small promises that nobody else sees. Their result is not a thrilling graph; it is a steady line.

Show, then name it. The steady line is the consistency advantage.

Explain it precisely. Consistency advantage emerges when the rate of repetition is stable enough that three things begin to happen at once. Output accumulates: more proposals sent, more pages drafted, more problems solved, more practice sessions completed. Feedback accumulates: more "no" responses, more objections, more small failures that teach exactly where the approach is weak. Trust accumulates: colleagues and clients start to assume the person will do what they said they would do, because the evidence is boringly abundant. The implication is not merely more work done. It is a change in how other people and systems respond. Opportunities tend to go to the person who lowers the risk of disappointment.

Risk is the hidden metric behind many professional decisions. A manager choosing who will lead an important project is not only choosing skill; they are choosing predictability under pressure. A client renewing a contract is not only choosing price; they are choosing the probability that emails will be returned, issues will be handled, and meetings will be prepared. Consistency advantage is the ability to make that probability high without making a song and dance about it. It transforms reliability from a personal virtue into a tangible asset.

A useful definition, stripped of motivational varnish, is this: consistency is the repeated execution of a behaviour at a frequency that makes it normal, not exceptional. The emphasis is on repeated and on normal. When an action becomes normal, it costs less to begin. The start-up pain drops. That reduction in start-up pain is why consistency tends to outperform talent over time. The talented person may produce better work on a good day. The consistent person produces work on more days. Quality has more chances to appear.

The ledger is ruthless about this. It does not care how gifted a person feels.

This is where many people misread what they are seeing. They encounter someone who looks "naturally disciplined" and assume a personality difference: some people have it, others do not. Often the difference is procedural. The consistent person is not necessarily tougher. They are less exposed to decision-making at the moment when decision-making is most fragile: the start. They begin with fewer negotiations. They do not ask themselves, each day, whether they are the kind of person who does the thing. They do the thing, and the ledger slowly rewrites the identity.

A second checkable example makes this more concrete, because it pulls the idea out of individual psychology and into organisational practice. In the early 1980s, the NUMMI plant in Fremont, California—then a joint venture between General Motors and

Toyota—became a case study in what repeatable process can do to performance. The plant had previously been one of GM's worst for quality and absenteeism. Under Toyota's production system, the same workforce began operating with dramatically improved quality and productivity; the story is documented and analysed in the manufacturing literature and in the MIT study published as *The Machine That Changed the World* (Womack, Jones & Roos, 1990). The fascination of NUMMI is not that Toyota imported "genius" workers. It did not. It changed the operating rhythm: standardised work, frequent feedback, and a culture where small problems were surfaced and addressed rather than patched over. Show, name, explain, implication again. The behaviour was repeatable; the system learned. The implication was not a one-off leap but sustained improvement that looked, from afar, like a miracle of competence.

That is the heart of the consistency advantage: it makes learning inevitable. When behaviour is repeated, the system—whether a person or an organisation—collects information. When information is collected, adjustments become possible. When adjustments are repeated, improvement compounds. Talent can accelerate the early stages of learning, but without repetition there is nothing to adjust. There is no stable baseline, only anecdotes.

Now return to the salespeople, because the dynamics are easiest to see there. The charismatic salesperson's biggest strength—improvisation—often becomes their hidden weakness. Improvisation feels alive. It also makes measurement difficult. If each pitch is different, it is harder to compare what worked. If activity comes in bursts, it is harder to diagnose whether a month's success was skill or timing. The dependable salesperson, by repeating a smaller set of behaviours, gains clarity. They can measure response rates. They can compare scripts. They can detect patterns in objections. They can run tiny experiments without needing a crisis to force them. Their confidence becomes less emotional because it is anchored to observable activity: contacts made, follow-ups completed, meetings booked. Trust, efficiency, and risk become visible in numbers and actions rather than in self-belief.

The longer the timeframe, the more punishing the comparison becomes. A bursty approach can produce spectacular quarters. It is also vulnerable to fatigue, mood, personal upheaval, and the inevitable drag of life. A repeatable approach is less exciting. It is also more survivable. Survivability matters because it keeps the person in the game long enough for the ledger to tilt. Many careers are not won by a single extraordinary year. They are won by avoiding the collapses that follow extraordinary years.

This is where "talent" reveals a second limitation: it can invite complacency. Early success teaches a dangerous lesson—"I can get away with this"—and that lesson becomes expensive later. A gifted person may skip the boring work because the boring work does not immediately appear necessary. They are not lazy in the cartoon sense. They are simply insulated. When resistance eventually appears, it feels like injustice. The person then reaches for what has always worked: more intensity, more improvisation, more self-belief. Sometimes that rescue attempt works. Sometimes it fails, and the failure is psychologically brutal because the person has tied their identity to being effortlessly good. Fragile confidence is not a personality quirk; it is often the by-product of success without process.

Consistency advantage does not require a person to abandon talent. It asks them to stop treating talent as the strategy. Talent becomes an amplifier rather than a steering wheel. The steering wheel is the repeated behaviour.

And yet, an honest definition must include a limitation, otherwise the idea turns into a moral creed. There are domains where a single act dominates outcomes: a breakthrough discovery, a hit song, a decisive goal in a final. In such fields, the distribution of rewards is not gentle. A person can be consistently competent and still be eclipsed by a rare, dazzling performance. Cultural history is full of these moments. The implication is uncomfortable: consistency is not a guarantee of stardom.

Reconcile it without flinching. Consistency advantage is not primarily an argument about fame. It is an argument about probability and control. Breakthroughs are real, but they are noisy, difficult to schedule, and often dependent on factors outside any one person's reach—timing, networks, funding, the appetite of a market.

Consistency governs what can be governed: the steady production of work, the steady collection of feedback, the steady reduction of avoidable errors. Even in hit-driven fields, consistent output increases the number of attempts, and attempts increase the odds of the rare event. The consistent person buys more lottery tickets, but with better odds because each ticket is informed by the previous one. Meanwhile, for most professionals, researchers, and students, the aim is not to be a cultural comet. It is to become reliably effective: to produce results that survive stress, boredom, and interruption; to earn trust; to keep learning; to avoid the collapses that ruin reputations and self-respect.

There is a quieter philosophical point here, too. We tend to worship talent because it allows us to imagine a clean hierarchy. Talent reassures us that the world is arranged by innate merit. Consistency complicates that story because it is democratic in the unsettling way: it suggests that many outcomes are built by people who simply keep going. That threatens the ego of the gifted and also the resignation of the discouraged. If consistency matters, then the future is not only assigned. It is negotiated.

The mechanism that turns repetition into advantage can be described without mysticism. Repetition reduces variance. Reduced variance increases predictability. Predictability makes planning meaningful. Planning makes learning efficient. Learning makes results compound. Each step is mundane. Together they are transformative.

Mundane is not the same as easy. Repetition is emotionally expensive because it refuses novelty. It asks a person to do work that may not produce immediate applause or even immediate visible progress. The mind tends to crave a sign that the effort is "working". Consistency often withholds that sign until much later. This is why the consistent person's relationship with time is different. They treat the ledger as the proof, not the mood. When a day feels unproductive, they still have a rep. When a week goes poorly, they still have data. The charismatic, erratic performer is more likely to experience each setback as a referendum on their identity because they lack the stabilising evidence of repetition.

A final return to the motif helps. Imagine two ledgers. In one, entries appear in clumps: several days of furious activity, then blank space, then another burst. In the other, entries appear almost daily, modest in size, sometimes smaller when life is crowded, but rarely absent for long. Over time, the second ledger becomes a kind of quiet authority. It is hard to argue with. It does not prove that the person is brilliant. It proves that the person is there. And being there, over and over, turns out to be the rarest advantage of all.

The tension that remains—and it is worth keeping unresolved because it forces honesty—is this: consistency is powerful precisely because it is unglamorous, yet most people still hunger for glamour. The question is not whether repetition works. The question is whether a person is willing to accept a trade: less dramatic self-image in exchange for more reliable outcomes. The ledger will record whichever choice is made. The diagnostic test is simple and uncomfortable: when nobody is impressed, what still gets done?

Limits of Raw Talent

In May 1990 in Paris, a fourteen-year-old Jennifer Capriati reached the semi-finals of the French Open, dismantling seasoned opponents with a kind of fearless speed that made adults reach for superlatives. The Stade Roland Garros crowd did what crowds always do when they glimpse a prodigy: it turned potential into destiny in real time. The ball came off her racquet with a bright, percussive crack; her movement looked effortless, almost insolent. A year later, in June 1991 at Wimbledon in London, she again reached the semi-finals, still a teenager, still carrying the strange burden of being "obviously" exceptional in public (tournament records are straightforward to verify). The story looked like a straight line. It was not.

Talent has a low ceiling.

That sentence sounds harsh until one asks what, exactly, "talent" buys. It buys early velocity. It buys attention. It buys the intoxicating sensation of being ahead without having to understand how. It does not, by itself, buy durability. It does not automatically produce the habits that keep a person improving once novelty evaporates and pressure becomes ordinary. Capriati's later career—its pauses, its turbulence, its eventual return to the top of the sport in the early 2000s—illustrates something uncomfortable but common: early advantage can outrun the systems that must eventually support it. When the systems are missing, talent does not simply plateau; it often becomes brittle.

Show the pattern closer to home, where the stadium lights are replaced by desk lamps and exam halls. A gifted student moves through school as if the curriculum were a thin mist. They read once and remember. They intuit solutions quickly. Teachers praise them for being "bright", a word that lands like a crown. They revise lightly, often at the last minute, and still collect high marks. The behaviour looks like confidence. The reality is simpler: the environment is not yet demanding enough to require method. What the student is practising, without realising it, is not learning. It is winning without preparation.

Name the mechanism. This is complacency-by-circumstance: the gradual belief that effort is optional because outcomes have been good without it.

Explain how it forms. Early success reduces friction. Reduced friction removes the need to build routines. Without routines, the student never learns how to start when they do not feel like it, how to break work into steps, how to return after a bad session, how to measure what they do not understand. Their identity fuses with their ease. They become the sort of person for whom struggle feels like shame. The implication is not merely academic. When they later enter a domain where difficulty is non-negotiable—university-level mathematics, laboratory work, a demanding professional qualification, a new language, a first job that requires sustained output—they face a problem that is procedural, not intellectual: they have no reliable way to produce effort.

There is evidence for how fragile "smart" identities can become when they are overemphasised. In a widely cited paper, Claudia Mueller and Carol Dweck (1998) found that praising children for intelligence rather than effort can lead to reduced persistence and lower performance when tasks become difficult. The point is not that praise is bad. The point is that a certain kind of praise teaches a child to protect an image rather than build a process. Show, name, explain, implication again. The child who has been told they are clever learns to avoid situations that threaten that label; they choose tasks where success is likely and withdraw when challenge implies the possibility of looking ordinary. The implication is a quiet tragedy: the person who could have become formidable becomes merely talented, because they stop collecting the reps that would have made them resilient.

Now put a concrete scene on the table, because abstraction lets the ego wriggle away. The gifted student sits down to study for an exam that matters. They open a textbook and feel a sudden, unfamiliar heaviness. The pages are dense. The concepts do not yield to intuition. Their attention skitters. They check their phone "for a minute", then again. They try to read faster, as if speed itself were a strategy. They highlight half the page, which feels productive and changes nothing. They tell themselves they will do a longer session tomorrow, because longer sessions are how serious people behave. Tomorrow arrives and the same thing happens, and now panic joins the room. The student has met the ceiling of raw talent: it is the point at which cleverness can no longer compensate for the absence of consistent execution.

This ceiling appears in professional life with different costumes. The charismatic manager who "just knows" what to do may thrive until the organisation scales, at which point intuition becomes a poor substitute for planning and measurement. The naturally persuasive salesperson may thrive until they enter a territory where relationships take months to mature and follow-up is the main job. The bright junior researcher may shine in seminars and struggle at the bench, where progress depends on repeatable protocols, clean notes, and patience with failure. In each case, the visible behaviour tells the truth. Who measures? Who reviews? Who documents? Who repeats the unglamorous action at a steady frequency? Skill without these behaviours is like a high-powered engine bolted to a frame with missing screws: impressive noise, unpredictable motion.

Name the deeper limitation. Raw talent often cannot *self-correct.*

Explain it. Correction requires feedback, and feedback requires repetition. If a person performs only in bursts, they generate too little data to diagnose what is working. They live on anecdotes. Anecdotes feel persuasive, especially to clever minds. They are also statistically unreliable. The implication is that the talented-but-inconsistent person may remain convinced of their high ability even as their outcomes wobble, because they can always point to a past peak and say, truthfully, "I can do it." The consistent person is less hypnotised by peaks because they live inside averages: they can see what happens most days, not only on the best ones.

This is why talent can create fragile confidence. Fragile confidence is not a lack of self-belief; it is self-belief that depends on conditions staying friendly. When conditions turn hostile—more competition, less time, higher stakes—the fragile confidence collapses or becomes defensive. Watch for the behaviours. The person avoids measurement because measurement might expose inconsistency. They avoid rehearsal because rehearsal feels like admitting they are not naturally excellent. They avoid accountability because accountability threatens the illusion of effortless competence. They may become sarcastic, dismissive, or bored in advance, which is a way of protecting the self from the possibility of trying and failing. The implication is severe: talent can turn into a shield against learning.

A second checkable example shows how the ceiling can be raised—if a person builds the missing scaffolding. Capriati's career did not end at fourteen with a semi-final in Paris. After years away from the sport, she returned and won three Grand Slam singles titles between 2001 and 2002, including the Australian Open and the French Open in 2001 and another Australian Open in 2002 (Grand Slam tournament records are public and easily verified). Whatever one believes about the personal details, the sporting fact is clear: sustained excellence arrived not merely from early giftedness, but from a later capacity to return, train, and compete consistently in a brutally demanding environment. The implication is not sentimental. It is mechanical. When a person adds disciplined execution to talent, the ceiling lifts.

At this point, a reasonable counter-example must be allowed into the room, otherwise the argument becomes dogma. Some people do appear to succeed through bursts of brilliance. History includes figures who seem to have produced extraordinary work with little formal structure, or who relied on rare cognitive gifts to leap past ordinary constraints. A classic example is Srinivasa Ramanujan, who produced remarkable mathematical insights in India before moving to Cambridge in 1914; his story is well documented in biographies and in the archival trail of his collaboration with G. H. Hardy. Ramanujan complicates any simple sermon about routines and discipline because his output appears, from the outside, like raw genius erupting through circumstance.

Reconcile the counter-example honestly. First, even the "burst" cases often contain hidden repetition. Ramanujan filled notebooks; he worked. The form of discipline may not look like modern productivity rituals, but the behaviour—sustained engagement with problems—was there. Second, rare gifts do exist, and in certain domains they can dominate. The argument here is not that talent is irrelevant. It is that talent is a volatile asset when it is not paired with repeatable execution. Most people do not live in the extreme tails of ability distributions, and even those who do still face the same laws of attention, fatigue, and time. For the majority, the most controllable way to raise the floor—and therefore the long-term outcome—is consistency.

The ceiling metaphor matters because it highlights a brutal asymmetry. Talent tends to improve your best days. Consistency improves your ordinary days. Ordinary days are most of them. When performance depends on best days, life becomes a lottery. When performance depends on ordinary days, life becomes a practice. The difference can be measured. In sales, measure weekly outreach volume and follow-up completion. In study, measure hours spent retrieving information from memory rather than merely re-reading, and measure the number of practice questions completed. In research, measure experiments run with clean documentation and the rate at which errors are traced and removed. In craft, measure drafts produced, revisions completed, and the frequency of deliberate practice rather than casual repetition. These are not romantic metrics, but they reveal whether a person is building a system or relying on mood.

There is also a social dimension to the ceiling of talent. Teams and institutions do not merely want brilliance; they want predictability. Predictability is a form of kindness. It reduces the cognitive load of everyone around you. A colleague who delivers consistently allows others to plan. A colleague who produces brilliant work unpredictably forces others into contingency mode. The second person may be admired; the first becomes indispensable. Indispensable is an odd compliment because it sounds less glamorous than "genius", yet it often leads to more responsibility, more autonomy, and more influence. The implication is quietly political: consistency builds trust capital, and trust capital changes what doors open.

A clever mind often resists this because it wants the world to be fair in a particular way: it wants rewards to map neatly onto visible intelligence. The world is not obliged to comply. Organisations reward risk reduction. Clients reward responsiveness. Examinations reward preparation. Craft rewards the patient accumulation of technique. In these environments, raw talent without disciplined execution does not merely underperform; it misleads. It creates a person who believes they are protected by their ability and then discovers—often late—that the protection was conditional.

The painful moment, for many, is not failure. It is the first time failure feels *personal.* The gifted student receives a poor mark and does not know how to interpret it. They cannot say, "I did the work and it didn't land," because they did not do the work. They cannot say, "I'll adjust my approach," because they do not have an approach. So they reach for the only explanation available: "Maybe I'm not actually smart." The implication is a false existential crisis created by a missing habit. The tragedy is that the person often retreats at exactly the moment when they should begin building consistency. They protect the identity of cleverness by avoiding the reps that would make them competent.

Research on expertise supports the central idea without turning it into a simplistic formula. Anders Ericsson and colleagues (1993) argued that expert performance is strongly associated with *deliberate practice*—structured, effortful repetition aimed at improvement, not mere time spent. The phrase is often misquoted in pop culture, but the serious point is relevant: consistent engagement with the right kind of practice builds capability that raw ability alone does not reliably deliver. The implication is that consistency advantage is not only about showing up. It is about showing up in a way that can learn.

This is where attachment to being clever becomes dangerous. Cleverness can become a narcotic. It feels good to be quick. It feels good to impress. It feels good to be the person who can rescue a conversation or ace an exam with minimal effort. But those pleasures can trap a person in a narrow version of themselves. They begin to choose environments that reward their existing strengths and avoid environments that would expand them. They become, in effect, consistent at avoiding consistency. The ceiling stays low, and the person blames the ceiling on circumstances rather than design.

The piece returns, quietly, to the motif of the ceiling because it forces a choice. One can keep living beneath it, polishing the surface where talent shines, collecting moments that prove one's giftedness. Or one can raise it by building the scaffolding that talent alone does not provide: repeatable effort, measurement, feedback, recovery after slips. This choice is rarely announced. It shows up in small decisions: whether to practise when nobody is watching, whether to prepare when improvisation would be easier, whether to run the rep when the rep feels beneath you.

The unresolved tension is not whether talent matters; it does. The tension is whether a person prefers the identity of being naturally brilliant or the freedom of being reliably effective. When the next difficult season arrives—and it will—what will matter more: a story about cleverness, or a record of consistency that raises the ceiling from the inside?

Compounding from Small Reps

In 1950 at Toyota Motor Company in Toyota City, Japan, a production engineer named Taiichi Ohno began shaping a way of working that looked almost offensively modest: notice a small problem, correct it, standardise the correction, repeat. No single adjustment was dramatic. The drama arrived later, when thousands of small corrections had accumulated into a system that could produce cars with a consistency and efficiency that startled competitors. The story is not folklore; it is documented in the history of modern manufacturing, including *The Machine That Changed the World* (Womack, Jones & Roos, 1990). What matters here is not cars. It is the underlying logic: tiny changes, repeated, can add up to a difference large enough to look like genius from a distance.

Compounding is usually explained with money because money behaves nicely in equations. Habits behave messier, because humans are not spreadsheets. And yet the basic phenomenon transfers with surprising fidelity. A small repeated action does not merely create a small repeated outcome; it changes the conditions under which the next action happens. Each rep is a tiny deposit into a system that will, if the deposits keep coming, start paying interest in competence, ease, trust, and momentum.

Small deposits earn quiet interest.

To understand this without turning life into arithmetic theatre, it helps to watch what repetition does at the level of behaviour. A person writes one paragraph. That paragraph becomes evidence that writing happened. Evidence changes identity more reliably than slogans. Identity changes willingness. Willingness changes the probability of writing again tomorrow. That is compounding in human form: not a magical multiplication of output, but a gradual shift in likelihood. Over months, likelihood becomes a baseline. Baselines are where careers are made and bodies are shaped.

Show it in a familiar arena. Two people decide to improve their writing. One waits for inspiration, because they have tasted the pleasure of a brilliant afternoon when language flows and the world seems obligingly quiet. When inspiration arrives, they produce something sharp. When it does not, they do nothing, because doing mediocre work feels like betrayal. The other writes a small, regular amount. Some days the sentences are clean, some days they are stubborn, but the rep happens. The difference, initially, looks trivial. A few hundred words are not a masterpiece. Yet after weeks, the second person has drafts to revise, patterns to study, a growing tolerance for imperfection, and a clearer sense of what "good" even means. Their improvement is not a sudden leap. It is the cumulative effect of having more contact with the craft.

Name what is happening. The rep is acting as both production and training.

Explain the mechanism. In most skills, the thing you are trying to create is also the thing that changes you. Writing produces text, and text reveals weaknesses you cannot think your way out of: clumsy transitions, vague claims, rhythm that drags, an argument that collapses when it meets a counterexample. Each new rep creates another opportunity to notice and correct. Without reps, the person remains in a realm of self-concept: "I could write if I had time." With reps, they acquire a realm of evidence: "This is what my writing looks like, and this is how it is changing." The implication is that compounding is less about heroic output and more about shortening the feedback loop between attempt and adjustment.

This is why small reps matter even when they look too small to impress. A rep that is easy enough to repeat is a rep that can compound. A rep that is large enough to require a special day is a rep that stays isolated. Isolated effort has its place—projects sometimes demand it—but it does not reliably build a trajectory. Trajectories come from frequency.

The same logic becomes stark in study, because the mind's illusions are so persuasive. A student reads a chapter and feels familiar with it. Familiarity is soothing. It is also a liar. Cognitive psychologists have repeatedly shown that retrieval practice—actively pulling information from memory rather than passively re-reading—produces stronger long-term learning (Roediger & Karpicke, 2006). The important point for compounding is behavioural: a tiny daily rep of retrieval (a few practice questions, a quick self-test, a short recall session) can outperform long sessions of re-reading because it produces better feedback. The rep tells the student what they do not know. Ignorance becomes visible. Visibility allows correction. The implication is that a small daily practice of the right kind can accumulate into competence that looks, on exam day, like natural cleverness.

Put a number to the idea without pretending numbers are life. If someone writes 200 words a day, five days a week, that is 1,000 words per week. Over fifty weeks it is 50,000 words—enough for a short book's worth of draft material, even allowing for deletions and rewrites. No advanced maths. Just a ledger. The point is not the exact total; it is the shift in imagination. Two hundred words feels negligible. Fifty thousand words changes what is possible. Compounding makes the small feel dishonest in the moment and undeniable later.

The same arithmetic applies to prospecting, a domain where the emotional weather can be savage. A person who makes ten outreach attempts in a single frantic day may feel industrious. They also create a problem: they have to recover from the effort and the rejection, and they have to remember to do it again. A person who makes one outreach attempt daily creates a different condition. Rejection becomes a small daily dose rather than a rare catastrophe. The activity becomes normal. Normal activities do not require motivational speeches. Over time, the person has more conversations, more information about which messages land, more opportunities to refine, and—crucially—a pipeline that is not dependent on adrenaline.

Name the compounding effect here. The system reduces emotional variance.

Explain how. When outreach is frequent and modest, the nervous system learns that discomfort is survivable and temporary. The person becomes less likely to interpret a rejection as a global judgement because rejection arrives as a data point in a stream. The implication is a competitive one: the individual who can continue contact-making without being thrown by each response has access to more learning and more opportunity than the individual who requires a "good mood" to begin.

This is also where compounding intersects with trust, which is often treated as a soft, sentimental idea when it is better understood as behavioural probability. Trust grows when promises are kept and communication is steady. A weekly report delivered on time. A follow-up sent when it was said it would be sent. A small error admitted quickly and corrected cleanly. These are reps. Each one is a tiny deposit into another person's expectation. Over time, the expectation hardens into a professional asset. People stop checking. They stop chasing. They begin to offer bigger work because the risk of disappointment is lower. The consistent person is not merely more productive; they are easier to work with. Ease is a currency that compounds.

A second named example, far from boardrooms and spreadsheets, makes the same point in a human register. In London on 1 January 1660, Samuel Pepys began the diary that he would keep for nearly a decade, recording daily details of life, politics, plague, and fire in a way that later became an invaluable historical document. The diaries did not become important because Pepys was struck by a single moment of genius. They became important because he returned to the page again and again, capturing small observations that, accumulated, offered an unusually rich view of an era. The rep created the archive. The archive created the value. The implication is that compounding is not limited to skill acquisition; it also governs the building of resources—notes, drafts, datasets, relationships, routines—that later appear, to outsiders, like extraordinary foresight.

Now introduce the limitation, because compounding is not a morality tale. Reps can compound in the wrong direction. Bad practice produces refined badness. A writer who repeats vague claims becomes skilful at sounding plausible without being clear. A runner who repeats poor form becomes efficient at injury. A salesperson who repeats manipulative scripts becomes quick at burning trust. The limitation is credible and severe: compounding does not care about virtue. It cares about repetition. Repetition will amplify whatever it is fed.

Reconcile the limitation with the thesis. The point is not to fetishise reps. It is to treat reps as investments that should be audited for return. A rep is not automatically good because it is done frequently. It becomes valuable when it is paired with feedback, adjustment, and a refusal to repeat obvious mistakes without interrogation. This is why small reps are so powerful when the unit is small enough to tweak. A tiny daily writing rep is easier to adjust than a once-a-month marathon session, because the person can test changes rapidly. A modest daily practice session allows errors to be corrected before they fossilise. A small daily outreach habit allows messaging to evolve in response to real replies. Compounding becomes safer when the cycle of repetition includes learning.

A quiet motif helps unify this. Think of the rep as a deposit, and the system—your skill, your health capacity, your professional credibility—as the account. Deposits can be good or bad. Some deposits are inflationary: they look large but buy little because they are unsustainable and followed by drought. Some deposits are small and steady. Those are the ones that earn interest because they keep the account active. They keep the system in motion. They keep feedback arriving. The question is not whether the deposit is heroic. The question is whether it is repeatable.

Repeatable is the hinge word.

There is a modern temptation to dismiss small reps as trivial because our culture prizes visible transformation. Small reps offend the impatient mind. They feel like a refusal to live loudly. Yet many of the most impressive achievements of adult life—writing a thesis, building a research programme, mastering a language, moving from novice to competent in a craft, building a client base that survives market swings—are not built by the dramatic week. They are built by what happens in the weeks when nothing dramatic happens. Compounding is the mechanism that makes those weeks matter.

It also clarifies why consistency beats talent in the long run. Talent can raise the quality of a single rep. Consistency raises the number of reps. When the number of reps rises, learning accelerates. When learning accelerates, quality tends to rise anyway. The consistent person does not need to win every day. They only need to keep adding deposits. Over time, even modest deposits outpace sporadic splendour because the sporadic approach keeps emptying the account with gaps, resets, and repeated re-starts.

This is where the concept of risk returns, not as abstract anxiety but as a measurable distribution of outcomes. The person who relies on big efforts carries high variance: some weeks are spectacular, some weeks are zeros. The person who relies on small reps carries lower variance: fewer spectacular spikes, fewer catastrophic gaps. In professional settings, low variance is often rewarded because it makes projects predictable. In study, low variance is rewarded because memory strengthens by repeated retrieval. In craft, low variance is rewarded because technique is built by repetition. In health-related behaviours, low variance matters because bodies adapt to regular signals more than to rare punishments. The implication is that compounding is not merely about producing more; it is about producing with less fragility.

There is also an emotional dividend. Small reps protect a person from the existential drama that follows inconsistency. When a person has not done the thing for weeks, beginning becomes loaded: it is no longer "a session", it is "a comeback". Comebacks attract the ego and the fear in equal measure. A small rep dissolves the drama. It is simply a deposit, not a reinvention. Over time, the person's self-story shifts from "I'm the sort who starts and stops" to "I'm the sort who returns". That identity shift is not decorative. It changes decisions under stress. It changes what a person believes is possible without needing a special mood.

And yet, compounding demands patience with invisibility. The account grows quietly. For a long while, it may not look like much. That invisibility is where most people abandon the project and retreat to intensity, because intensity produces immediate sensation. Sensation is not the same as progress. The disciplined mind learns to measure progress with the ledger rather than the adrenaline.

So the forward test is not philosophical; it is practical and slightly uncomfortable. When the next choice arrives—make a small deposit today or wait for a day that feels important—what will be valued more: the satisfaction of a dramatic effort or the interest earned by a rep that can be repeated tomorrow? The answer is not revealed in a single decision. It is revealed in the balance of the account a year from now.

Principles of Reliable Execution

In April 1971 at the Apollo 15 training site in Flagstaff, Arizona, NASA's crew spent days rehearsing tasks that, to an outsider, would have looked absurdly small: repeated checklists, repeated tool handoffs, repeated sequences for contingencies that everyone hoped would never occur. The surface glamour of spaceflight lives in photographs and launch footage; the machinery of success lives in rehearsal rooms and procedural manuals. When Apollo 15 landed on the Moon in July 1971 and carried out complex surface operations with the first Lunar Roving Vehicle, it did not do so by improvising heroically in the moment; it did so by executing what had been made repeatable through disciplined practice and explicit systems (NASA mission documentation and public transcripts for Apollo 15 are straightforward to verify). The lesson is not that ordinary lives should be run like a spacecraft. The lesson is that reliability is built long before it is needed, and it is built by shrinking tasks into sequences that can be executed when attention is imperfect.

Small beats dramatic.

Reliable execution is the craft of making desired behaviour happen under ordinary conditions: fatigue, distraction, competing obligations, unpredictable interruptions. It is not the pursuit of constant intensity. Intensity is exciting. Intensity is also fragile. It creates a dependency on a particular emotional state—anger, ambition, panic, inspiration—none of which can be scheduled with any certainty. Reliability, by contrast, is schedule-friendly. It assumes that moods will wobble. It designs around that fact rather than denying it.

The guiding principles that follow can be stated bluntly because they are not mystical. They are rules of engineering applied to human behaviour. *Smaller than you think, easier than you think, more often than you think.* Each phrase is an antidote to a common failure mode.

Show the failure mode first. A professional decides to "get serious" about a skill: writing, a qualification, coding, language learning, fitness, prospecting. They draft a plan that flatters their self-image. It is ambitious, detailed, and slightly theatrical. The first week goes well because novelty supplies energy and the person is temporarily living inside a new identity. Then reality arrives: a late meeting, a disrupted night, a family problem, a stressful deadline. The plan begins to crack. The person misses a session, then another. The plan becomes a reminder of failure. Because it was designed at the scale of an idealised life, it cannot survive a normal one.

Name what happened. The plan was not wrong about what matters. It was wrong about what is executable.

Explain it. Most breakdowns in consistency are not caused by laziness. They are caused by over-sized steps, over-reliance on mood, and an absence of mechanisms for recovery. The implication is liberating: if the breakdown is structural, it can be redesigned. Reliable execution treats the self as a system under constraints. It does not romanticise willpower. It measures constraints and works with them.

Begin with "smaller than you think". The consistent person makes the unit of work deliberately modest. This feels counterintuitive to high performers because they associate seriousness with size. Yet the most reliable units are the ones that create the least resistance at the start. Resistance is not merely dislike. It is the accumulation of tiny costs: the time required to set up, the uncertainty about what to do next, the fear of not doing it well, the exhaustion of a long day. When the unit is small, those costs shrink. The behaviour becomes easier to begin, which is the real bottleneck in most habits.

A concrete example keeps this honest. A researcher plans to write every weekday. If "write" means producing 1,000 polished words, the unit contains hidden costs: finding two uninterrupted hours, managing perfectionism, marshalling complex arguments, facing the blank page with high stakes. The start becomes heavy. If the unit is "produce one paragraph that states a claim and a reason," the start cost is lower. The paragraph can be wrong. It can be revised. It can be discarded. But the rep happens. The implication is not lower standards. It is higher reliability, which over time produces more material to refine and therefore a better final standard.

This is the logic behind minimum viable habits, a term that sounds modern but describes an old human trick: shrink the action until the self stops fighting it. Minimum viable does not mean meaningless. It means the smallest honest version of the behaviour that keeps the identity of "I show up" intact. A person who reads one page still reads. A person who does a short mobility sequence still moves. A person who sends one outreach message still prospects. The rep is not impressive; it is repeatable. Repeatable is the point.

Now "easier than you think". Ease is often misunderstood as indulgence. In reliable execution, ease is a design parameter. A behaviour that requires constant self-confrontation will not survive. The goal is not to remove effort from life; it is to remove unnecessary friction so that effort is spent on the work itself, not on the wrestling match required to begin.

Show friction in the wild. The professional who intends to study in the evening but keeps their materials scattered across devices, logins, and rooms. The writer who begins each session by searching for notes. The salesperson who begins each day unsure whom to contact and what to say. The exerciser who realises, at the moment of action, that their shoes are in the car and the bag is half-packed. These are not moral failings. They are practical obstacles. Each obstacle adds a small delay. Delays invite distraction. Distraction becomes non-action.

Name the remedy. Friction audits.

Explain it. A friction audit is a deliberate inventory of everything that stands between intention and action. It treats "I didn't do it" as a signal to investigate, not a reason to condemn. The audit lists physical barriers (distance, clutter, missing tools), cognitive barriers (unclear next step, perfectionism, fear), and social barriers (competing expectations, environments that cue other behaviours). The implication is measurable: if the number of barriers drops, the probability of behaviour rises. People like to imagine they need more motivation. Often they need fewer obstacles.

A second checkable example from outside self-help clarifies why ease is not weakness. Toyota's production system, as documented in manufacturing history, emphasised making problems visible and reducing waste—extra movement, extra waiting, extra steps that did not add value (Womack, Jones & Roos, 1990). A factory that requires heroic effort to function is a poorly designed factory. A work system that requires heroic willpower every day is similarly poorly designed. Ease is not laziness; it is efficiency applied to behaviour.

The third principle—"more often than you think"—addresses a different misunderstanding. Many people try to compensate for inconsistency with intensity. They miss several days and then attempt a marathon session. The marathon feels righteous. It also rarely builds a stable habit because frequency is the engine of normalisation. The brain treats repeated cues and repeated actions as a pattern worth automating. Rare, dramatic sessions do not create the same automation. They remain events rather than routines.

Frequency also improves learning because it shortens the gap between attempt and feedback. In education research, the benefit of retrieving information over time, rather than cramming, is well established; spacing and testing effects are discussed in classic work such as Roediger & Karpicke (2006). The behavioural implication generalises: more frequent contact with a skill means more opportunities to notice errors, adjust, and continue. Longer gaps allow skills to cool, requiring re-start energy each time. High-frequency reps reduce re-start costs.

Here the motif that runs through the book returns as a practical image: the metronome. Reliable execution is about keeping a beat that the week can sustain. The beat does not need to be loud. It needs to be steady. The metronome is what allows a musician's practice to shape technique. It is what allows a researcher's writing sessions to accumulate into papers rather than promises. It is what allows a salesperson's outreach to become a pipeline rather than a periodic panic. The metronome is also what keeps identity stable when life becomes noisy.

Now add the principle that sits beneath all three: systems over moods. Mood is information. Mood is not command. People often behave as though motivation must precede action. In reality, action often precedes motivation because action changes physiology, attention, and perception. The person who begins a small rep frequently finds that the mind follows. This is not a mystical claim; it is observable. The feeling of resistance is strongest before starting. Once started, the task becomes more specific and therefore less threatening. Systems exploit that fact. They remove the need to debate with oneself. They turn "should I?" into "it is time".

This is where tracking and streaks enter, not as moral scorekeeping but as feedback. A streak makes the beat visible. Visibility reduces self-deception. A person who believes they are "pretty consistent" can check the record. The record may flatter or correct. Either way, it provides data. The danger, of course, is brittleness: a streak can become a fragile idol, shattered by one disruption. That is why reliable execution includes the concept of a streak shield: a pre-defined, smaller version of the habit that can be executed during disruption—travel, illness, deadlines—so the identity of showing up remains intact. The shield is not a loophole. It is an acknowledgement that life has seasons.

And yet, a credible limitation must be faced. Systems can become cages. There are people who turn routine into a form of control, clinging to it as anxiety management rather than as a means to growth. They punish themselves for deviation. They treat flexibility as failure. This is not reliable execution; it is rigidity disguised as discipline.

Reconcile it. The difference is learning over perfection. Reliable execution is not about never missing. It is about returning intelligently. Systems are meant to be revised in response to evidence. A habit that was appropriate in one season may need shrinking or reshaping in another. A routine that worked in a quiet month may fail in a chaotic one; the failure is a design signal. Perfectionism treats the signal as shame. Learning treats it as information. The implication is humane and practical: a person can keep the metronome without becoming its servant.

Learning requires measurement, but measurement need not be elaborate. The consistent person measures leading indicators—reps completed, minutes spent, contacts made—because these are controllable. They avoid tying identity to outcomes that are partly luck, such as deals closed in a given week or external recognition for a piece of work. This distinction matters in high-variance environments. A researcher cannot control when a paper is accepted, but they can control whether they drafted, revised, and submitted. A salesperson cannot control every "yes", but they can control outreach volume and follow-up completion. A student cannot control the exact curve of an exam cohort, but they can control the frequency of retrieval practice. The visible behaviour is where reliability lives.

At this stage, the principles begin to sound almost too plain. That is their power and their insult. Many people want discipline to feel like a personality upgrade, a dramatic self-reinvention. Reliable execution is closer to housekeeping. It is the daily maintenance of a life that can produce results without needing to be rescued by mood. The person who accepts this becomes oddly free: they stop waiting to feel like the right person, because they have built mechanisms that make the right action the default.

NASA's training culture offers a final useful image. The checklist is not a confession of incompetence. It is a protection against the predictable fragility of human attention under stress. At stake in a mission is not the brilliance of an individual in a single moment; it is the avoidance of preventable errors across hundreds of small moments. In most adult lives, the stakes are lower than a lunar mission, but the structure is similar. Careers, health, craft, and learning are not usually destroyed by one dramatic failure. They are eroded by small inconsistencies and preventable friction: the missed follow-up, the week without practice, the repeated decision to delay, the habit of only working when it feels satisfying. Reliable execution is the art of removing those preventable losses.

The metronome, again, keeps time. The question is what tempo is chosen. Too fast and the system collapses; too slow and nothing accumulates. The principles point towards a tempo that can survive: small enough to begin, easy enough to repeat, frequent enough to compound, structured enough to outlast mood, flexible enough to learn.

The forward test is deliberately unsentimental. When the next plan is made—whether for a project, a skill, a qualification, a sales target, a creative practice—will it be designed for the person one wishes to be, or for the person who will wake up on a tired Wednesday and still have to act?

Chapter 2
How Habits Really Work

At 07:18 on an ordinary weekday, a hand reaches for a phone before the mind has fully arrived. The screen lights the room with a cold, obedient glow. There is no ceremony, no decision spoken aloud. Thumb, glass, scroll. A small jolt of interest, then another. Minutes disappear without having been spent on anything that would stand up in court as a "choice". The body knows what to do. The mind catches up afterwards, often with a faint irritation that feels moral: *Why did I do that again?* It is a familiar scene because it is not a personal failing. It is a loop running as designed.

The strange thing about habits is that they are both intimate and impersonal. They feel like "me"—my cravings, my comforts, my quirks—yet they behave more like mechanisms than like personality. They run with the blunt efficiency of a kettle switching on: cue, routine, reward. That is their genius and their danger. They save effort. They also steal agency in tiny, cumulative amounts. The point of understanding habits is not to become puritanical about behaviour. It is to stop treating repeated actions as mysteries of character when they are often patterns of wiring.

A great deal of human misery comes from arguing with mechanisms as though they were morals.

The previous chapter established a quiet truth: repetition builds outcomes. This chapter goes closer to the machinery. If repetition is the engine, habit is the gearbox. It determines what power reaches the wheels when the road is rough, when the driver is tired, when distractions multiply. People who imagine discipline as a permanent state of willpower are like drivers who think they can coast uphill forever. The question is not whether willpower exists. The question is what happens when it predictably fades—late afternoons, stressful weeks, lonely evenings, overfull calendars. Habits answer that question. They decide what happens next when nobody is feeling heroic.

Begin with something deliberately small, because habits are built from smallness. Tea is a good example precisely because it does not feel dramatic. Someone walks into the kitchen. The kettle is there. A mug waits in the same place it always waits. The hand reaches, the switch clicks, water begins its rising hiss. Perhaps the person adds milk without thinking, or chooses the same brand because it is familiar. The action sequence is so rehearsed that the mind can wander elsewhere. This is the ordinary miracle of automation: the brain offloads routine behaviour so it can spend attention on other problems. Habits are not primarily about self-control. They are a labour-saving device.

The labour saved is real. So is the cost.

The modern environment, however, is engineered to exploit this labour-saving tendency. Notifications, snack packaging, algorithmic feeds, commuter patterns, workplace norms—all of them provide cues that invite routines. A cue is not only a sound; it can be a time of day, a location, a feeling, a social situation, a visual trigger on a desk. The routine is the behaviour that follows. The reward is whatever the brain learns to expect: relief, stimulation, social connection, the sense of completion, the numbness of distraction. None of this requires moral language. It requires observation.

That observation matters because the consistent life is not built by grand decisions but by repeated defaults. The person who steadily writes, studies, practises, trains, prospects, or shows up for relationships is often not more virtuous than anyone else. They are simply living inside loops that support the behaviour. The loops do not guarantee perfection. They do make action more likely. Once habits are understood as loops, change becomes less theatrical. One does not need to win an internal argument every day. One needs to reshape a mechanism.

Environment is the first and most underestimated lever. People speak of "self-discipline" as though the self were sealed in a jar. In reality, the self is porous. The shape of a room influences what a person does in it. A bed beside a phone encourages late-night scrolling; a phone outside the bedroom changes the probability of sleep. A desk associated with study becomes a cue; a sofa associated with mindless entertainment becomes a cue. Gym clothes laid out by the bed are not motivational theatre; they are a physical prompt that reduces start-up friction. A notebook left open to the next blank page is not an aesthetic gesture; it is a cue that makes writing the path of least resistance.

Even time functions as environment. Many people have predictable energy patterns: a sharper morning, a foggier afternoon, a restless late evening. Habits that align with these patterns feel "natural". Habits that fight them require more willpower. The point is not to become enslaved to one's rhythms. It is to notice that a habit loop often begins not with an inspirational thought but with a predictable context. Change the context and the loop changes.

Social context is the most powerful environment because it supplies cues and rewards simultaneously. A colleague who always offers biscuits at the same time each day is creating a cue. A friend who expects a weekly run is creating a cue and a reward: the reward is connection, the mild pressure of being expected, the shared story afterwards. Teams, too, have habits: meetings that begin late, emails that go unanswered, procrastination that is tacitly accepted, or routines of follow-up that make a group unusually effective. Culture is a set of shared loops. It shapes what feels normal.

Emotion is the other hidden driver. Many people picture habits as rational routines—brush teeth, make bed, study, exercise—as if the brain were a tidy administrator. The brain is not tidy. It learns through feeling. Reward, in the habit sense, is not always pleasure; it is often relief. Checking a phone can relieve boredom or anxiety. Snacking can relieve stress. Avoiding a difficult task can relieve dread. The problem is that relief rewards avoidance, and the brain learns quickly. Negative emotion, repeated, can wire in a pattern of escape. This is why habits often have a strange emotional logic: the behaviour that makes life worse in the long term can feel better in the short term because it soothes something immediate.

This is where small celebrations and rituals matter—not as childish gimmicks, but as emotional signals to the brain. A tiny win paired with a tiny reward can make repetition more likely. The reward might be as small as marking a completion, or attaching a pleasant ritual to a hard task: a particular piece of music before writing, a specific tea after study, a brief walk after sending outreach. The point is not indulgence. The point is to teach the brain that the desired behaviour leads to something it values. The brain is a pattern detector, not a moral philosopher.

The fragile nature of willpower sits inside all of this like a truth nobody wants to admit. Willpower is useful. It can get a person through a moment of temptation, a difficult conversation, a day of fatigue. But it is a scarce resource because it is entangled with attention, sleep, stress, and decision load. When a person has made hundreds of small decisions already—emails, meetings, family logistics, social cues—the capacity to resist an easy routine tends to drop. This is not a personal insult. It is a predictable feature of human cognition. Willpower works best as a bridge, not a foundation: it can help install a habit loop, but it is a poor strategy for running a life indefinitely.

This matters now for a simple reason: the average person's day contains more cues, more micro-rewards, and more decision friction than almost any day in human history. That is not melodrama; it is an observation about digital life and contemporary work. The phone provides thousands of cues. The workplace provides constant switching. Social networks supply endless metrics of comparison. Under such conditions, asking a person to "just be disciplined" is like asking them to navigate a city without street signs. They need a map of the mechanisms. Habits provide the map.

The chapter's deeper promise is not self-control. It is emotional relief. When people understand habit loops, they stop interpreting every lapse as evidence of moral weakness. They begin to see the pattern: cue, routine, reward. They begin to ask different questions. What is the cue? What need is the routine serving? What reward is being collected? What would happen if the routine changed but the reward stayed? What would happen if the cue were redesigned? The tone shifts from self-attack to investigation. Investigation is not soft. It is precise. It is the beginning of agency.

Agency does not mean constant vigilance. It means designing defaults.

There is also a philosophical element worth naming. Many people have been taught to treat the mind as a sovereign ruler, issuing commands to the body and expecting compliance. Habits reveal a different picture: the mind is more like a parliament with many factions, some ancient and impatient, some calm and strategic. The "decision" to check a phone or procrastinate is often a coalition of fatigue, boredom, and learned reward, with the rational self arriving late to the vote. Understanding this is not an excuse. It is a diagnosis. Once diagnosed, one can build systems that reduce the number of moments in which the impatient factions win by default.

The motifs of the book return here in a new form. In the previous chapter, reliability was described as a metronome: a steady beat that produces results without requiring drama. Habits are the internal metronome settings. They determine what beats exist in the day at all. If the cue for study is vague—"sometime after dinner"—the metronome slips. If the cue is concrete—"after the kettle clicks, sit at the desk and open the notes"—the beat becomes easier to keep. If the reward for study is only distant—future success, future exams—the brain may not feel it. If there is a small immediate reward—completion marked, a brief pleasant ritual—the brain begins to cooperate. The day becomes less a battlefield and more a sequence.

This chapter will move through the habit loop in its most practical form, using examples so ordinary they are almost insulting: phones, tea, desks, commutes, the moment when a person sits down to work and reaches for anything except the work. From there it widens into environment, not as interior design, but as behavioural architecture. It examines how objects and spaces cue routines, how time and social context act as triggers, and why small changes to surroundings often outperform grand promises. It then moves into the emotional chemistry of reward and memory—why tiny celebrations matter, why avoidance becomes sticky, and how to attach a better emotional signal to a hard behaviour without pretending the behaviour will always be fun. Finally, it addresses willpower with respect and scepticism: what it can do, when it fails, and why treating it as the main engine of discipline is a recipe for fatigue.

The payoff is subtle but substantial. A person who understands habits begins to see their own behaviour with less shame and more clarity. They can locate the moments where repetition is being quietly sabotaged—not by lack of ambition, but by cues that pull them elsewhere and rewards that teach the wrong lessons. They can stop demanding that their best self show up daily and instead build loops that produce decent behaviour even when the self feels mediocre. That is reliability. That is how consistency becomes possible for people who do not wish to live like monks or machines.

The chapter ends, not with a slogan, but with a question that haunts every attempt at change. When a behaviour repeats, what is it really doing for you: providing a reward you can name, or simply providing an escape you have never examined? The answer determines whether the next rep serves the life you want, or merely repeats the life you already have.

Habit Loops in Practice

In the winter of 1903, inside the Imperial Institute of Experimental Medicine in St Petersburg, Ivan Pavlov watched dogs begin to behave as though the future were audible. A door creaked, a tray shifted, a footstep approached, and saliva arrived before food did. The lab was all enamel and order: glassware, clipped notes, the faint metallic smell of instruments warmed by hands. Pavlov's gift was not sentiment but method. He measured what most people moralise. He treated anticipation as a physical event with a repeatable trigger, and by doing so he made a strange claim testable: much of what looks like "choice" is often a learned response to a cue. The bell meant food was coming.

That bell is still with us, though it rarely rings. It buzzes. It lights up. It sits in a pocket. It takes the form of a kettle's click, a calendar alert, a colleague's tone, a particular chair, a familiar corridor, the moment the work becomes difficult and the hand drifts towards a screen. These are not grand dramas. They are small signals. The brain notices them anyway.

The temptation is to make all this about virtue. People call themselves undisciplined, weak, addicted, easily distracted. They tell stories about character because stories are what humans do when they cannot see the machinery. But habit is machinery. The moral vocabulary obscures it. Once the mechanism is visible, shame becomes a poor tool—too blunt, too inaccurate, too expensive.

A habit loop is simple in outline and slippery in real life. It begins with a cue: something that reliably precedes the behaviour. The cue can be external (a sound, a place, an object) or internal (a feeling, a thought, a bodily state). It is followed by a routine: the behaviour itself, often quick and often automatic. Then comes a reward: the brain's pay-off signal, which might be pleasure, relief, stimulation, social connection, or the satisfaction of completion. The loop exists because it saves effort. A brain that had to decide everything from scratch would be paralysed. Automation is efficiency, and efficiency is adaptive.

Show it, plainly. A person walks into a kitchen and switches on the kettle. They do not run a committee meeting inside their head about whether boiling water is a good idea. The hand goes where it always goes. The sound of the switch is oddly comforting. The kettle begins its rising hiss, and the mind drifts elsewhere. A few minutes later, the click. Tea happens. The cue may be the time of day, the entry into the kitchen, the sight of the mug. The routine is the sequence of boiling, pouring, stirring. The reward is not only the taste; it is the small sense of order restored, the warmth, the tiny pause that divides one part of the day from another. The implication is that the habit is not merely about tea. It is about a predictable transition.

Now show a modern loop that carries more sting. A hand reaches for a phone. The cue may be boredom at a traffic light, the discomfort of an awkward pause, the micro-anxiety of an unread email, or the first friction of beginning work. The routine is the same thumb-on-glass choreography: unlock, scroll, refresh. The reward is often not pleasure in any rich sense but *relief*—relief from uncertainty, from effort, from the feeling of being unoccupied. Relief is a powerful teacher. The implication is sobering: the phone habit is not primarily about information. It is about emotion management delivered through a fast, repeatable sequence.

The "save effort" logic is why habits are not moral successes or failures. They are solutions the brain has adopted, sometimes excellent, sometimes disastrous, often both depending on context. A habit that saves effort in one arena can steal effort in another. The tea ritual can be a gentle anchor. The scrolling loop can amputate attention in five-minute slices. But both run for the same reason: the brain has learned that a certain cue predicts a reward, and it prefers not to deliberate if it does not have to.

Name what changes when a loop forms. The shift is from decision to default.

Explain it without mythology. When a behaviour becomes a default, the brain reduces the cognitive cost of starting it. The action feels more "natural" not because it is virtuous but because it is rehearsed. This is why people so often describe habits as if they were personality. "I'm just the sort of person who…" is frequently a retrospective explanation for "I have rehearsed this loop a thousand times." The implication matters for consistency: if a desired behaviour can be made default, it becomes less vulnerable to mood, fatigue, and the ordinary chaos of life.

The evidence for this is not confined to Pavlov's dogs and anecdotal introspection. In 2002, researchers including Wendy Wood studied habit as it appears in everyday life, showing that much routine behaviour is cued by context rather than by conscious intention (Wood, Quinn & Kashy, 2002). The details of any single paper are less important than the general pattern it describes: context stability predicts habit strength. Put more simply, people do what their environments and repeated situations have trained them to do. The implication is not that humans are robots. It is that a large portion of daily behaviour is outsourced to learned context-response patterns, and that is precisely why small environmental cues carry such power.

Context, here, does not mean only physical surroundings. It includes time, social setting, and internal state. The same person who has no urge to snack in a meeting may snack automatically when they sit on a particular sofa at 21:30. The cue is not hunger. It is a location married to a time, reinforced by repetition. The routine—snacking—

has been linked to that cue. The reward might be comfort, distraction, a ritual punctuation to the day. The abstraction "self-control" is too vague to be useful here. The visible behaviour—where the person sits, what time it is, what is on the table—contains the real causal chain.

If habit loops are so mechanical, why do they feel so personal? Because the brain recruits narrative after the fact. A person checks their phone, then tells themselves they "needed" to, or that it was a break, or that they were waiting for something important. Sometimes those reasons are true. Often they are post-hoc rationalisations—stories layered over a loop to preserve the sense of agency. The loop itself is not offended by the story. It keeps running.

The moment one begins to watch loops in real time, the atmosphere changes. A person notices the cue before the routine completes. That is a small shift, but it is a structural one. It is the difference between being dragged and being aware of being dragged. Awareness does not instantly stop the behaviour. It does something more valuable: it gives the person a lever. Without the lever, the only strategy is force: "Don't do it." Force is exhausting. A lever allows redesign.

A practical way to see the loop is to track the first few seconds. The cue is often a tiny sensation of discomfort. The work becomes hard; the mind wants escape. That discomfort is the cue. The routine is the reach, the check, the scroll. The reward is the softening of discomfort. The implication is that the habit is not about the screen. It is about not feeling what the work makes you feel. This also explains why people can switch the object of the habit—phone, email, snack, conversation—without changing the underlying loop. The cue and the reward stay the same; the routine changes costume.

This is also why moralising habit is counterproductive. Shame adds discomfort. Discomfort strengthens the cue. The loop tightens. People then declare themselves hopeless and seek more dramatic solutions, which typically fail because they never addressed the cue-reward structure. The "mechanical" perspective is not cold. It is merciful. It says: the loop is doing something for you, even if it is doing it badly. Identify what it is doing, and you have a chance to replace the routine without waging war on yourself.

A second named example, from a very different domain, shows the same logic. In manufacturing, Taiichi Ohno's work at Toyota in the 1950s emphasised making small problems visible and correcting them repeatedly, rather than relying on heroic bursts of effort (Womack, Jones & Roos, 1990). The analogy is not superficial. A factory that relies on heroism is fragile. A person who relies on heroism for daily discipline is fragile. In both cases, reliability comes from designing repeatable sequences that require less improvisation and generate fast feedback. The implication is that habit loops can be treated as processes: identify the trigger, observe the routine, examine the reward, adjust one element, repeat.

Now introduce a limitation that deserves respect. Not all repeated behaviour is a habit in the strict sense. Some actions remain deliberately chosen because they occur in variable contexts or carry high stakes. A surgeon does not "habitually" improvise on a patient; they execute protocols with conscious attention. A researcher confronting a novel problem cannot outsource the work to automaticity; novelty requires deliberation. Even in everyday life, sudden changes in context—travel, a new job, an illness, a move to a different city—can disrupt cues and weaken loops. The implication is important: habit does not explain everything. Humans remain capable of reflective choice, especially when conditions change or when the stakes are made explicit.

Reconcile that limitation with the central claim. Habits do not abolish agency; they shape its workload. When a person automates the right routines, they free attention for problems that genuinely require thought. When the wrong routines dominate, they spend agency on constant repair. Reliable execution depends on protecting agency by reducing the number of daily decisions that have to be won through willpower. Habit is the tool for that reduction.

This is why the cue matters more than people expect. Many assume the battle is in the routine: "I need to stop doing the thing." But routines are sticky because they reliably deliver rewards. The more efficient move is to examine cues and rewards. A person who always scrolls after opening their laptop might discover that the cue is a few seconds of uncertainty about what to do first. The reward is clarity—any clarity, even trivial. The routine is the scroll. The behavioural metric here is visible: how many times per day does the person begin the work session with a detour? How long does the detour last? What precedes it? Once measured, the pattern becomes less mystical. It becomes a process with inputs and outputs.

The tea example can be used for this kind of diagnosis without defensiveness. The cue might be the kettle's click. The routine is making tea. The reward might be warmth and a pause. If someone wanted to change that pattern—perhaps to reduce caffeine or to reclaim time—they would need to understand what the tea is *doing* beyond taste. Is it marking a transition? Is it providing comfort? Is it creating a socially acceptable break? Replace the tea without replacing the reward, and the loop will likely reassert itself with a different routine. Replace the reward with something equally satisfying—warmth, pause, transition—and the loop becomes easier to reshape. This is not a guarantee. It is a better map.

A habit loop can also be assessed by its "risk profile", to borrow a term from earlier arguments about reliability. High-risk loops are those that scale easily and invisibly: they can consume hours without feeling like hours. Phone checking is high-risk because the reward arrives quickly and the routine is easy to repeat. Low-risk loops are those with natural limits: making tea takes time and ends when the mug is empty. The implication is not moral hierarchy but strategic awareness. Some loops require more careful design because their cost is harder to notice in the moment.

The motif of the kettle's click returns here as a reminder that cues are often banal. People search for dramatic triggers—childhood trauma, deep personality flaws—when the cue is sometimes simply a sound, a place, a time, a feeling of friction. The click is not destiny. It is data. Once cues are treated as data, change becomes less emotional and more experimental. That shift is the intellectual heartbeat of this chapter: to replace self-judgement with pattern recognition, because pattern recognition makes consistency possible.

The forward test is therefore not about motivation. It is about observation. When the next automatic reach begins—towards the phone, the snack, the avoidance, the familiar detour—can you identify the cue before the routine completes, and can you name the reward you are actually collecting? The answer determines whether the loop remains an invisible engineer of your days, or becomes a mechanism you can finally redesign.

Environment and Triggers

In 1994 at Geneva University Hospitals in Switzerland, Didier Pittet began a hospital-wide hand-hygiene campaign that treated infection control not as a matter of lecturing clinicians into virtue, but as a matter of redesigning what was within reach at the moment care was delivered. Alcohol-based hand rub was placed where hands already went; reminders and feedback made the behaviour visible. The clinical stakes were not abstract. Intensive care wards do not forgive polite intentions. When Pittet and colleagues later reported the programme's results in *The Lancet* (Pittet et al., 2000), the striking feature was not merely that compliance improved, but that the improvement was made plausible by changing the environment in which staff acted under pressure. A hospital is an extreme setting, yet it exposes a rule that governs ordinary life as well: when attention is scarce, proximity and cues win.

The room decides for you.

That sentence sounds insulting until one watches what the room does. A phone placed face-up on a desk is not just an object; it is a trigger waiting to happen, a small rectangle that can turn any sliver of boredom into a routine. A pair of gym clothes folded by the bed is not just fabric; it is a prompt that shortens the distance between waking and movement. A particular chair, a particular mug, a particular corridor in an office—these are not merely background. They are thresholds. Cross the threshold, and the body begins to run an old script.

Environment is often miscast as décor, when it is better understood as behavioural infrastructure. People like to believe they act from intentions. They do, sometimes. Yet much of life is executed from cues: objects, times, places, and social settings that repeatedly precede certain actions. When the cue appears, the routine becomes the path of least resistance. The cue does not have to be dramatic. It can be a notification ping, the sight of a biscuit tin, the end of a meeting, the moment the kettle clicks, the slump of 15:40, the awkward pause after sending a difficult email. The brain's preference is efficiency: if a sequence has worked before, it tries it again. That is not a moral failure. It is a design constraint.

Show how this plays out in the smallest possible theatre. A person sits down to study at a desk that also hosts their entertainment: games, streaming tabs, social feeds, messages. The cue is not "study"; the cue is "sit here". The routines available from that cue are many, and the fastest rewards belong to distraction. Compare that to the person who uses a particular desk only for study and nothing else. Over time, the desk itself becomes a trigger. The moment they sit, the mind begins to orient towards work because the environment has been trained to mean one thing. Name the concept without fuss: cue control. Explain it: the same intention placed in two different environments produces different behaviour because cues steer attention and lower the cost of starting one routine rather than another. The implication is practical and slightly unsettling: "discipline" often looks like a person who lives among better triggers.

The research literature supports this commonsense observation with an unromantic clarity. Habits, as psychologists have argued for decades, are frequently cued by stable contexts rather than by conscious goals; when contexts repeat, the brain learns to respond automatically (Wood & Neal, 2007; Wood & Rünger, 2016). This is why people can sincerely decide to change and still find themselves repeating the old behaviour in the old setting. The cue is doing its work beneath the level of self-image. The trigger arrives, and the routine follows before the mind has time to narrate what is happening.

Objects are the most literal triggers because they occupy space and attract the eyes. A bowl of fruit on a counter is a cue; so is a jar of sweets. A book left open on a table is a cue; so is a television remote within arm's reach. A notebook beside a laptop can cue writing; a second screen with notifications can cue task-switching. These cues are not magical. They are simply present, and presence matters more than intention when a person is tired. In this sense, "willpower" is often a story told after the fact. A person who does the desired behaviour has frequently removed a physical obstacle or placed a physical prompt. A person who fails has often placed the wrong prompt in the most visible location.

Time is a trigger in a different way because it is not seen but felt. Certain hours arrive with predictable states: the alertness of early morning for some, the mental grit of late evening for others, the post-lunch dip that turns ambitious plans into a negotiation. People tend to treat these rhythms as personality—"I'm a morning person"—when they can be treated as recurring contexts. The same person who writes fluently at 07:00 may procrastinate at 22:30, not because their values change, but because their cognitive resources have. This is why a recurring time can become a cue: not only because it is on the clock, but because it carries a bodily state that the brain associates with certain routines. The implication is quietly strategic: when a behaviour is anchored to a time that reliably includes low energy, it will demand more self-control than the same behaviour anchored to a time that reliably includes adequate energy.

Place, too, carries its own weight. In 1975, psychologists Duncan Godden and Alan Baddeley conducted a now-famous study of context-dependent memory with scuba divers in Scotland, showing that recall improved when learning and retrieval occurred in the same environment—underwater or on land (Godden & Baddeley, 1975). The experiment is often summarised as a curiosity about memory, but its deeper relevance is broader: environments do not merely host behaviour, they shape what comes to mind within them. A library cues quiet focus; a café cues social awareness; a bedroom cues sleep or scrolling depending on what has been rehearsed there. When a place is repeatedly paired with a routine, the place begins to call the routine forward, like a scent that drags a memory out of hiding. The implication is not that people are prisoners of location. It is that location is a trigger that can be trained, for good or ill.

Social context is the most complex trigger because it contains both cues and rewards. A team that begins meetings on time cues punctuality and respect for the schedule; a team that drifts into meetings late cues slackness, even if nobody says it aloud. A friend who always offers a drink after work cues a routine; the reward is belonging. In these cases, "environment" is not a room but an expectation. Humans are exquisitely sensitive to the behaviour that is normalised around them, and this sensitivity is not only conscious. It sits in micro-signals: laughter, eye contact, shared rituals, mild disapproval. Social triggers can be powerful enough to override private intentions because social rewards are ancient and strong.

The most famous modern demonstrations of social cues often come from public policy rather than self-improvement folklore. The UK's Behavioural Insights Team, established in 2010 and active in large-scale trials by 2011, showed that small changes to communications—such as telling late taxpayers that "most people in your area pay their tax on time"—could increase payment rates (Behavioural Insights Team, 2012). The striking element is not the wording itself; it is what the wording does. It provides a cue about what is normal. It turns compliance into a social identity rather than a private chore. The implication is not that people are sheep. It is that norms are triggers, and triggers steer behaviour when attention is thin.

At this point, a moralist might object: surely this reduces human agency to furniture arrangement and peer pressure. That objection is healthy. It is also incomplete. Environment is influential, not omnipotent. There are moments when values, commitments, or acute consequences override cues. People can resist a trigger. People can also choose environments—moving cities, changing friend groups, leaving a job—precisely because they recognise that surroundings shape behaviour. The credible limitation is this: environment works best when contexts are stable. When contexts change abruptly, triggers weaken. Travel breaks routines. A new job dissolves old cues. A new baby makes time-based triggers chaotic. In such seasons, relying solely on environment can fail because the environment itself is in flux.

Reconcile the limitation without retreating into motivational slogans. The honest view is that stable environments *amplify* consistency, and unstable environments *test* it. When cues disappear, the brain does not automatically know what to do next. The implication is diagnostic: if a behaviour collapses whenever context changes, the behaviour was likely heavily context-cued. That is not a condemnation; it is information. It suggests that a person's "discipline" was partly the product of a particular setting. In a stable season, that may be enough. In an unstable season, additional scaffolding becomes necessary—portable cues, simpler routines, clearer starting steps—so that repetition can survive without its usual environmental props.

This is why triggers should be treated as a design language rather than a motivational accessory. A trigger is not only something that nudges behaviour; it is something that reduces the need to remember. Remembering is expensive. It requires attention, and attention is already being taxed by work, social life, and the constant ping of modern stimuli. A well-designed trigger substitutes for memory by placing the beginning of a routine directly in the line of sight, or by attaching it to something that already happens. The difference between "I must remember to study" and "When I sit at this desk, I open the notes" is the difference between a fragile intention and a repeatable loop.

Notice, too, how triggers alter risk. Earlier chapters treated risk as something that can be measured: missed deadlines, inconsistency in outreach, lapses in practice. Triggers change the probability distribution of those outcomes. A person with clear, stable cues is less exposed to high-variance behaviour. They do not need a perfect day to do the work; they need a familiar cue. This is one reason consistent people can appear calm: their systems create fewer moments of existential choice. The cue arrives; the routine begins. The metronome keeps time.

The motif of thresholds is useful here because triggers are often thresholds in disguise. A doorway between kitchen and desk. The moment the kettle clicks. The act of placing a notebook on a chair the night before. The moment a meeting ends and a colleague turns to chat. These thresholds are where the day's direction is quietly decided. They are also where small environmental changes can have outsized effects, because a threshold is a bottleneck: tiny steering inputs produce large route changes downstream.

This is not a call to micromanage life. It is a call to see what is already micromanaging it. Environments are never neutral. They are always cueing something. If the cues are left to chance, chance becomes the author of daily behaviour. If cues are deliberately shaped, behaviour becomes easier to predict, and predictability is the substrate of consistency.

The forward test, then, is not whether one can summon more motivation. It is whether one can identify the thresholds that reliably precede the behaviours that matter, and then ask a blunt question that refuses self-deception: are the cues in those thresholds aligned with the person you mean to be, or with the person your environment has quietly trained you to remain?

Emotion, Reward and Memory

In September 1953 at McGill University in Montreal, Brenda Milner began working with a patient known in the literature as H.M., whose severe amnesia became one of the most consequential windows into how memory actually functions. The clinical details are often retold for their drama, but the behavioural facts are the useful part. H.M. could not form new declarative memories in the ordinary way—he could not reliably remember events or facts from day to day—yet he could still improve at certain tasks with practice, showing learning without conscious recollection (Milner, 1962). The mind, it turned out, keeps more than one kind of ledger. And one of those ledgers is heavily influenced by feeling and reward, not by narrative self-understanding.

Emotion writes the ledger.

That is not metaphor so much as mechanism. Memory is not an impartial archive. The brain is a prediction machine with limited storage, and it prioritises what seems useful for future behaviour. "Useful" is often tagged by emotion. Pleasant outcomes and relief are marked as worth repeating. Pain, embarrassment, dread, and boredom can be marked as worth avoiding. The result is that many habits are less about values than about reinforcement: the brain learns what to approach and what to flee. If disciplined behaviour repeatedly feels punishing, it becomes associated with threat. If disciplined behaviour repeatedly feels satisfying, even in small ways, it becomes associated with return. This is why consistency is not merely a matter of planning; it is also a matter of emotional bookkeeping.

Show it in a room with no diagnosis and no drama. A person sits down to write after a day of meetings. The first sentence comes slowly. The mind produces a familiar critique: "This is rubbish." The chest tightens. The person feels a small flush of incompetence. The hand drifts towards the phone. The cue is not the phone itself; it is the discomfort. The routine is escape. The reward is relief. The implication is blunt: the brain has just been taught that writing equals discomfort and avoidance equals relief. Repeat that sequence enough times, and "writer's block" becomes less a mysterious creative condition and more a learned avoidance loop.

Name what is happening. Negative reinforcement.

Explain it without jargon. When a behaviour stops something unpleasant, the stopping itself becomes rewarding. The person does not scroll because scrolling is wonderful. They scroll because it removes the feeling of being stuck, judged, or overwhelmed. Relief is an efficient reward. The implication is that many of the behaviours people resent in themselves are not really "bad habits" in the moral sense; they are coping routines that have been trained by repeated emotional relief. Moral disgust does not break that loop. It often strengthens it by adding more discomfort for the routine to relieve.

Now consider the opposite: small celebrations. To a sophisticated mind, celebration can sound childish, like a sticker chart. Yet the brain is not persuaded by sophistication. It is persuaded by experience. A tiny win followed by a tiny positive marker teaches the brain, "This action leads somewhere good." The marker does not have to be applause. It can be a private signal: a tick on a record, a brief moment of satisfaction, a ritual that feels pleasant. The point is not vanity. The point is reinforcement.

Make it concrete. A student completes a short retrieval session—pulling key ideas from memory rather than re-reading—and marks it immediately. The mark is visible: a line in a log, a small note, a completed box. The emotional effect is subtle but real: completion has been registered. The brain likes closure. If the student then returns to other tasks without acknowledging the rep, the rep may evaporate into the general fog of the day. If they register it, the rep becomes a memory that carries a small reward. Over time, that reward can become part of the loop. The implication is that tiny celebrations are less about motivation and more about memory: they increase the chance that the brain will file the behaviour as worth repeating.

This is not mere folk psychology. Dopamine, often simplistically called the "pleasure chemical", is more accurately linked with reward prediction and learning: it signals that something important has occurred, especially when outcomes are better than expected, helping to strengthen future behaviour. A classic account of dopamine's role in reinforcement learning and prediction error comes from work by Wolfram Schultz and colleagues (Schultz, Dayan & Montague, 1997). The relevance here is not biochemistry trivia. It is the behavioural implication: when a small reward follows a behaviour, the brain becomes more likely to repeat the behaviour in similar contexts. If the reward is immediate and clear, the loop strengthens faster.

Immediate matters. The brain learns from proximity.

This is why many disciplined actions struggle to become habits. Their rewards are often delayed. Writing today may not yield publication for months. Studying today may not yield exam results for weeks. Training today may not yield visible change for a long time. Outreach today may not yield a meeting until next week. Meanwhile the rewards for distraction are instant: a new message, a funny clip, a snack, a hit of novelty. The competition is asymmetrical. A person who relies solely on distant rewards is fighting a learning system that prefers quick feedback.

This is where ritual enters as a practical bridge. A ritual is not superstition. It is a deliberately placed immediate reward that can be attached to a behaviour whose "true" reward arrives later. Show it in a realistic scene. A researcher has to read dense papers each morning. The work is valuable but not immediately pleasant. They create a ritual: the same good coffee, the same quiet corner, the same opening act—perhaps underlining one key sentence and writing a single-sentence summary in the margin before continuing. The coffee is not a bribe. It is a cue and a reward. The corner is a cue. The first summary sentence is an early completion signal. Together they alter the emotional profile of beginning. The work still requires effort. The start stops feeling like punishment. The implication is that rituals can change what the brain associates with the behaviour: not dread, but a predictable sequence that contains small comforts and small wins.

At this point, it is tempting to overstate the role of positive emotion, as if life could be engineered into constant pleasantness. That would be dishonest. Some tasks remain difficult, boring, or uncomfortable even with rituals. There are also people for whom celebration feels artificial or irritating, and in some cultures overt self-reward can feel self-indulgent. This is a credible limitation. Emotional design must respect temperament and context. A forced celebration can create a new discomfort, which becomes a cue for avoidance.

Reconcile the limitation. The principle is not "make everything fun". The principle is "make the learning signal clear". A reward need not be exuberant. It can be quiet. It can be *relief in the right direction*: the relief of having begun, the relief of having finished a small unit, the relief of having kept a promise. A person does not have to clap for themselves. They can simply acknowledge the rep as complete. The behavioural metric here is visible: whether the rep is recorded, whether it is closed, whether it is allowed to count. What counts gets repeated.

Negative emotion, too, has to be treated with realism. Sometimes discomfort is simply the cost of growth. The brain can learn to tolerate discomfort when it is predictable and bounded. What turns discomfort into avoidance is often not the discomfort itself but the sense that it is endless, aimless, or identity-threatening. If each writing session begins with "prove you're good", the emotional stakes become unbearable. If the session begins with "produce one rough paragraph", the stakes drop. The discomfort becomes manageable. The implication is that emotional memory can be shaped not only by reward but by *reducing threat*: shrinking tasks, clarifying the next step, limiting perfectionist standards that turn practice into a trial.

Here the earlier motif of the kettle click becomes a useful unifier. When the kettle clicks, the brain expects tea. That expectation is a reward prediction. If tea reliably follows, the loop strengthens. If the kettle clicks and chaos follows—no tea bags, no mugs, a spill, scolding—the kettle click might become a cue for irritation rather than comfort. Humans are trained in the same way. If the cue "sit at desk to study" reliably produces confusion, shame, and failure, the desk itself becomes a trigger for avoidance. If the cue reliably produces a small win and a registered completion, the desk becomes a trigger for starting. The environment provides the cue; emotion decides what memory will be attached to it.

A second named example grounds this in a domain that professionals respect because it is measured. In 2006, psychologists Henry Roediger and Jeffrey Karpicke published work showing that retrieval practice improves long-term retention compared with repeated studying (Roediger & Karpicke, 2006). The connection to emotion is indirect but crucial. Retrieval practice can feel harder and less fluent than re-reading, which misleads students into avoiding it. The unpleasant feeling is not evidence that it is ineffective; it is evidence that the brain is being asked to work. If the student interprets that feeling as failure, they will avoid the technique that works best. If the student learns to pair retrieval practice with a small immediate reward—a clear record of completion, a brief ritual afterwards—they are more likely to repeat the practice despite its discomfort. The implication is that emotion can either sabotage learning or support it, depending on what it is allowed to mean.

This brings us back to memory. Memory is not only an archive of facts; it is also a catalogue of tendencies. The brain stores, often outside awareness, whether a behaviour "pays". When it pays quickly, it becomes sticky. When it pays slowly and feels punishing, it becomes fragile. Small rewards act like interest on a delayed-return investment: they keep the behaviour financially viable in the brain's accounting system until the larger returns arrive.

There is also a subtle social dimension. Praise from others, even mild, can serve as reward, but it is unreliable. It arrives on someone else's schedule and can distort the behaviour towards performative outputs rather than meaningful reps. Private rewards—self-recorded completion, a ritual that does not require an audience—are more stable. They make the loop less dependent on external validation. In the long run, this stability is a form of risk reduction. A person who requires applause to repeat a habit is vulnerable to silence. A person who can register their own completion is less so.

None of this should be mistaken for medical or therapeutic instruction. It is an educational lens: how reinforcement shapes repetition. The practical consequence is that when a person wants consistency, they must take emotion seriously, not as a tyrant but as a signal. If the behaviour repeatedly produces dread, the loop will resist. If the behaviour produces a small sense of completion and a small reward, the loop will cooperate. The work is not to eliminate feeling. The work is to stop letting feeling write the ledger by accident.

The forward test is a simple diagnostic question that does not flatter the ego. After the next rep—writing, studying, practising, outreach—what emotional marker will the brain record: *pain relieved by escape*, or *effort rewarded by completion*? The answer determines whether the loop strengthens in the direction you want, or continues to train you, quietly and faithfully, to avoid the very work you claim to value.

Why Willpower Is Fragile

In October 1998 at Case Western Reserve University in Cleveland, psychologist Roy Baumeister and his colleagues ran a now-famous experiment that looked almost comically domestic: participants sat in a room with warm chocolate cookies and radishes. Some were instructed to eat the cookies; others had to resist them and eat only radishes. Afterwards, everyone attempted a difficult task and the radish group gave up sooner (Baumeister et al., 1998). The scene is easy to picture—the smell of chocolate hanging in the air, the faint bitterness of raw radish, the small humiliation of being watched while you resist. The conclusion was not that radishes are tragic. It was that self-control seems to draw on a limited resource that can be depleted by prior acts of restraint.

Willpower runs out.

That sentence has been treated as gospel and as nonsense, sometimes in the same conversation. The right stance is neither worship nor dismissal. Willpower exists. It also behaves badly under realistic conditions. It is a short-term tool with a long-term reputation. People rely on it because it feels like agency: a heroic "no" spoken into temptation, a noble refusal to procrastinate, a decisive moment in which the self takes command. Those moments are real. They are also expensive. A life designed around repeating expensive moments will eventually bankrupt itself.

The idea of "ego depletion" has been debated intensely in psychology, with later replication attempts producing mixed results and a broader reconsideration of how to model self-control (for overviews and discussion, see Inzlicht & Schmeichel, 2012; Hagger et al., 2016). The debate matters because it reminds us of something that the self-help market often forgets: humans are complex, and single metaphors can mislead. Yet the everyday observation remains stubbornly true, regardless of which theoretical model one prefers. Self control is not equally available at all times. It is altered by sleep, stress, cognitive load, and emotion. A person who plans to "just be disciplined" after a day of high-stakes decisions is planning to perform surgery with trembling hands.

Show it in a real day rather than a laboratory. A professional begins the morning with decent intentions. They respond to messages, make judgement calls, negotiate priorities, deal with a colleague's frustration, hold a difficult boundary with a client, then sit through a meeting where everyone wants an answer. Each decision is small, but each extracts a cost: attention, restraint, emotional regulation. By late afternoon, the person is not morally weaker. They are simply taxed. When they finally face the choice that matters to them—write, study, practise, prospect—they discover that the mind behaves like a tired committee. The easiest motion wins: checking the phone, snacking, drifting into low-friction tasks that feel productive without demanding anything. The cue is fatigue. The routine is default behaviour. The reward is relief. The implication is that willpower is not failing; it is being used as if it were infinite.

Decision overload is the name people give to this experience, and it is a useful phrase if it stays attached to visible behaviour. What does overload look like? It looks like slower email replies. It looks like avoiding complex work. It looks like deferring choices. It looks like seeking immediate reward. It looks like the quiet irrationality of a tired brain that chooses a trivial task because it can be finished quickly and therefore produces a small hit of completion. In professional life, these behaviours are misread as laziness or lack of ambition. More often they are a signal that the person has built a day that consumes too much self-control before the important work begins.

Stress amplifies the problem. Under stress, attention narrows. The brain prioritises immediate threats and immediate rewards. That is not a modern pathology; it is an ancient pattern. The stressed person is more likely to choose what soothes quickly and less likely to choose what pays later. This is why so many discipline plans fail precisely when they are most needed. People attempt to use willpower to counteract stress at the very moment stress is eroding the conditions required for willpower to work well. The implication is not despair. It is design: the plan must assume stress will happen and must not require extraordinary self-control to survive it.

Sleep, similarly, is not a lifestyle decoration. It is a cognitive resource. Researchers have shown that sleep loss impairs attention, decision-making, and emotional regulation, all of which shape self-control (for a review, see Killgore, 2010). The details of mechanisms—prefrontal control, reward sensitivity, attentional lapses—can be left to the journals. The behavioural consequence is simple and measurable. When people sleep badly, they reach for the easiest routines more often. They make more impulsive choices. They start fewer difficult tasks. They are also more likely to interpret their diminished control as a character flaw, which adds shame, which adds stress, which further diminishes control. The loop is vicious and entirely predictable.

This is why the book insists on systems over moods. It is not anti-willpower. It is anti-dependence. Willpower is valuable at the beginning of change, when a new behaviour has not yet been made easier by cues, routines, and rewards. It is valuable in emergencies, when something must be resisted or initiated despite poor conditions. It is valuable as a bridge. But bridges are not houses. Building a life on constant willpower is like deciding to commute by sprinting: possible for a few days, humiliating soon after, and eventually impossible.

Show what happens when people mistake willpower for a strategy. They set rules that require repeated heroic choices. "I will never check my phone during work." "I will study for two hours every night." "I will exercise intensely six days a week." These rules create drama because they create repeated moments of high-stakes restraint. The environment is unchanged. The cues remain. The rewards of old routines remain immediate. The new routine has delayed benefits and high starting costs. The person uses willpower to force compliance for a short time, then inevitably misses a day, and then the system collapses because it had no slack. The implication is that failure is built into the design. It is not an accident. It is an engineering issue disguised as a moral struggle.

A second named example from outside psychology helps here because it shows how high-stakes systems treat human fallibility. In aviation, checklists are not a luxury. They are an acknowledgement that attention and memory fail under stress, even among highly trained pilots. The modern cockpit checklist culture is associated with developments in the twentieth century, including responses to early aircraft accidents that revealed the limits of relying on memory and improvisation. The Boeing Model 299 crash in 1935 near Wright Field, Ohio, is frequently cited in aviation history as a catalyst for the widespread adoption of checklists, after the aircraft was deemed "too much airplane for one man to fly" without procedural support (accounts appear in multiple aviation histories and are easy to verify in broad outline). The implication is not that the pilot lacked willpower. The implication is that complex systems must be designed for predictable human limitations. No one expects a pilot to will themselves into perfect recall under pressure. They build procedures that reduce reliance on the fragile parts of the mind.

Treat daily discipline with the same respect for reality and the same refusal to moralise. If a behaviour matters, it should not depend on a daily duel between intention and temptation. It should depend on default pathways, reduced friction, and cues that make the desired action more likely than the undesired one. This is why friction audits matter: they identify the concrete barriers that force a person to spend willpower just to begin. This is why minimum viable habits matter: they shrink the action so that starting requires less negotiation. This is why streak shields matter: they preserve continuity when conditions deteriorate, rather than demanding perfection and collapsing at the first disruption.

There is, however, a credible counterpoint that deserves to be taken seriously. Some researchers argue that willpower is not a finite "fuel" in a simple sense and that beliefs about willpower can influence performance—if people think willpower is limited, they may conserve it; if they think it is not, they may persist longer. Work by Veronika Job, Carol Dweck, and Gregory Walton (2010) suggested that implicit theories about willpower can shape self-control outcomes. The implication is that the story one tells oneself about willpower can matter, and that framing willpower as fragile could, in some cases, become a self-fulfilling excuse.

Reconcile the counterpoint without losing the plot. The purpose of calling willpower fragile is not to excuse inconsistency. It is to stop designing systems that require heroism. Even if willpower is partially shaped by belief, it is still shaped by sleep, stress, attention, and context—variables that remain stubbornly influential in real life. A person may be able to persist longer by adopting a different belief. They will still perform worse when exhausted, overwhelmed, and surrounded by cues for distraction. The practical stance is therefore: respect willpower, but do not build your life on it. Use it to install better defaults. Use it to cross short bridges. Then let systems carry the weight.

This reframing also changes how self-control failures are interpreted. Instead of asking, "Why am I weak?", the more useful question becomes, "What conditions made the desired action expensive?" Conditions can be measured. How many high-stakes decisions happened before the planned work? How many interruptions occurred? Was the environment cueing distraction? Was the next step unclear? Was the reward for the desired task delayed and invisible? Did the person end the last attempt with frustration, teaching the brain to avoid the routine? Each of these questions points towards a design adjustment rather than a character verdict.

Notice how this shifts the emotional tone. Shame is heavy. Design is lighter. Design treats failure as data. Data can be acted upon. This is why willpower-based discipline so often feels exhausting: it turns every lapse into a referendum on the self. Systems-based discipline turns lapses into signals about friction, cues, and recovery mechanisms. The person does not become indulgent. They become precise.

Precision matters most for people who are already capable. Many professionals, researchers, and students are not failing because they lack ambition. They are failing because they have placed their most important work at the end of days that consume their cognitive resources. They have built environments rich with triggers for distraction and poor in triggers for focus. They have linked disciplined work with negative emotion by demanding perfection in early drafts or by treating practice as a test of worth. They have then tried to solve the resulting mess with more willpower. That is like trying to fix a leaky roof by shouting at the rain.

The motif worth threading through this piece is the bridge. Willpower is a bridge. It gets you from one bank to another: from old defaults to new ones, from impulse to pause, from avoidance to beginning. Bridges are essential. They are also finite spans. A person who tries to live on the bridge will become weary. A person who uses the bridge to reach solid ground—habits shaped by cues, routines, and rewards—can stop fighting the same battle every day.

The forward test is therefore not a moral vow. It is a design choice disguised as a question. When the next period of stress arrives, when sleep is poor, when the calendar becomes crowded and attention fragments, will the plan depend on a heroic act of willpower at exactly the wrong time, or will it depend on a structure that makes the next right rep almost embarrassingly easy to begin?

Chapter 3
Designing Minimum Viable Habits

At 06:02, the alarm goes off and a familiar negotiation begins. The mind offers a deal: *start on Monday*. The body, heavy with sleep, prefers the simplest solution, which is to do nothing and call it rest. Somewhere between those two voices sits the real problem of discipline: not ambition, not intelligence, not even effort, but the moment of beginning when the cost feels disproportionate to the reward. Most people do not fail because they lack a plan. They fail because the plan asks for a version of them that only exists in bright, imaginary mornings.

The smallest actions escape that negotiation. They slip past the bouncers.

There is something quietly radical about doing less than you feel you "should". It offends pride. It offends the part of a conscientious person that equates seriousness with difficulty. Yet smallness has a property intensity does not: it is repeatable under mediocre conditions. A one-minute stretch can happen on a day that would never tolerate a full workout. One sentence can be written on a day when the mind feels like wet wool. One sales call can be made on a day when confidence is low and the inbox is snarling. These are not substitutes for deeper work; they are entrances into it. The great lie of self-improvement is that the entrance must be grand.

The previous chapters have already tightened the screws: repetition wins because it keeps happening; habits run as loops and are sculpted by cues, rewards, and environments; willpower is useful but unreliable, especially when life becomes crowded. Chapter 3 takes that logic and turns it into a design discipline. The unit of work becomes the central question. Not the dream outcome. Not the heroic schedule. The unit. What is the smallest version of a behaviour that still counts, still trains identity, still keeps the ledger moving in the right direction?

The phrase "minimum viable habit" sounds like something borrowed from product development, and in a sense it is. It treats behaviour change as an experiment rather than a confession. A minimum viable habit is the smallest honest action that preserves continuity. It is the lowest bar that can be crossed even on days when the self is unremarkable. This is not an argument for mediocrity. It is an argument against fragility. A habit that requires a perfect day is not a habit. It is an occasional performance.

People resist this for a reason that deserves respect: they suspect smallness cannot matter. They fear they will cheat themselves, that a tiny rep is a lie disguised as discipline. The fear is understandable. It is also often based on a misunderstanding of what habits actually do. The primary function of a habit, especially in the early stage, is not to generate a large outcome. It is to make the behaviour normal and to make starting cheap. The first purpose is identity. The second is mechanics. Once the behaviour is normal and starting is cheap, scale becomes possible. Without normalisation, scale becomes brittle and collapses into guilt.

This chapter therefore asks the reader to trade a kind of ego-pleasure for a kind of freedom. The ego-pleasure is the satisfaction of setting a bold standard and feeling serious. The freedom is the ability to keep moving when life is not impressed by your standards. Seriousness is not what changes outcomes. Repeatability does. The most effective people are not those who promise the most; they are those who keep their promises to themselves in small ways so consistently that the self stops arguing.

Minimum viable habits also force clarity. Many people claim to want to "get healthier", "be more productive", "improve at sales", "study better", "write more". These are not behaviours; they are aspirations. A minimum viable habit cannot hide behind aspiration. It must name a visible action: stretch for one minute, write one sentence, review yesterday's notes for five minutes, send one outreach message, read one page, practise one scale, do one set, open the textbook and answer one question. The action is small enough to be hard to excuse away, which is precisely why it is powerful. It exposes where resistance really lives.

Then comes the more strategic question: which small action is worth repeating? This is where high leverage matters. Busywork is seductive because it feels like motion without risk. Organising notes, colour-coding calendars, reading about improvement, tinkering with tools—these can become elaborate avoidance routines that generate the pleasant sensation of being responsible. High leverage actions are less soothing. They touch the work itself. In sales, it is contact and follow-up rather than endlessly rewriting a pitch deck. In study, it is retrieval and review rather than passive highlighting. In craft, it is deliberate practice rather than endless consumption of other people's output. In health, it is regular movement and simple routines rather than occasional punishment sessions.

A minimum viable habit is therefore not merely small. It must be *meaningful.*

This is why the chapter will place emphasis on choosing keystone behaviours that move outcomes. A single daily sales call can, over months, change a pipeline more than any number of motivational podcasts. Ten lines of code written daily can, over a year, create a portfolio that hiring managers can actually assess. One page of reading can, over time, rebuild the identity of someone who learns. Five minutes of review can rescue a student from the false comfort of familiarity by forcing recall. These are modest actions. They are also actions that touch the core of the domain rather than the ornamental edges.

To make this concrete, the chapter will introduce short sketches: a professional who wants to become consistent in outreach but keeps waiting for "big prospecting days" that rarely arrive; a student who keeps planning revision schedules but avoids the unpleasantness of testing themselves; a creative who dreams of writing a book but treats writing as something that should happen only when it feels profound; a busy parent who wants strength but cannot afford a routine that collapses whenever a child is ill. In each sketch, the question is the same: what smallest rep could be executed almost regardless of circumstances, and what would that rep do over time? The answer will not be dramatic. It will be workable.

There is also a psychological elegance to minimum viable habits that is easy to miss. When the bar is small, failure becomes rarer. When failure becomes rarer, shame recedes. When shame recedes, the brain becomes less likely to avoid the behaviour. This is not a therapeutic claim; it is simple behavioural logic. People avoid what makes them feel bad. If the habit design repeatedly produces a feeling of missing the mark, it trains avoidance. If the design produces frequent completion, it trains approach. Completion is not the same as success, but it is the necessary condition for repetition. Repetition is the necessary condition for improvement. Improvement is the thing people were chasing all along.

Of course there is a danger here, and it must be faced early. Small habits can become comfortable. A person can hide inside minimums and call it a system. They can keep their identity intact—"I'm consistent"—without ever increasing challenge. This is a real risk, particularly for intelligent people who can rationalise elegantly. The chapter therefore treats minimum viable habits as a floor, not a ceiling. The floor exists to protect continuity. Once continuity is stable, the question becomes how to expand without breaking the system. Expansion is not a burst of ambition. It is a gentle increase in load that preserves repeatability.

This is the art of shrinking steps safely and expanding them wisely. It requires a kind of humility that the culture rarely teaches: the willingness to begin embarrassingly small, and the willingness to judge progress by what can be repeated rather than by what sounds impressive. The same humility can later support growth: not by leaping to intensity, but by adding one small increment at a time. A micro-workout can become a routine. A sentence can become a paragraph. A five-minute review can become a study session. A single sales call can become a daily block. The growth is real, but it is earned by protecting the beat.

The chapter's modern relevance is obvious to anyone living under digital distraction and time pressure. Many people now operate in a state of constant partial attention. They have less uninterrupted time than they imagine, and more micro-friction than they notice. Grand habit plans collapse in this environment because they require long, pristine stretches of focus. Minimum viable habits respect the fragmented reality. They allow progress in small pockets. They stop waiting for the mythical day when life becomes calm. They make use of the real day: the five minutes before a meeting, the short pause after dinner, the quiet moment before sleep, the first minute after waking.

There is also something quietly ethical about this approach. It refuses the cruelty of perfectionism. It refuses the false hierarchy in which only intense effort counts. It creates a discipline that can coexist with health, relationships, and unpredictable responsibilities. It does not demand that life become smaller so that habits can be bigger. It asks habits to fit inside life so that life can become richer.

A motif worth carrying through the chapter is the doorway. The minimum viable habit is not the room; it is the doorway. It is the act of crossing from intention into action with the least possible friction. Many people stand outside the room of their own ambitions, rehearsing, planning, waiting for the feeling that would make entry graceful. The minimum viable habit is an ungainly step over the threshold. It is not elegant. It is effective.

By the end of this chapter's opening movement, the reader should feel a shift in what seems respectable. It should begin to feel more respectable to write one sentence every day than to write a thousand words once a fortnight. More respectable to do one small movement rep daily than to punish the body occasionally. More respectable to make one contact daily than to depend on the rush of sporadic effort. Respectable, here, does not mean socially praised. It means likely to work.

The page turns with a certain tension. Lowering the bar can feel like losing. It can also be the first intelligent move in a long campaign. The forward question that hangs over everything that follows is simple enough to be inconvenient: if the goal is not to look disciplined but to *be* consistent, what is the smallest action you are willing to count as a real rep—today, on a day that is not special?

Minimum Viable Habits Defined

In January 2009 in Bahrain, Kenya's Samuel Wanjiru attacked the World Marathon Majors circuit with a style that looked like raw fire, yet his Olympic title the previous summer in Beijing had not been built from heroic race-day feeling. It had been built from training logs: repeated runs, repeated drills, repeated early mornings that would never be televised. The race is what people remember. The log is what produced it. This pattern—visible outcome built on invisible repetition—is familiar in sport because sport keeps receipts. It is just as true in craft, study, and professional work, where the receipts are quieter and easier to ignore. The question, for most people, is not whether the log matters. It is how to keep a log when life refuses to cooperate.

Small is the entry.

A minimum viable habit is the smallest version of a behaviour that still counts as a rep. "Counts" is the operative word, because it forces honesty. A minimum viable habit is not wishful thinking dressed as progress; it is a deliberately tiny unit of action that preserves continuity. It is the rep you can do on a bad day without needing to negotiate with yourself for an hour. It is the behaviour you can execute when your calendar is crowded, your sleep is poor, your mood is sour, and your environment is unhelpful. It is not the behaviour that will transform you in one go. It is the behaviour that keeps you in motion long enough for transformation to occur.

Show the difference in a scene that does not flatter anyone. A person wants to write consistently. They set a goal of an hour a day. The first week is fine, because novelty supplies energy and the ego enjoys the story of becoming disciplined. In week two, a late meeting and a tired evening break the chain. The person misses a day. They now face an ugly psychological tax: returning to the habit feels like admitting they are not who they claimed to be. They wait for the next "proper" day. That day does not arrive. Two weeks later, the person says they have "fallen off". The failure was not a lack of desire. It was a unit too large to survive ordinary disruption.

Name what went wrong. The habit was designed for an ideal week.

Explain it. Large units require large blocks of uninterrupted time, high energy, and high tolerance for imperfect output. They also create a steep "start-up cost": the moment of beginning feels heavy because it commits you to a long period of effort. When start-up cost is high, the brain will look for escape, especially under stress. The implication is grimly practical: the bigger the unit, the more likely the habit becomes an occasional performance rather than a consistent behaviour.

Now show the alternative. The person defines the habit as *one sentence*. Not a good sentence. Not a paragraph. One sentence placed on a page. The action is almost insulting in its modesty. It also has a crucial property: it can be completed quickly, and therefore it has a low start-up cost. The person can do it even when tired. The rep remains. The identity remains: "I am someone who writes daily." The implication is that minimum viable habits preserve the most important asset in behaviour change—continuity—without requiring heroism.

This is why starting tiny bypasses resistance. Resistance is not always laziness. It is often self-protection. A large commitment carries risk: risk of failure, risk of discovering you are not as good as you hoped, risk of wasted effort, risk of discomfort. The brain treats these risks as threats. It produces avoidance. A tiny commitment carries less perceived threat. There is little to lose. The threat signal drops. Action becomes easier. The behavioural mechanism fits what we already know about habits: stable cues, small routines, immediate completion signals strengthen repetition (Wood & Neal, 2007; Wood & Rünger, 2016). A minimum viable habit is not a motivational trick; it is a way to create stable repetition in the presence of normal human threat responses.

"Counts" also means that the habit must be observable. It must show up in the ledger. Many people claim a habit without a measurable rep. "I thought about writing." "I planned my workout." "I read an article about sales." These are not reps. They may be preparatory or reflective acts, but they do not train the target behaviour. A minimum viable habit insists on a visible unit: one sentence written, one minute of stretching, one page read, one outreach message sent, one practice problem answered. The unit can be small, but it must be real. The implication is clarifying: the mind can no longer substitute intention for action.

The immediate objection arrives quickly, especially among intelligent, time-conscious people: surely this is just lowering the bar. Surely it is a way to feel good without doing the work. The objection deserves to be taken seriously because it protects against self-deception. Yet it confuses two different bars. There is the bar of *outcome*, which should remain high if the person has ambition. Then there is the bar of *entry*, which must be low enough to make repetition reliable. Minimum viable habits lower the entry bar, not the outcome bar. They protect the route to the outcome by ensuring that movement continues.

The distinction becomes more obvious when we borrow a familiar idea from skill acquisition. Expertise is built through repeated engagement with feedback. Anders Ericsson's work on deliberate practice emphasised that improvement requires structured effort and correction over time (Ericsson, Krampe & Tesch-Römer, 1993). A person who never practises cannot benefit from correction. A person who practises sporadically receives too little feedback to learn reliably. Minimum viable habits increase the frequency of engagement, which increases opportunities for feedback, which increases learning. The aim is not to stay tiny forever. The aim is to make practice frequent enough that improvement becomes inevitable.

Identity change is the second mechanism and, in many ways, the more profound. People do not only do habits; they become the kind of person who does them. This is not mystical identity work. It is behavioural evidence accumulating in the mind: "I did the thing again." The smallest rep can carry disproportionate identity weight because it is a vote cast in the direction of a self-concept. One sentence is not much text, but it is proof of writing. One minute of stretching is not much exercise, but it is proof of movement. The proof is what matters when motivation is thin. The implication is that minimum viable habits allow identity change without the trauma of constant failure. They build confidence by record, not by pep talk.

This is where the phrase "strategic move" earns its place. Lowering the bar is strategic when it increases the probability of repetition. A person who insists on high-intensity behaviour as the only behaviour that counts is choosing a fragile strategy, because it depends on rare conditions. A person who accepts a smaller unit is choosing a robust strategy, because it can operate under common conditions. The strategy is not about laziness. It is about risk management. It reduces the risk of complete collapse.

Collapse is costly. It is not only the missed days. It is the psychological residue: shame, self-distrust, the sense that you cannot rely on yourself. Minimum viable habits are designed to reduce that residue by reducing the probability of a full break. They keep the chain alive. They keep the metronome beating. They prevent the habit from becoming a referendum on your character.

The motif of the doorway is useful here, because minimum viable habits are doorways. They are not the room of deep work, mastery, or fitness. They are the threshold that allows you to enter more often. Many people stand outside the room, rehearsing, waiting for the right mood or the right uninterrupted block of time. The doorway is crossed quickly. Once inside, something interesting happens: starting often creates momentum. A person who writes one sentence sometimes writes more. A person who stretches for one minute sometimes continues. This is not guaranteed and should not be relied upon as the main mechanism. But it is common enough to matter. The minimum viable habit gets you through the door. The room may keep you longer.

A second checkable example, from a different angle, illuminates why "tiny" is not trivial. In 1960, psychologist Edwin Locke began publishing work that would later develop into goal-setting theory, emphasising that specific, challenging goals can improve performance (Locke, 1968). The popular misuse of this literature is to assume that harder goals always work better. The more careful reading is that goals influence behaviour when they are both clear and accepted, and when feedback is available. A minimum viable habit does not reject ambitious goals; it creates an accepted, clear, and repeatable behavioural unit that generates feedback daily. It is, in effect, a micro-goal with high acceptance and low resistance. The implication is that tiny units can serve large ambitions by keeping behaviour in motion and feedback flowing.

Now acknowledge a credible limitation. Not every domain respects tiny reps in the same way. Some tasks have fixed minimums: you cannot meaningfully practise a complex surgical procedure for one minute, or draft a legal brief in a single sentence, or run a chemistry experiment in thirty seconds. The unit of work has constraints. The minimum viable habit must therefore be defined at the level of what can be honestly completed and reviewed. For a surgeon, the minimum might be a short review of a protocol or a simulation step, not a token gesture. For a lawyer, it might be drafting one paragraph of an argument or reviewing one case citation. For a chemist, it might be preparing a reagent list or documenting an experimental plan. The reconciliation is simple: minimum viable does not mean absurdly small. It means the smallest *honest* unit that advances the behaviour and preserves continuity.

There is a second limitation: minimums can become hiding places. A person can cling to the minimum forever, using it as a shield against the discomfort of scaling. This is where the definition must remain sharp. Minimum viable habits are not meant to be the whole of one's effort; they are meant to be the minimum that prevents zero. They are an insurance policy against the days when zero would otherwise occur. Once the habit is stable, the person can add optional "more" without threatening the baseline. The minimum is the floor. The ceiling remains open.

This distinction also prevents a common misunderstanding. People think minimum viable habits are a trick for beginners. In practice, they are often most valuable for high performers because high performers are prone to all-or-nothing standards. They do not want to do a small rep because a small rep offends their self-image. Yet that self-image is precisely what makes them fragile: if "real" work requires perfect conditions, then life will win. Minimum viable habits are a disciplined person's humility practice. They force a trade between pride and consistency. Consistency is usually the better bet.

The educational angle is now clear. Habit formation is not a competition to see who can tolerate the most pain. It is a design task: choose a unit, make it repeatable, make it count, protect it against disruption. Minimum viable habits solve the most common failure mode in behaviour change: the gap between intention and initiation.

They shrink the gap until action can occur even when willpower is low.

The forward test that follows from the definition is slightly uncomfortable, because it refuses flattering fantasies. If the day is bad—late meetings, low sleep, strained attention—what is the smallest rep you are willing to count as real, not as a loophole, and will you still count it when nobody is watching?

Choosing High Leverage Actions

In October 2002 in Oakland, California, the Oakland Athletics won 103 games with one of Major League Baseball's lowest payrolls, turning a front-office philosophy into a season-long provocation. Billy Beane's organisation did not discover a secret training method or a new kind of athlete. It chose a different *lever*: it valued on-base percentage as a core signal, then recruited and managed accordingly, even when the aesthetic of the sport scoffed. The outcome is checkable in the standings; the deeper lesson is behavioural. When resources are constrained, choosing what to repeat matters more than how heroically one repeats it. A hundred disciplined reps spent on the wrong thing become a well-organised waste.

Find the fulcrum, then press.

Minimum viable habits solve the entry problem: they get the behaviour to happen at all. High leverage actions solve the direction problem: they ensure the behaviour, once repeated, actually moves the needle. Without leverage, consistency becomes a treadmill. People exhaust themselves being reliably busy while their real outcomes remain stubbornly unchanged. The modern workplace is particularly good at producing this kind of elegant futility—calendars full, inboxes emptying, status updates immaculate—while the work that truly matters sits untouched because it is uncomfortable, uncertain, or socially risky.

"High leverage" can sound like corporate jargon until it is tied to visible behaviours and measurable consequences. A high leverage action is a behaviour that, when repeated, produces outsized downstream effects: skills that unlock further skills, outputs that generate feedback, contacts that compound into relationships, routines that reduce variance. It is not always the hardest action. Often it is simply the most *causal* one. The key is that it changes the system rather than decorating it.

Show how people usually miss it. A thoughtful student wants better grades and spends an evening rewriting notes into neat summaries, colour-coding headings, feeling industrious. A salesperson wants more deals and spends an afternoon perfecting a slide deck rather than contacting anyone new. A writer wants a body of work and rearranges their workspace, buys a notebook, reads about craft. A professional wants better health and buys equipment, downloads apps, and thinks about their ideal routine. These activities are not evil. They are busywork when they substitute for the action that creates learning and feedback. Busywork feels safe because it avoids exposure. Core work exposes you to reality: ignorance, rejection, awkward drafts, physical discomfort, the sharp edge of not being good yet.

Name the mechanism. Busywork is a low-risk routine with a fast emotional reward.

Explain it. The brain prefers quick closure and low threat. Organising and planning create a pleasant sense of control. They also often delay the very actions that would produce real change. The implication is not to ban preparation; it is to see preparation for what it is: a support act. If the support act becomes the main show, progress stalls while the person remains convinced they are "working hard".

High leverage actions are the opposite: they tend to feel slightly uncomfortable precisely because they touch the real constraints of the domain. In study, leverage often lives in retrieval—pulling knowledge from memory and discovering what cannot be recalled—rather than in re-reading, which can create familiarity without competence. In a classic demonstration, Henry Roediger and Jeffrey Karpicke (2006) showed that retrieval practice can improve long-term retention compared with additional studying. The behavioural implication is sharp: if a student makes a minimum viable habit of answering a small number of questions from memory, that tiny habit can produce more learning than longer sessions of comfortable review. Leverage here is not time. Leverage is the type of effort and the quality of feedback.

In craft, leverage often lives in deliberate practice: targeted repetition of specific sub-skills with feedback, rather than mere time spent "doing the thing". Anders Ericsson and colleagues (1993) argued that expert performance is strongly related to structured practice designed for improvement, not just experience. The phrase has been popularised and distorted, but the core remains useful. A musician repeating a difficult bar slowly, correcting errors, is using leverage. A programmer building the same kind of toy project repeatedly without stretching is not. A writer revising weak paragraphs with a specific aim—clarity, rhythm, argument structure—is using leverage. The implication is that the smallest habit that counts should not only be small; it should be a *good bet.*

In sales, leverage lives in contact and follow-up, because those actions generate the only data that matters: how real people respond. Everything else is theatre until it meets a customer. A minimum viable habit of one outreach message per day can look laughably small, yet it touches the causal chain. It produces rejection, questions, objections, interest, silence—each of which is information. Information is leverage because it allows adjustment. A perfect pitch with no prospects is a closed system. Outreach turns it into an open one.

In health-related domains, leverage is often misunderstood because people chase dramatic effort rather than reliable signals. The high leverage behaviour is frequently the one that reduces variance—making movement normal, establishing a predictable sleep window, creating routines that prevent long gaps—rather than the one that generates the most pain per minute. This is educational rather than prescriptive: the point is that bodies adapt to repeated signals. A small, repeatable signal tends to beat a rare, punishing signal because it produces a steadier training effect and a steadier identity: "I move." Identity is a lever; it changes what feels normal.

A useful way to choose high leverage actions is to ask a brutally practical question: which behaviour produces feedback fastest with the least room for self-deception? In study, retrieval exposes ignorance immediately. In craft, producing output exposes weaknesses immediately. In sales, outreach exposes market reality immediately. In health-related behaviour, consistency exposes patterns immediately—whether movement is truly happening, whether it is stable across weeks, whether it survives disruption. The metric need not be elaborate. It should be hard to manipulate. "Minutes spent writing" is harder to fake than "thinking about writing". "Number of prospects contacted" is harder to fake than "updating a CRM field". "Questions answered from memory" is harder to fake than "time spent highlighting".

This is where the motif from the opening returns: the fulcrum. The wrong behaviour is like pushing directly on a heavy door; you can strain and still fail. The right behaviour is like finding the handle and applying steady pressure. High leverage is not glamour. It is mechanics. The shameful secret is that many people love strain because strain feels like virtue. Leverage feels almost indecent because it looks too easy. That is why it works.

Short sketches make this real without turning it into a sermon. A doctoral student has limited time and a mind trained to seek intellectual comfort. They love reading. They feel virtuous when they read. Yet their bottleneck is not reading; it is producing clear arguments that can survive critique. The high leverage habit is not "read more papers". It is "draft one claim and one supporting reason each day", because drafting forces clarity and creates material for feedback from supervisors. The visible behaviour shifts: fewer tabs, more paragraphs. The risk is social—showing imperfect work. The payoff is competence.

A mid-career professional wants to move into a more technical role. They buy courses, watch lectures, collect bookmarks. Months pass. They can talk *about* the subject but cannot build anything that runs. The high leverage habit is "write ten lines of code daily that actually execute", because running code provides immediate, unflattering feedback. The behaviour produces error messages, which are a form of instruction. The metric is plain: lines that run, not hours consumed. The person stops feeling "busy learning" and starts accumulating solved problems.

A salesperson wants consistency but keeps waiting for the right mood. They polish scripts. They reorganise their contacts. They read about persuasion. Their pipeline remains thin. The high leverage habit is "make one real contact attempt daily", because the attempt is the causal action. The rejection is not failure; it is data. Over weeks, they learn which messages get replies and which sink. They discover that confidence is a by-product of activity, not a prerequisite. The metric is visible: contacts attempted, follow-ups completed.

A person who cares about health wants to regain basic fitness without turning life into a project. They have previously tried intense routines and then collapsed. The high leverage habit is not "destroy myself in the gym". It is "establish a tiny daily movement rep that survives bad weeks", because survivability is what changes the long-term curve. The metric is behavioural: days moved, not calories burned. The person is no longer performing health; they are building it.

These sketches share a common structure. The lever is chosen by identifying the bottleneck, then selecting the smallest repeatable action that directly attacks it. Bottlenecks are not the most dramatic problem; they are the constraint that limits progress. In study, the constraint is often retrieval. In craft, the constraint is often feedback on output. In sales, the constraint is often volume of contact and quality of follow-up. In health-related behaviour, the constraint is often continuity. The implication is that a minimum viable habit should be designed at the bottleneck, not at the edges.

Now introduce a credible limitation, because leverage can become a new form of self-deception. Some domains resist a single keystone action because the system is genuinely multi-causal. Sales performance can be constrained by product-market fit, territory, and timing; outreach alone may not rescue a flawed offering. Study performance can be constrained by foundational gaps so severe that retrieval practice feels like repeatedly failing; without scaffolding, the habit may become an avoidance trigger. Craft improvement can be constrained by lack of feedback; producing output in isolation can harden bad habits. Health-related consistency can be constrained by injury, disability, or life circumstances that make certain routines inappropriate or unsafe. The implication is that "high leverage" is not a magic key. It is a hypothesis.

Reconcile the limitation honestly. A high leverage action is not chosen once and worshipped. It is chosen, measured, and revised. If the lever does not move the system, it is either the wrong lever or it is being applied in a context where another constraint dominates. That is still useful information. The point of focusing on leverage is not to guarantee success. It is to avoid spending months on behaviours that cannot plausibly produce the outcome. When leverage is treated as an experiment, it becomes resilient. When treated as ideology, it becomes another trap.

A second named, checkable example from public policy illustrates why behaviour selection matters as much as effort. In 2012, the UK's Behavioural Insights Team reported results from trials showing that small changes to communications—such as social norm messages in letters—could measurably improve compliance behaviours like tax payment (Behavioural Insights Team, 2012). The lesson is not about letters. It is about choosing an intervention point with leverage: a moment where a small input produces a large behavioural shift. Many institutions waste effort by pushing in places with low leverage—grand campaigns, vague exhortations—when a small change at the right trigger point moves outcomes. Individuals do the same with habits: they grandly overhaul lifestyle rather than selecting a small action at the bottleneck.

This brings us back to minimum viable habits with sharper criteria. The minimum is not merely about size. It is about position. A tiny habit placed at the bottleneck compounds. A tiny habit placed in the decorative periphery stays decorative. That is why this chapter insists on distinguishing between the satisfying work of preparation and the sometimes awkward work of causation. The causal action is the one that makes the system respond.

The motif of the fulcrum has one more use. A lever is only as good as where it rests. If the fulcrum is placed on sand—an unstable environment, unclear triggers, no feedback—the lever slips. This is why high leverage actions must be paired with the earlier mechanics of habits: cues, environment design, small rewards, and protection against willpower fatigue. Leverage chooses the right direction. Habit design makes the direction repeatable. Together they produce what looks, from the outside, like effortless discipline.

The forward test is a trade-off disguised as a question. When the next habit is chosen, will you select the action that feels safest and most respectable in the short term, or the action that produces the fastest feedback and therefore carries the most leverage—even if it exposes you to a little discomfort?

Shrinking Steps Safely

In April 1997 at Deep Blue's match site in New York City, IBM's chess machine did something that looked, to spectators, like uncanny intelligence: it beat Garry Kasparov over six games. The headlines were about man versus machine, genius versus computation. The less theatrical truth was about decomposition. Deep Blue did not "understand" chess the way a human grandmaster understands it; it evaluated positions by breaking the game into countable possibilities and comparing them at speed, then selecting moves based on search and heuristics documented by the engineers and analysts who built it (contemporary reporting and IBM's published accounts are easily checked). The lesson for habit design is not to behave like a chess computer. It is to respect the power of breaking a complex task into small, executable steps that remove the need for heroic intuition at the moment of action.

Reduce the move. Then move.

Most people fail at consistency not because they chose the wrong goal, but because they chose a unit of action that was too large to execute reliably. They make "study" mean two hours and "exercise" mean an intense session, so the first step becomes a negotiation with fatigue, anxiety, and time. Shrinking steps safely is the craft of turning a chosen behaviour into a sequence of actions so small they feel almost embarrassing. Embarrassing is a useful indicator here. It signals that the ego is protesting: "This doesn't count." The ego's protest is not evidence of inefficacy. It is evidence that you have escaped the domain of performance and entered the domain of repeatability.

Show the familiar failure mode. A student plans to study every evening. They get home late, eat, and open a book. The material looks dense. Their mind protests: "This will take ages." The work feels like a cliff. They check messages for a moment, then for another. The evening evaporates. They feel guilty, so they plan an even bigger session tomorrow to compensate. Tomorrow arrives with the same cliff. This cycle is not laziness; it is a predictable response to high start-up cost. The first step is too large, so the brain avoids it.

Name the mechanism. Start-up cost.

Explain it. Start-up cost is the friction and perceived threat at the beginning of a task: uncertainty about where to begin, fear of not doing it well, discomfort with difficulty, and the time required to set up tools and attention. High start-up cost demands willpower. Willpower is fragile. The implication is mechanical: if the first step can be reduced, the task becomes more likely to start, and once started it becomes more likely to continue.

This is why the "five-minute study block" works when grand plans fail. Five minutes is small enough to be imaginable at 21:30. It is also small enough to be bounded. Boundaries matter because the brain treats open-ended effort as threat. A short session has a clear end. That reduces dread. Once dread drops, action becomes easier. The deeper point is not the duration itself; it is the shift in perception. "I must study for two hours" is a demand. "I will do five minutes" is a rep. Reps are easier to repeat.

A quiet piece of cognitive science sits behind this. People are poor at predicting how they will feel in the future and tend to overestimate the difficulty of starting unpleasant tasks. Behavioural economists and psychologists have written extensively about present bias and temporal discounting—the tendency to overweight immediate costs and undervalue distant benefits. This is why long sessions with delayed rewards provoke avoidance, whereas tiny sessions with immediate completion signals provoke less. The implication is that shrinking steps does not merely save time; it changes the brain's cost-benefit calculation.

Shrinking steps safely means decomposing the behaviour until the next action is concrete. "Study" is vague. "Open the notes and answer one question from memory" is concrete. "Exercise" is vague. "Put on trainers and do one set of a simple movement" is concrete. "Write" is vague. "Write one sentence that states the next claim" is concrete. Concrete steps reduce cognitive friction because they remove decision-making. Decision-making is expensive late in the day. This is why people feel "more disciplined" when their routines are explicit: they are spending less self-control choosing what to do and more energy doing it.

Show it with writing, because writing punishes vagueness. A person who intends to write a report sits down and thinks, "I need to write the introduction." The introduction is a cloudy, high-stakes object. The mind resists. If, instead, the person defines the first step as "write one ugly sentence that states the problem", the task becomes smaller and less threatening. Once that sentence exists, the next step becomes clearer: "add one reason the problem matters". The work becomes a chain of small actions rather than a single intimidating block. The implication is not that the report writes itself. It is that starting no longer requires a dramatic act of courage.

This is the first rule of shrinking: shrink the beginning, not the ambition.

Now address the fear that small steps cannot matter. This fear is rational at a certain level: a five-minute session does not cover much content, and a micro-workout does not look like serious training. Yet the fear mistakes visible effort for cumulative effect. Compounding does not care about whether a rep looks serious; it cares whether it repeats. Five minutes of retrieval practice repeated daily can accumulate into far more learning than sporadic long sessions, because retrieval strengthens memory and reveals gaps. The spacing and testing effects in learning research show that distributed practice and retrieval can improve long-term retention compared with cramming or passive review (Roediger & Karpicke, 2006). The implication is that small reps can matter more than large ones when they are the right kind and occur at the right frequency.

The same logic applies to micro-workouts, without slipping into health advice. Bodies adapt to repeated signals. When movement becomes normal, the person lowers the start-up cost of movement and becomes more likely to continue. The short session also teaches identity: "I move daily." That identity is not sentimental; it changes the probability of the next rep. Over months, probability becomes a trajectory. The issue is not that micro-workouts are secretly miraculous. The issue is that they keep the system alive. A system that stays alive can be scaled. A system that collapses cannot.

Here is where "safely" matters. Shrinking steps is not the same as shrinking standards. It is a method for preventing the most common failure: all-or-nothing collapse. "Safely" means the step is small enough to preserve consistency but large enough to remain honest. It must still touch the lever chosen in the previous section. A student who wants to improve by retrieval practice cannot shrink into merely looking at notes; that becomes busywork. A salesperson who wants to improve by outreach cannot shrink into merely reorganising contacts. The step must retain the causal behaviour. The implication is that shrinking is constrained by leverage: the smallest step must still be the right step.

This also clarifies when to shrink further. A useful diagnostic is behavioural, not emotional. If the habit is being skipped more often than it is completed, the step is too big for the current life conditions or too expensive in start-up cost. Shrink. If the habit is being completed reliably but with significant dread, shrink the start even more. Dread is a cue for avoidance. A smaller start reduces dread. If the habit is completed reliably and feels almost automatic, the system is stable. Stability is the precondition for gentle expansion.

Gentle expansion is the second half of the craft, and it is where many people sabotage themselves through impatience. They build a small habit, feel early momentum, then leap to intensity and break the system. A better approach treats expansion as adding weight to a bridge without collapsing it. Add a minute. Add a second question. Add a second sentence. Add a second set. Expand only when the baseline remains intact. The implication is that growth becomes a controlled process rather than a series of self-inflicted boom-and-bust cycles.

A named example outside self-improvement illustrates the logic of incremental expansion. The Toyota Production System, associated with Taiichi Ohno's work in the mid-twentieth century, emphasised continuous improvement through small, repeatable changes rather than occasional overhauls (Womack, Jones & Roos, 1990). The manufacturing analogy is not decorative. A factory that changes everything at once creates chaos and hides what caused improvement. A person who changes everything at once creates chaos and hides what caused failure. Small adjustments preserve learning. The implication is that shrinking and expanding are methods for keeping the feedback loop clean.

Now face a credible limitation. Some tasks have minimum effective doses that cannot be reduced without losing meaning. A laboratory procedure may require a fixed setup time. A complex legal analysis may require a sustained period of concentration. A musical performance may require longer rehearsals to be coherent. In such cases, shrinking the core action too far can become performative, a way to tick a box without doing the work. The reconciliation is to shrink *the gateway step* even when the full session has a minimum. If the full task requires an hour, the minimum viable habit might be "set up the workspace and begin the first five minutes," because beginning is the bottleneck. The full session may follow more often once the start is cheap. The step retains honesty because it initiates the real work rather than substituting for it.

There is another limitation that matters for thoughtful people: embarrassment can turn into contempt. Intelligent professionals sometimes sneer internally at small steps, seeing them as beneath their capabilities. That contempt is dangerous because it reintroduces the ego's need for drama. The point of shrinking is not to pretend you are incapable. It is to accept that consistency is easier when the start is trivial. A person can be capable and still be tired. Capability does not remove human constraints. The implication is a kind of maturity: doing small reps is not an admission of weakness; it is an admission of reality.

The motif worth threading through this piece is the chess move. When Kasparov faced Deep Blue, each move mattered because each move constrained the next. Habit design works the same way. The first step constrains the rest of the session. If the first step is vague and heavy, the next move is often avoidance. If the first step is concrete and small, the next move is available. Over time, the sequence becomes easier because each move reduces uncertainty. The day becomes less of a negotiation and more of a chain.

This is why shrinking steps safely is not a self-help trick. It is a discipline technology. It takes the work out of the realm of heroic intention and places it in the realm of executable design. It respects the earlier truth that willpower is fragile and that environments cue behaviour. A shrunken step reduces reliance on willpower and increases the chance that cues will lead to action rather than avoidance.

The forward test is therefore not whether you can do a big session. The question is whether you can identify the next smallest honest move—the move so small it feels silly—and then decide whether you are willing to let that move *count*, even when it does not satisfy the ego's appetite for grandeur.

Examples Across Life Areas

In March 2014 in San Francisco, a small company called GitHub watched an unglamorous behaviour become a cultural artefact: the commit. The green squares on a profile's contribution graph were not invented as a moral scoreboard, yet they became one—an ambient reminder that progress in software is often the sum of tiny, frequent submissions rather than heroic late-night rescues. The detail is checkable in the platform's history and design, but the more important point is behavioural. A commit can be small. It still counts. Once "counts" becomes visible, repetition becomes easier to sustain.

Small reps leave fingerprints.

This section's purpose is not to sell a lifestyle. It is to make the concept of minimum viable habits concrete across the domains people actually inhabit. The challenge is always the same: pick a unit so small it survives normal life, yet so honest it touches the work that matters. The unit is not the end state. It is the rep that keeps the ledger alive. That ledger can be physical, a log, or simply the accumulating evidence in the mind: "I did it again." Evidence is what changes identity. Identity is what makes repetition less negotiable.

Begin with craft, because craft punishes fantasy. Consider writing. "Write for an hour" is noble and brittle. "Write one sentence that makes a claim" is humble and survivable. The leverage is clear: a sentence is actual output, which can be revised, critiqued, expanded, and stitched into paragraphs. The reason this unit is chosen is not that one sentence is enough to produce a book. It is that one sentence is enough to preserve the identity of a writer and to reduce start-up cost to almost nothing. The action bypasses the perfectionist trap, because no one expects a single sentence to be finished art. Once the sentence exists, the next step becomes visible. Scaling later is also straightforward because the unit contains a built-in ramp: a sentence can become two, then a paragraph, then a short timed session. The rep remains the same type—produce text—while the quantity expands when reliability permits.

Move to coding, where the equivalent of a sentence is a small, running change. "Build an app" is an aspiration. "Write ten lines of code that run" is a rep. The "that run" matters because it anchors the behaviour to feedback. A person can type ten lines of nonsense and call it work. Running code is less easy to fake. The unit is chosen because it is small enough to do even on a demanding day and because it yields an immediate response from reality: the programme executes or it does not. That response is a form of instruction. The scaling path is natural: ten lines become a small function, then a small feature, then a larger block of work. The identity shift is subtle but powerful: from "I learn about programming" to "I write code daily." That shift is not motivational. It is evidential.

The same logic works in design and other creative crafts, though the output is less binary than code. A minimum viable habit for a designer might be "make one deliberate iteration on a single component": redraw an icon once, revise one layout with a specific constraint, rewrite one line of microcopy with a single aim such as clarity. The unit is chosen because it creates a finished, reviewable artefact. Reviewability is crucial. It invites feedback and makes learning visible. Scaling later can mean adding a second iteration, then an entire screen, then a weekly portfolio piece. The rep remains "make and revise", which is the heart of craft.

Now consider study, where the most seductive mistake is mistaking familiarity for knowledge. A minimum viable habit that respects learning science would be "answer one question from memory" or "recall three key points without looking". This unit is chosen because it triggers retrieval, not recognition. Retrieval is often uncomfortable and therefore avoided, yet it is linked with stronger long-term retention in research on the testing effect (Roediger & Karpicke, 2006). The unit's power is that it makes ignorance visible quickly. Visibility is a form of feedback. Scaling later might involve answering more questions, increasing spacing, adding brief review sessions, or integrating a short cycle of self-testing and correction. The rep remains "retrieve, then check", a loop that produces learning rather than the comforting illusion of learning.

A second study example fits the time-poor professional who is learning outside formal education. "Read one page" can sound insultingly small, yet reading one page consistently can rebuild the identity of someone who learns daily. The unit is chosen not because one page creates expertise, but because one page creates continuity. Continuity creates a relationship with a subject rather than a sporadic flirtation. Scaling later can occur by adding a page, adding a summary sentence, or by choosing a slightly denser text once the reading behaviour is stable. A page can also become a cue: the open book becomes a prompt that reduces the start-up cost of beginning again tomorrow.

Sales and outreach require a different kind of courage: social risk rather than cognitive effort. Here the minimum viable habit might be "one real contact attempt a day": one call, one personalised message, one follow-up sent to a specific person. The unit is chosen because it touches the causal chain. A salesperson can spend hours polishing messages, updating CRM notes, and reading about persuasion without ever generating the only data that matters—response. The contact attempt produces immediate feedback, even when the feedback is silence. Silence is still data. Scaling later can be gradual: one becomes two, then a small timed block, then a structured daily outreach session with a simple tracking metric such as attempts made and replies received. The rep remains "initiate contact", which is the work most people avoid because it exposes them to rejection and uncertainty.

In sales, there is also a high-leverage review habit that can be made minimum viable: "review one conversation and extract one objection and one response". This unit is chosen because it converts experience into learning. Many people repeat outreach without improving because they never mine their own interactions. A single review creates a small upgrade in message and approach. Scaling later might involve a weekly review block, a shared feedback loop with a colleague, or a simple library of objections and tested replies. The rep remains "learn from contact", which turns activity into competence.

Health-related habits must be handled with care, not because the body is fragile, but because the culture around health often collapses into punishment and fantasy. Minimum viable habits in this domain are best treated as educational examples of consistency design rather than prescriptions. A one-minute mobility sequence, a short walk to the end of the street, or a brief set of a simple movement can function as a rep because it preserves continuity. The unit is chosen because it is hard to argue with. A minute is small enough to fit into almost any day, yet it is still a signal: "I moved." That signal matters because bodies adapt to repeated signals and because identity follows evidence. Scaling later might include increasing duration, adding a second set, or introducing variety once the behaviour is reliable. The rep remains "move intentionally", not "punish myself". Punishment creates avoidance cues. Intentional movement creates approach cues.

Sleep and recovery can also be framed as minimum viable behaviours without giving health advice. The unit could be "begin a wind-down cue": dim lights, close a laptop, or perform a short end-of-day closure ritual that signals a shift. The reason such units matter is that they are triggers; they reduce reliance on willpower at the moment when willpower is weakest. Scaling later might involve extending the ritual or aligning it more consistently with time. The rep remains "signal the transition", which is an environmental cue for behaviour rather than a heroic act of restraint.

In professional work—especially knowledge work—minimum viable habits often live in the realm of start-up friction. A minimum viable habit for a person who struggles with procrastination might be "open the document and write the first line of the next section" or "define the next visible action in ten words". This unit is chosen because it collapses ambiguity. Ambiguity is a cue for avoidance. A named next action reduces threat and therefore reduces the impulse to escape into easier tasks. Scaling later can mean extending the session, adding a timer, or building a stable sequence. The rep remains "begin with clarity".

Across all these domains, the logic of selection is consistent. The unit must be small enough to survive fatigue, stress, and disruption. It must be concrete enough to measure. It must be close enough to the core work to generate feedback. It must be modest enough that the ego cannot demand a special day. These properties are why minimum viable habits differ from motivational slogans. They are engineered for the reality of human cognition: attention fluctuates, willpower depletes, emotion drives avoidance, and environment cues routine.

A credible limitation must be faced, because examples can mislead by simplicity. Not every domain allows absurdly small units. Some tasks have fixed setup costs. A laboratory experiment may require preparation that cannot be compressed into a minute. A legal brief may demand sustained concentration to be coherent. A musical rehearsal may need longer to be meaningful. The reconciliation is to choose minimum viable habits at the level of what can be honestly completed and reviewed. If the core task requires an hour, the minimum might be the first preparatory step that reduces start-up cost—setting up materials, outlining the next section, reviewing a protocol—so that beginning is guaranteed even when the full session cannot be completed. The rep is still real because it moves the causal chain forward.

There is another limitation, more psychological. Some people will try to turn the minimum into a hiding place. They will do the smallest possible thing forever and call it consistency. The minimum is not meant to be the whole story. It is meant to prevent zero. Scaling is the natural next question once the baseline is stable. The best minimum viable habits are designed with scaling in mind: they contain a natural "more" that can be added without changing the identity of the rep. A sentence can become a paragraph. A question can become a set. A contact attempt can become a block. A minute of movement can become a routine. The core remains intact.

The motif of fingerprints returns here for a reason. A rep that counts leaves evidence. Evidence builds trust—with oneself first, and then with others. A person who writes daily has drafts. A person who studies daily has recall records. A person who contacts prospects daily has a pipeline. A person who practises daily has technique that does not vanish under stress. These are not motivational claims; they are the ordinary consequences of repeated observable behaviour.

The forward test is now unavoidable, because a menu of examples is only useful if it forces a choice. When you decide what to do daily, will you choose a rep that flatters your self-image—grand, ambitious, impressive in theory—or will you choose a rep that leaves a fingerprint you can verify tomorrow, even if it feels almost too small to mention?

Chapter 4
Removing Friction from Behaviour

At 08:11, the decision has already been made, though nobody has said it out loud. The shoes are somewhere under the bed, the charger is missing, the notes are in the wrong bag, the document is not where it "should" be, the gym is across town, the script for the call is half-finished, the desk is a mess of cables and crumbs. A person stands in the doorway of their own intention and feels a familiar heaviness. They interpret the heaviness as laziness. They interpret the delay as weakness. Then they drift into something else—email, tidying, scrolling—because drifting requires no setup.

Friction is the invisible author.

The story people tell about discipline is usually psychological: motivation, grit, confidence, self-belief. Those words can be useful. They are also often a way of not looking at the obvious: the practical obstacles between wanting and doing. Most failures of consistency are not dramatic collapses of character. They are small mechanical failures: the missing item, the unclear next step, the awkward transition, the decision you have to make again because it was never made properly the first time. These failures accumulate until the action becomes expensive. When action is expensive, avoidance looks rational.

The earlier chapters have tightened the logic. Consistency wins because it repeats. Habits run in loops, cued by environment and reward. Willpower helps, but it is fragile under stress and decision load. Minimum viable habits solve the entry problem by shrinking the unit until starting becomes cheap. Chapter 4 does something slightly different: it targets the cost of starting itself. It treats resistance as a signal that the system contains unnecessary drag. If minimum viable habits are the doorway, friction removal is what stops the doorway from sticking.

Friction is not only physical. It is mental. It is social. It is logistical. It is the accumulated "little too hard" that turns a good intention into a deferred one. A person might be fully committed to studying, yet their study materials are scattered across devices and logins; each session begins with a hunt, and the hunt becomes the cue for procrastination. A person might be fully committed to writing, yet each session begins with the question "where do I even start?", and the ambiguity becomes dread. A person might be fully committed to outreach, yet they have to decide whom to contact, what to say, and how to log it each time; the decision load becomes the barrier. None of this is solved by more self-lecture. It is solved by design.

Design begins with diagnosis, which is where the friction audit enters. A friction audit is a deliberate inventory of obstacles between intention and action. It is not therapy. It is not confession. It is a practical map. One sits down and traces the route from "I intend to do the behaviour" to "I am doing the behaviour" and lists every snag: missing tools, unclear steps, poor timing, awkward transitions, social interruptions, environmental cues pulling in the wrong direction. The audit's great virtue is that it relocates the problem from the self to the system. That relocation is not an excuse. It is accuracy.

Accuracy changes the emotional tone. When people believe the obstacle is personal weakness, they respond with shame or with grand vows. Both are brittle. When they see the obstacle as friction, they respond with curiosity and adjustment. Curiosity leads to iteration. Iteration leads to reliability. The aim is not to become a person who never feels resistance. The aim is to remove the unnecessary resistance so that the remaining effort is spent on the work itself.

From there the chapter moves into the physical and logistical barriers that are easiest to observe and often the easiest to fix. Distance matters. Clutter matters. Timing matters. Tools matter. A gym bag packed the night before is not an optional flourish; it is part of the habit. A sales script written in advance is not extra work; it is friction removed. A dedicated study space is not aesthetic; it is a cue that reduces start-up cost and protects attention. These are small changes, and they can feel almost stupidly mundane. Their mundanity is precisely their power. They are the difference between a habit that requires a daily motivational speech and a habit that begins almost by accident.

Then comes mental friction, which is often more decisive than physical barriers and far more often misinterpreted. Perfectionism is friction wearing a respectable suit. Fear is friction that feels like prudence. Unclear next steps are friction that masquerades as complexity. The mind resists not because it is lazy but because it cannot see a safe first move. A person says "I should write" and feels dread. The dread is not proof they are unfit to write. It is a signal that the first action is too vague or too loaded. When the first visible action is defined—ridiculously concrete, almost laughably small—the dread often reduces. Not because the work has become easy, but because the threat has become bounded.

Checklists belong here for the same reason they belong in aviation and medicine: they reduce reliance on fragile attention under stress. They are not a confession of incompetence. They are a respect for reality. A checklist turns a vague task into a sequence of actions that can be executed even when the mind is tired. It reduces decision load. It reduces the number of opportunities to abandon the task. It also creates a small rhythm of completion, which feeds the habit loop with reward signals. The chapter will treat checklists and "first visible actions" as tools for turning cognitive dread into solvable design.

The final movement is about default pathways: making the desired behaviour the easiest behaviour available, not through moral heroism but through choice architecture. People think discipline should feel like pushing a boulder uphill. Effective discipline often feels like sliding—because the system has been arranged so that the path of least resistance leads somewhere valuable. A default calendar block for deep work is a pathway. A prepared prospect list is a pathway. A pre-decided set of meals is a pathway. These defaults do not remove choice; they reduce the number of times choice must be fought for. They protect attention for higher-order work.

This matters now because modern life is built to create friction and distraction at scale. The inbox is endless. The phone is an always-on cue machine. Work has become more fragmented, with more switching and more micro-deadlines. Under those conditions, insisting that discipline must be a constant internal battle is not noble; it is inefficient. A person who treats their day as a system to be designed will outlast a person who treats their day as a test of virtue. This is the same point that manufacturing and safety engineering have learned repeatedly: when human attention is the bottleneck, the system must compensate. The person should not be asked to be superhuman.

A subtle motif threads through this chapter: drag. Drag is what slows a cyclist even when the road is flat; it is the invisible force that makes forward motion cost more energy than it should. Human habits have drag too. The drag is the small obstacle, the unnecessary step, the hidden decision, the missing tool, the poorly placed cue. Remove drag and the same effort produces more movement. Leave drag in place and even motivated people stall. The beauty of drag as a motif is that it shifts blame away from character and towards mechanics, without denying responsibility. You are still responsible for moving. You simply stop insisting on moving through treacle.

There is also a philosophical undercurrent worth naming. People tend to take pride in the idea of rugged individual agency: the self as a sovereign will that should triumph over circumstances. That is an appealing story. It is also an incomplete model of human behaviour. The environment shapes cues. Emotion shapes avoidance. Decision load shapes self-control. Recognising these influences is not surrender. It is a more accurate picture of the human animal. Accuracy is power.

The chapter ends with momentum because friction removal has a peculiar emotional payoff. It makes discipline feel less like a moral project and more like a craft. A person begins to experience what high performers often know quietly: when systems are well designed, the "hard part" is not doing the habit. The hard part is designing the habit so that doing it becomes normal.

The forward question that hangs in the air is diagnostic and slightly unsettling. When a habit keeps failing, is it truly a problem of desire, or is it simply a problem of drag—and if it is drag, which single point of friction would change the odds most if it were removed?

Running a Friction Audit

In December 1988 at Stanford University in California, Donald Knuth released TeX Version 3.0 and, with it, a quiet manifesto about reliability. He did something unusual for a celebrated computer scientist: he offered a monetary reward for each bug found, and he used the feedback to improve the system until it became remarkably stable. TeX is not famous because it is flashy. It is famous because it behaves predictably under pressure, which is why it became foundational in academic publishing and scientific typesetting. Knuth's method was not motivational. It was diagnostic: surface the faults, map them precisely, then remove them one by one. A friction audit applies the same logic to habits. Instead of treating failure as personal weakness, it treats it as a bug report.

Start with the bug.

A friction audit is a systematic way to identify everything that makes a behaviour hard to execute. It is not a pep talk. It is not a moral evaluation. It is closer to an engineer's inspection, except the "machine" is a human day with all its ordinary constraints: fatigue, distractions, competing obligations, emotional states, and environments that cue the wrong routines. The audit asks a deliberately unromantic question: between intending to do a habit and actually doing it, what obstacles appear, in what order, and with what force?

Show why this matters. A person decides to study nightly. They do not. They conclude they are undisciplined. That conclusion is easy because it is global; it explains everything and therefore explains nothing. Another person decides to study nightly, fails, then runs an audit. They discover that the failure point is not "discipline" but a sequence: the materials are scattered across devices; the desk is cluttered; the first step is unclear; the act of beginning triggers dread; the phone is face-up and lit; the session is planned for the hour when attention is lowest. These are not character flaws. They are friction points. Name the concept: friction is the small cost that accumulates until action becomes unlikely. Explain it: the brain chooses the path of least resistance when tired or stressed; friction raises resistance; raised resistance shifts behaviour towards easier routines. The implication is liberating and exacting: if you can locate friction, you can reduce it. If you reduce it, the behaviour becomes more probable without requiring a nobler personality.

The audit's power lies in its granularity. Humans love stories. Stories are seductive and imprecise. "I'm just not a morning person." "I can't focus." "I'm bad at consistency." These statements sound like insight. They often conceal the true causes. A friction audit refuses those abstractions. It asks for specifics: what time did you intend to start? Where were you? What were you doing five minutes before? What tool did you need first? What was missing? What decision had to be made? What felt unclear? What emotion arrived? What distraction was easiest? Each question drags the problem back into the realm of observable behaviour.

A five-word truth belongs here. Details beat self-blame.

To run a friction audit properly, it helps to treat it like a worksheet even when it is not written on paper. The structure is simple. Choose one habit—one. Not an entire life. One behaviour that matters and that is currently unreliable. The audit begins with a baseline description: the intended behaviour stated in plain terms ("read and self-test for five minutes", "write one sentence", "send one outreach message", "prepare study materials and answer one question"). Then you trace the route from intention to completion as a sequence of steps. The audit does not only record what you wish happened. It records what actually happens on a day when the habit fails or is resisted.

Begin with "the moment before". What is the immediate cue that is supposed to trigger the habit? A time of day, a location, the end of a meeting, the moment the kettle clicks, the act of opening a laptop. If there is no cue, that itself is friction—because without a trigger, the habit relies on memory and motivation. Name this friction: cue ambiguity. Explain it: when the trigger is vague ("sometime after dinner"), the brain must decide repeatedly whether now is the time; repeated deciding is costly; cost invites avoidance. The implication is that good habit design begins by attaching the behaviour to a clear, stable cue.

Then trace the first physical step. Not "start studying". What is the first visible action? Sit at the desk. Open the notebook. Put on trainers. Dial the number. If the first physical step is unclear, the brain experiences cognitive friction: "Where do I begin?" That question, if unanswered, becomes a cue for escape. When people say they feel "overwhelmed", the audit often reveals that overwhelm is not a mystical emotion but a practical confusion: too many options, too many steps, too much uncertainty. The implication is that clarity is not a motivational luxury. It is friction removal.

Now identify the practical obstacles. The audit asks, with almost tedious honesty: what was missing? A pen. A charger. A quiet space. A document. A script. A list of prospects. A login. A stable internet connection. These can sound trivial, which is precisely why they matter. Trivial obstacles are the ones people refuse to take seriously, and therefore they persist. In aviation and medicine, trivial errors kill because complex systems magnify small failures. Life is less dramatic, but the logic holds: missing tools create delays; delays invite distraction; distraction becomes abandonment. The implication is not to obsess over minutiae, but to acknowledge that small obstacles can decide the day.

Then look for timing friction. When is the habit scheduled relative to energy and obligations? A person may plan to do deep work after a day full of meetings. The audit makes the absurdity visible. The plan depends on high-quality attention at the hour when attention is most depleted. That is not a moral issue. It is a scheduling issue. The behavioural metric is clear: how often does the habit succeed when placed at that time? If the answer is "rarely", the time itself is a friction point. The implication is that reliability often improves not through more determination but through moving the behaviour to a lower-friction window.

Social friction deserves its own lens. Who is around? What expectations are present? Is the environment one where the habit is socially awkward or easily interrupted? A person who intends to study at a kitchen table in a busy household may find that the friction is not internal at all; it is interruption. Interruptions are not merely annoyances; they reset attention and raise start-up cost repeatedly. The implication is not to blame others. It is to recognise that social context is part of the system and must be designed around if consistency matters.

Now examine emotional friction. This is where most people revert to self-blame, because emotions feel personal. The audit treats them as data. What emotion reliably appears when the habit is about to begin? Dread, boredom, fear of failure, irritation, shame. What does that emotion cue? Checking the phone, tidying, snacks, "just one more email", a sudden urge to plan rather than act. The pattern is often predictable. Emotion is a cue. Avoidance is a routine. Relief is a reward. The implication is not to eliminate emotion; it is to stop pretending emotion is random. If dread appears reliably at the start, the start is too vague, too large, or too identity-threatening. Shrink it. Clarify it. Reduce the perceived threat by defining an embarrassingly small first move.

A friction audit also includes a question that is easy to avoid: what is the "temptation alternative"? When the habit fails, what replaces it? This matters because replacement behaviour reveals what reward is being sought. If the replacement is scrolling, the reward may be novelty or relief. If the replacement is tidying, the reward may be control and closure. If the replacement is planning, the reward may be the feeling of progress without exposure. By naming the replacement, the audit makes the habit loop visible. The implication is strategic: if you want to reduce friction, you must understand what the easier alternative is offering and either remove it from reach or offer a competing reward for the desired behaviour.

Two named examples help anchor this beyond personal anecdote. In infection control, Didier Pittet's work at Geneva University Hospitals showed that compliance improved when the environment made the desired action easier—placing alcohol-based hand rub at the point of care, reducing friction for clinicians operating under time pressure (Pittet et al., 2000). The principle is not confined to hospitals. The audit approach—identify where the behaviour fails, locate the friction at the point of action, redesign the system—explains why environment changes often outperform exhortations. A second example comes from public policy: the UK's Behavioural Insights Team reported in 2012 that small changes to communications and defaults could shift behaviour measurably

(Behavioural Insights Team, 2012). Again, the lesson is not about letters. It is about using diagnosis to locate the moment where a small adjustment yields a large shift.

Now face a credible limitation. Some friction is irreducible. Difficult work remains difficult. Learning requires effort. Outreach involves rejection. Craft involves producing imperfect drafts. A friction audit cannot make the work painless without turning it into something else. If an audit is used as an endless quest to remove all discomfort, it becomes avoidance in a new costume. This is a real risk for smart people: they can endlessly optimise systems to avoid the sensation of work. The reconciliation is to distinguish between *unnecessary friction* and *the necessary difficulty of the domain*. Unnecessary friction is missing tools, unclear steps, poor timing, and environments that cue the wrong behaviour. Necessary difficulty is the effort of thinking, practising, and being exposed to feedback.

The audit therefore has a stopping rule. Once the obvious mechanical obstacles are removed and the first action is clear, what remains is the domain's honest difficulty. That difficulty should be met with the tools already established: minimum viable reps, cues, small rewards, and protected streaks. The audit is not an alternative to effort. It is a way of ensuring effort is not wasted fighting avoidable drag.

Return to the motif of the bug report. A bug report is valuable because it is specific. It says: when I do X in conditions Y, Z happens. A friction audit aims for that same specificity. "When I sit down to write at 21:30 after three hours of meetings, I cannot find my notes, I feel dread, I check my phone, and the session ends." That is not a confession. It is a diagnostic statement. Once it is written, it can be acted upon: notes moved, time shifted, first step clarified, phone displaced, session shrunk. The person stops being a mystery to themselves.

The forward test is therefore simple and slightly confronting. The next time a habit fails, will you reach for the comforting story—"I'm just not disciplined"—or will you write the bug report: what cue appeared, what obstacle intervened, what routine replaced the habit, and which single friction point, if removed, would change the odds tomorrow?

Fixing Physical Barriers

In April 2000 at Geneva University Hospitals in Switzerland, Didier Pittet and colleagues reported a hand-hygiene programme that succeeded not by pleading for better intentions, but by altering the physical reality of the ward. Alcohol-based hand rub was made readily available at the point of care; compliance improved, and rates of hospital-acquired infection fell over the period studied (Pittet et al., 2000). The story is often told as a triumph of public health. It is also, more quietly, a triumph of logistics. When the tools are where the hands already are, behaviour changes. When the tools are missing or distant, even conscientious people fail.

Distance is a verdict.

Physical barriers are the most underestimated reason habits do not happen. People prefer psychological explanations because they flatter the self: either they are strong-willed or weak-willed, motivated or lazy. Physical explanations are less theatrical: the shoes are not packed, the desk is cluttered, the document is buried in folders, the prospect list is out of date, the gym is a twenty-minute detour, the printer has no ink, the password is forgotten, the kitchen is full of cues for the wrong routine. Yet it is precisely because these obstacles are mundane that they are powerful. Mundane obstacles repeat daily. Daily obstacles compound.

A physical barrier is any concrete, logistical friction between intention and action. It includes distance (how far you must travel, physically or digitally), clutter (how much you must clear before beginning), tools (whether the necessary objects are available and ready), and timing (whether the environment at the chosen moment supports the behaviour). These barriers are not "excuses". They are costs. Costs change probability. When a habit depends on a sequence of small costs being paid at precisely the moment you are tired, the habit becomes unreliable.

A five-word truth belongs here. Setup is part of work.

Show the mistake in an ordinary scene. Someone plans to exercise after work. At 18:40 they remember. They search for clean kit. The bag is half-packed. The water bottle is missing. The headphones are dead. They cannot find their membership card. By the time everything is assembled, the person is irritated and time has narrowed. The irritation becomes a cue for abandonment—"I'll go tomorrow"—and the person drifts into something that requires no setup. The failure is then interpreted as lack of discipline. In reality, the system asked the person to solve six small problems at the worst time of day.

Name the concept. Start-up friction.

Explain it. Start-up friction is the time and attention required before the real behaviour begins. High start-up friction turns habits into projects. Projects invite procrastination because they require planning, decisions, and effort before any reward arrives. The implication is simple: if you reduce start-up friction, you reduce the number of reasons the brain can plausibly generate to avoid starting. You do not make the work effortless. You make starting less expensive.

This is why "packing the gym bag" is not an optional extra. It is a behavioural intervention. It moves the cost from the fragile moment—late, tired, distracted—to a more stable one—earlier, calmer, pre-committed. The bag becomes a cue and a shortcut. It collapses multiple decisions into one prior decision. In habit terms, it shifts the burden from willpower to environment. The implication is profound: many people do not need more determination; they need to pay the costs in advance.

The same logic applies to study. A person says they will study each evening. At the moment of beginning, they realise their notes are scattered across tabs, folders, and devices. They spend ten minutes searching, another five minutes remembering where they left off, and then they feel "too behind" to begin. A dedicated study space—one desk, one chair, materials left in place—reduces these costs. It does not guarantee focus, but it reduces the threshold cost of entry.

It also creates context stability, which research on habits suggests strengthens automaticity: repeated behaviour in stable contexts becomes more likely to run without deliberation (Wood & Neal, 2007; Wood & Rünger, 2016). The implication is that environment is not scenery. It is behavioural scaffolding.

Distance is not only about geography. It is also digital distance. A file buried in a labyrinth of folders is far away in the only sense that matters: it costs time and attention to reach. A prospecting list in a clunky CRM that requires multiple logins is far away. A textbook left in a different room is far away. Each extra step adds delay, and delay is fertile ground for distraction. If a person must walk downstairs, open a laptop, find a charger, locate a file, log into a platform, then decide what to do first, the habit begins to resemble an expedition. Expeditions require a particular mood. Habits should not.

Show how small digital adjustments change behaviour. A writer who keeps the next document pinned and opened to the exact point of return reduces the "where was I?" friction that can kill a session. A salesperson who keeps a small list of today's contacts visible reduces the decision cost of choosing whom to contact. A student who keeps a single set of materials in one place reduces the temptation to "just organise things first". These changes sound almost embarrassingly simple. That is the point. The brain does not care how sophisticated the fix is. It cares whether the fix reduces the cost of beginning.

Tools are another barrier masquerading as personality. People often say, "I'm not consistent with outreach," when the true issue is that they do not have a ready script. Each time they try to start, they must invent language. Inventing language is cognitively expensive, especially under stress, and it introduces the risk of sounding foolish. That risk provokes avoidance. Pre-writing scripts—simple starting lines, a set of questions, a brief follow-up template—reduces both cognitive cost and emotional threat. It turns "contact someone" from a vague social performance into an executable routine. The implication is not to become robotic. It is to remove the barrier that prevents practice.

This connects to a broader principle: pre-commitment is physical. People think of commitment as a mental promise. In many cases, the most effective commitment is embodied in objects and arrangements. A packed bag is a pre-commitment. A document left open is a pre-commitment. A meal prepared is a pre-commitment. A calendar block is a pre-commitment. These are not expressions of willpower. They are structural choices that reduce future decision load. They are the practical expression of the earlier argument that willpower is fragile and should not be the foundation.

Timing is the final physical barrier, and it is often ignored because it feels less tangible. Yet timing is physical in the sense that it governs what resources are available: quiet, energy, social interruptions, access to tools. Studying at the kitchen table at 20:30 in a busy household is a different physical environment from studying at 07:00 before the day begins. Outreach planned for the hour after back-to-back meetings is a different environment from outreach planned at the start of the day before decision fatigue accumulates. The goal is not to produce an ideal schedule. The goal is to recognise that timing creates a physical context, and context cues behaviour.

A named example from policy helps underline that small physical adjustments can change behaviour at scale. The UK's Behavioural Insights Team reported in 2012 on trials where changing defaults and simplifying processes altered outcomes in areas such as tax compliance (Behavioural Insights Team, 2012). The mechanism is the same: reduce friction, increase compliance. The implication, when brought back to personal habits, is that "simplifying" is not childish. It is powerful.

A credible limitation deserves acknowledgment. Physical fixes can become a form of procrastination. People can spend weeks perfecting a workspace, buying equipment, and arranging systems, all while avoiding the work itself. The environment becomes an altar. This is a real danger for conscientious people because setup feels productive and safe. The reconciliation is to treat physical fixes as targeted interventions drawn from a friction audit. Fix what blocks action most. Fix it quickly. Then test whether behaviour occurs. If the behaviour still does not happen, the barrier is not physical alone. The audit continues. The point is not to build a beautiful system. It is to build an executable one.

Physical barriers are also constrained by circumstance. Not everyone can create a quiet study room. Not everyone can commute less. Not everyone can control shared spaces. The implication is not defeat. It is to work within constraints by moving the tool placement, reducing steps, and preparing in advance. Even in constrained environments, small reductions in friction often produce large gains because they change the probability of starting. Probability is the currency of consistency.

The motif that threads through this section is the threshold. Physical barriers live at thresholds: the moment you would begin, the moment you would leave the house, the moment you would open the document, the moment you would make the call. Thresholds decide the day because they are bottlenecks. A tiny obstacle at a bottleneck has disproportionate power. Remove it, and the behaviour flows more easily. Leave it, and the behaviour stalls.

The forward test is therefore practical rather than inspirational. The next time a habit fails, will you ask whether you lacked motivation, or will you ask which single physical barrier at the threshold—distance, clutter, missing tools, awkward timing—quietly raised the cost of starting until avoidance became the easiest option?

Fixing Mental Barriers

In September 2004 at the University of Amsterdam, psychologists Roy Baumeister and colleagues published a paper with a title that sounded almost quaint—"Losing Control"—yet it captured a harsh everyday truth: self-regulation fails in patterned ways under certain conditions, particularly when people are tired, stressed, or cognitively overloaded (Baumeister et al., 2004). The interesting part, for our purposes, is not the laboratory framing. It is the implication that "I just couldn't make myself do it" is often not a mysterious moral collapse. It is a predictable interaction between the task and the mind's limited resources. Mental barriers are not ghosts. They are frictions.

The mind needs a handle.

Physical barriers are visible: missing tools, distance, clutter. Mental barriers are subtler because they live inside language and feeling. They often arrive dressed as personality—"I'm a perfectionist", "I overthink", "I work best under pressure", "I'm not confident"—when they are better understood as design problems. The mind avoids what feels threatening. Threat can be obvious, like social rejection. It can also be abstract: the threat of being exposed as incompetent, the threat of producing something mediocre, the threat of confronting ambiguity. When threat appears, attention narrows, and the easiest escape route becomes attractive. This is why mental barriers often present as procrastination. Procrastination is not a single behaviour. It is a family of avoidance routines.

Show the moment it happens. A writer opens a document. The cursor blinks. The topic matters. The stakes feel real. The writer thinks, "I need to write the introduction," and the mind instantly produces a counter-voice: "If you get this wrong, you'll look foolish." The body tightens slightly. The hand reaches for email. The cue is not laziness. The cue is threat. The routine is avoidance. The reward is relief. The habit loop is intact; only the costume has changed.

Name the first mental barrier. Perfectionism.

Explain it in behavioural terms. Perfectionism is often not a love of excellence but an intolerance of imperfect beginnings. It turns early drafts into identity tests. If each attempt is treated as evidence of worth, the mind protects itself by avoiding the attempt. The implication is severe: the more a person wants to do something well, the more likely they are to avoid starting when perfectionism is high. That is why talented people stall. They are not "lazy". They are frightened of producing anything that does not match their self-image.

A five-word sentence belongs here. Make it safely unfinished.

"Safely unfinished" is not a motivational mantra. It is a design requirement. The first visible action must be defined so that it cannot plausibly threaten identity. "Write an excellent introduction" threatens identity. "Write one rough sentence that states the problem" does not. The former invites judgement; the latter invites motion. When the first action is safe, the mind is less likely to trigger avoidance. This is why defining the first visible action is one of the most effective ways to fix mental barriers: it replaces vague ambition with a handle.

The phrase "first visible action" matters because it forces the action to be concrete, observable, and physically executable. "Work on the report" is not executable. "Open the document and write a heading" is executable. "Study for the exam" is not executable. "Answer one question from memory and check the answer" is executable. "Improve sales" is not executable. "Send one follow-up to a named person using a prepared opening line" is executable. The visible action is a behavioural atom: small enough to execute, clear enough to remove decision load, and safe enough to reduce threat.

Fear is the second mental barrier, and it is often mislabelled as lack of confidence. Confidence, in practice, is often the by-product of repeated exposure and feedback. Fear arises when the outcome is uncertain and the perceived cost of a bad outcome is high. In sales, fear is fear of rejection and awkwardness. In study, fear can be fear of discovering you do not know what you thought you knew. In craft, fear is fear of producing something mediocre. In each case, the mind behaves rationally from its own perspective: it avoids exposure. The implication is that "overcoming fear" is not primarily about bravery. It is about reducing the perceived cost of exposure by shrinking the unit and by creating a process that makes exposure routine rather than exceptional.

Unclear next steps are the third barrier, and they may be the most common. People often say they feel overwhelmed. Overwhelm is frequently the sensation of having too many possible actions with no obvious starting point. When the mind cannot see the next step, it defaults to a familiar routine that provides quick closure: messages, tidying, planning, consuming information. These routines are not random. They are behaviours with immediate rewards. The implication is that clarity is not a luxury. It is friction removal.

This is where checklists enter, and they deserve to be treated with respect rather than condescension. Checklists are a tool for reducing cognitive load. They externalise the sequence of steps so that the mind does not have to carry them while also doing the work. In high-stakes domains, checklists exist because human attention fails under stress. In 2009, surgeon Atul Gawande and colleagues reported on the World Health Organization's Surgical Safety Checklist in *The New England Journal of Medicine*, noting reductions in complications and deaths across diverse hospitals after implementation (Haynes et al., 2009). The medical details are not the point here. The behavioural principle is: when complexity and stress are high, external structure prevents predictable failures. If experienced surgical teams benefit from checklists, the idea that personal habits should be managed purely by memory and willpower begins to look like arrogance.

Checklists are not only for safety-critical fields. They are also for work that triggers mental friction. A writer who stalls at "write the chapter" can use a checklist that begins with absurdly small steps: open the document, write the working title, paste the outline, write one sentence under the first subheading, highlight the next gap, stop. The checklist is not a prison. It is a handle. It turns a vague task into a sequence of visible actions, each of which is too small to provoke the full force of dread.

A short example makes the technique concrete without becoming theatrical. Consider a blocked writer who has to produce a report and keeps failing to start. The writer's internal language is grand: "I have to make this sharp, convincing, and comprehensive." Each word raises stakes. The writer sits down, feels threat, and escapes. Now the writer runs an audit on the mental barrier and discovers the bottleneck is the first five minutes. The solution is not to increase willpower. The solution is to redesign the first five minutes as a list of visible actions that are almost insultingly concrete: open the document; type a working title that can be changed later; write a one-sentence statement of the problem; write three bullet fragments of evidence without worrying about phrasing; copy one relevant quote or data point from the source material; stop. The purpose of these steps is not to finish the report. It is to lower start-up cost and to produce a small artefact that makes the next step easier tomorrow. The implication is that "writer's block" often dissolves when the mind is given a handle it can grasp without fear.

This approach also respects the earlier work on minimum viable habits. The minimum viable unit is not just small in time; it is small in threat. A person can technically do a small rep and still trigger dread if the rep is framed as a test. "Write one sentence that must be brilliant" is still a test. "Write one ugly sentence that gets the idea onto the page" is a rep. The difference is psychological framing with behavioural consequences. The mind is sensitive to what the action means. If the action means judgement, avoidance rises. If the action means practice, avoidance falls. The implication is that mental barriers are often created by meaning, not by effort.

A credible limitation must be faced, because mental barriers cannot always be solved by a checklist and a small first step. Some problems are genuinely complex and require sustained engagement. Some fears are rooted in real consequences—public scrutiny, professional stakes, institutional pressure. Some people face environments that punish early drafts or mistakes harshly. In such contexts, asking for "safe imperfection" can sound naive. The reconciliation is that the techniques here do not remove consequences; they reduce unnecessary threat signals so that action becomes possible. Even in high-stakes work, the early stages of thinking can be made less identity-threatening by separating drafting from judgement, by defining intermediate artefacts, and by externalising steps so that the mind is not holding the whole risk at once.

There is also a subtler limitation: smart people can use checklists as avoidance, endlessly refining systems rather than doing the work. The checklist becomes a shrine. This is where the "first visible action" remains the anchor. A checklist is only useful if it produces a rep quickly. The measure is behavioural: did the person produce an output, however small? If not, the checklist is another layer of friction. The implication is that structure must serve action, not replace it.

Mental barriers, then, are best treated as design constraints. If perfectionism is present, the rep must be framed as practice. If fear is present, the rep must reduce exposure to a manageable dose. If uncertainty is present, the rep must be defined as a visible action that can be executed without further planning. If cognitive load is high, the rep must be guided by an external sequence. These are not inspirational principles. They are engineering decisions.

Thread the motif once more. The handle is not the work itself; it is how you pick it up. A heavy suitcase is unmanageable without a grip. The same suitcase becomes carryable when the handle is sturdy and well placed. Work is similar. The task may remain heavy. The handle determines whether you lift it at all.

The forward test is therefore not whether you can summon courage. It is whether you can name, in plain behavioural terms, the next visible action that would make starting possible—so small, so clear, so safely unfinished that the mind has no reasonable excuse to avoid it.

Designing Default Pathways

In 2012 in London, the Behavioural Insights Team published results from field trials showing that small changes to choice architecture—defaults, prompts, and simplified steps—could shift behaviour at scale, including in areas such as tax payment and charitable giving (Behavioural Insights Team, 2012). The striking feature was not the cleverness of any single letter or form. It was the quiet brutality of the lesson: people do not reliably do what they *intend*; they do what is *easy to do next*. When the next step is frictionless, behaviour flows. When the next step is tangled, behaviour stalls.

Default beats desire.

A default pathway is the route your day takes when you are not paying close attention. It is the behaviour that happens when you are tired, distracted, rushed, or emotionally flat. For most people, that route has been designed accidentally—by workplaces, by devices, by social norms, by the layout of a kitchen, by the calendar's demands, by what is within reach. Designing default pathways means taking authorship of that accidental route. It is not about forcing yourself to choose well every time. It is about reducing the number of times you must choose at all.

A five-word truth belongs here. Ease writes the routine.

This section sits on the foundation built earlier. Habits run as loops, cued by environment and rewarded by relief or satisfaction. Willpower is fragile under stress and decision load. Minimum viable habits lower the entry bar so action becomes possible. Friction audits locate the points where behaviour breaks down. Physical fixes remove obvious drag. Mental fixes provide handles when dread and ambiguity appear. Default pathways are the final integration: they turn all those insights into a daily architecture that guides behaviour by gravity rather than by force.

Gravity is the right metaphor because defaults are not usually experienced as coercion. They feel like the natural flow of the day. People check email first because the inbox is open and demanding, not because they truly believe it is their highest purpose. They scroll because the phone is in reach and boredom is uncomfortable, not because scrolling aligns with their values. They skip practice because beginning requires too many steps, not because they consciously prefer stagnation. Defaults are not always bad. Many are useful. The problem is that unchosen defaults often express someone else's priorities.

Show how this works in a mundane professional morning. A person opens their laptop and the first thing visible is a stream of messages. The cue is the screen lighting up. The routine is checking and responding. The reward is immediate relief—problems solved, people answered, small closures achieved. By the time the person considers their own deep work, their attention has been fragmented and their willpower taxed. The default pathway has already carried them away. The behaviour is understandable. It is also expensive. The abstraction "productivity" is too vague to help here. The visible behaviours are clear: what opens first, what is visible, what is demanded, what is rewarded. The implication is that a default pathway can be redesigned by changing what appears first and what demands attention.

Name the concept that ties these changes together. Choice architecture.

Explain it in human terms. Choice architecture is the arrangement of options and steps that shapes what people do without requiring constant deliberation. It includes defaults (what happens if you do nothing), friction (how many steps are required), and salience (what is most visible). In personal discipline, choice architecture is often the difference between "I keep failing" and "it almost happens by itself". The implication is the central promise of this section: effective discipline often feels like sliding, because the system has been shaped so that the path of least resistance leads towards the desired behaviour.

Calendar blocks are a clean example because they turn time into architecture. A person who says "I'll find time to practise" is relying on an unstable resource: spare time. Spare time is rare and politically contested. A person who has a default calendar block for the behaviour has changed the environment. The behaviour now has a place in the day before the day is filled by others. This is not a guarantee—calendars can be overridden—but it changes the baseline. It turns the question from "Will I do it?" to "Will I protect it?" Protection is still effortful, but it is a different kind of effort: less about starting from zero, more about defending a pre-committed pathway. The behavioural metric becomes simple: how often does the block occur as intended? When it fails, what displaced it? The implications are measurable, which is why calendars can be powerful.

Default pathways also matter in sales and outreach, where inconsistency is often a function of decision friction. If a salesperson must decide each day whom to contact, what to say, where the last conversation left off, and how to track it, the task becomes cognitively heavy and emotionally threatening. A default pathway would reduce decisions by pre-building a short prospecting list, pre-writing a small set of opening lines, and creating an automatic follow-up queue. This is not about becoming robotic. It is about removing the "blank page" problem from social work. The blank page is a fear trigger. A prepared list is a handle. The implication is that the salesperson's daily rep becomes easier to start, which makes it more likely to happen, which increases exposure to feedback, which increases competence.

Study defaults work similarly. Many students rely on hope: hope that they will feel motivated later, hope that they will remember what to revise, hope that they will not be interrupted. A default pathway might involve a single, consistent location used only for study and a predictable opening action such as retrieving one concept from memory before looking at notes. The key is that the first step is automatic. When the environment and time cue the same opening action repeatedly, the habit loop strengthens (Wood & Neal, 2007). The implication is that studying becomes less a heroic event and more a scheduled, cued routine, which is precisely how competence is built.

Food and health-related behaviours often demonstrate default pathways vividly because physical convenience is so powerful. When people are tired and hungry, they do not make philosophical decisions; they reach for what is easiest. A default pathway could be a set of pre-decided meal options or a prepared ingredient routine that reduces the decision load at precisely the moment decision load is least available. This is not advice about nutrition. It is an example of behavioural mechanics: the easiest option becomes the chosen option. The implication is that if you care about a behaviour, you must ensure the default option aligns with it, because real life reliably returns you to default.

Defaults also live in devices. A phone that sleeps beside the bed creates a default pathway: wake, check, scroll. A laptop that opens to email creates a default pathway: respond, react, fragment. A notification system that interrupts constantly creates a default pathway: switch tasks, lose attention, seek closure. These defaults are not neutral. They are designed. Often they are designed by someone else's incentives. Designing your own default pathways means taking control of what your environment cues first. This is not anti-technology. It is pro-agency. The implication is that attention is a limited resource and should not be handed away by default settings.

A named example from research helps clarify why defaults can be so powerful. Richard Thaler and Cass Sunstein popularised the idea of "nudges" and the influence of defaults on behaviour, including in retirement savings, by highlighting how small design choices can lead to large shifts in participation (Thaler & Sunstein, 2008). The book is not an academic treatise, but its central point is robust: defaults matter because people often stick with them. The implication for habits is that the most reliable behaviour change is often achieved not by trying harder but by changing what happens when you do nothing. If the default when you do nothing is distraction, you will be distracted. If the default when you do nothing is the beginning of a rep, you will more often do the rep.

Now introduce a credible counter-example. Defaults can be oppressive. They can reduce flexibility. A calendar block can become a cage if life changes. A rigid routine can break under travel, illness, or caring responsibilities. An over-designed system can create resentment, especially if it treats human variation as a bug rather than a feature. The reconciliation is that default pathways should be designed with slack. They should include small versions that survive disruption and allow conscious overrides without collapsing. A default pathway is not an iron law. It is a baseline route that can be adjusted when reality demands it.

There is also the risk of confusing default pathways with avoidance of effort. People can spend weeks redesigning calendars, apps, lists, and environments without doing the work. This is the same danger seen in physical setup and checklists: system design becomes another procrastination ritual. The reconciliation is again behavioural. A default pathway is only real if it produces reps. The test is not how elegant the system looks. The test is whether the behaviour becomes easier to start and more likely to occur. Design must be iterative and grounded in actual execution.

Thread the motif of sliding once more. Sliding is not the absence of effort; it is effort placed earlier, in calmer moments, to reduce future effort at the moment of action. This is the deep logic of discipline. The disciplined person is often not pushing harder than everyone else in the moment; they have arranged their world so that pushing is rarely required. They have invested in rails, not in heroism. When the day is difficult, they still move, because the rails remain.

The forward test is therefore not a moral challenge. It is a design decision that exposes your true priorities. When you do nothing—when you are tired, distracted, or rushed—where does your day naturally go, and what would it cost to redesign that default so that the first easy step leads towards the work you claim matters?

Chapter 5
Stacking Habits into Systems

At 09:03, a person opens a laptop, and a small tragedy repeats itself with the smoothness of a well-rehearsed play. The inbox is already there, bright with demands. A notification blinks. A colleague's message arrives with a question that feels urgent. The person answers. Another message arrives. The morning becomes a chain of reactions, each perfectly reasonable, each stealing a little more agency. By lunchtime, the work that actually mattered—the practice, the study, the outreach, the craft—has not been touched, not because it was forgotten, but because it never found a place to land.

Days do not fail randomly. They fail by default sequences.

That line is not pessimism; it is a clue. If behaviour is shaped by loops, by friction, by cues and rewards, then a day is simply a larger loop—an architecture of one behaviour leading into the next. People tend to think in isolated actions: one workout, one study session, one call, one paragraph. Life rarely presents itself in isolation. It presents itself in transitions: waking to coffee, coffee to commute, commute to laptop, laptop to meetings, meetings to fatigue, fatigue to the easiest available reward. The discipline problem, in practice, is often a transition problem.

Habit stacking is the craft of shaping transitions so that one behaviour naturally cues the next. It is the difference between a set of isolated good intentions and a sequence that runs with minimal negotiation. It is not multitasking, which fractures attention. It is not a vague "morning routine" fantasy that collapses the first time a child is ill or a train is delayed. It is a deliberate linking: after this, then that; when this happens, I do that. The stack turns the day into rails. You do not have to push as hard. You slide.

Modern life makes stacking unusually valuable because modern life is unusually chopped up. Work arrives in pings and messages. Study competes with the endless availability of information that feels like learning but often isn't. Health and movement compete with fatigue and convenience. Craft competes with the seduction of consumption. In such conditions, relying on "finding time" is a losing strategy. Time does not appear; it is taken, and taking it repeatedly demands willpower, which we have already established is an unreliable source of energy. Stacks, by contrast, borrow strength from what is already happening.

This is why anchors matter. Anchors are stable behaviours that already occur with high reliability: making coffee, brushing teeth, commuting, eating lunch, opening a laptop, returning home, putting children to bed. They are the fixed points in a day that otherwise feels like a storm. The art is to attach a new rep to one of these fixed points so that the cue is automatic. The person does not need to "remember" to do the new behaviour. The anchor remembers on their behalf.

The chapter begins by making the concept sharp, because many people misuse it. A habit stack is not a long list of aspirational behaviours arranged in an optimistic order. It is a short sequence of actions that can run under ordinary conditions. "After I make coffee, I review my sales list, then send one message" is a stack because it uses an existing cue and keeps the sequence brief and executable. "After coffee, I meditate, journal, run, read, plan my day, and eat a perfect breakfast" is not a stack; it is an audition for a different life. Stacks are defined not by how ideal they look but by how reliably they survive.

Survival is the measure.

From there, the focus shifts to finding anchor behaviours with care. Not every daily event is a good anchor. Some are unstable. Some are emotionally charged. Some occur in contexts full of interruption. A commute may be a powerful anchor for listening and reviewing, but it may also be chaotic and unpredictable. Meals can be stable anchors, but they can also be social and therefore poor moments for deep focus. Opening a laptop is stable, but it is also the moment when distractions are strongest. The anchor must be chosen with an eye for stability and for what tends to follow it. Anchors are not only time markers. They are context markers. They contain cues, constraints, and social expectations.

Then comes sequencing, which is where stacking becomes a serious discipline rather than a cute trick. Order matters because the brain does not have the same resources at every moment, and because different tasks have different levels of fragility. Fragile tasks—those that require attention, courage, or emotional steadiness—are more likely to be skipped if placed after draining tasks. This is why people who "plan to write later" often do not. By later, the mind has been sanded down by meetings and decisions. Sequencing means placing the fragile rep earlier in the stack, or attaching it to an anchor that occurs before the day's friction accumulates. It also means grouping similar tasks to reduce context switching, because switching carries cognitive cost. A person who stacks "open laptop → draft one paragraph → review notes" may find it easier than "open laptop → check messages → draft paragraph → check messages again", not because their virtue has increased, but because their attention has not been torn apart.

The chapter's realism comes alive in a specific kind of example: the busy parent whose mornings are not a sanctuary but a sprint. The romantic version of stacking would demand silence, candles, and an hour of uninterrupted time. The workable version uses the actual anchors present: boiling the kettle, waiting for toast, school drop-off, the moment the house becomes briefly quiet. It finds tiny reps that can be attached to those anchors without demanding a new life. It also accepts that some days will be messy and designs stacks that can bend without snapping.

Because stacking's greatest temptation is also its greatest danger: overload. The moment people understand stacking, they often attempt to design their perfect day in one ambitious chain. They create a stack so long and intricate that it cannot survive a single disruption. Then, when the stack fails, they interpret the failure as proof that they are incapable of discipline. In truth, the failure is a design error: the stack exceeded the day's carrying capacity. Overload has signals—dread, frequent skipping, constant "catching up", resentment towards the routine. The chapter will treat these signals as diagnostic data rather than moral verdicts. A good stack should feel like a groove. A bad stack feels like a choreographed performance that requires applause to sustain.

There is a deeper philosophical point beneath all this, and it is worth making explicit because it shapes how people relate to their own lives. Many people treat discipline as an inner battle, a private drama of desire versus duty. That drama can be intoxicating. It also keeps the person trapped in self-judgement, because every day becomes a verdict on character. Stacking shifts the frame. It treats behaviour as a designed sequence within a designed environment. The hero of the story is not the person who wins the battle every morning. The hero is the person who rearranges the morning so the battle happens less often.

This is not about becoming mechanical. It is about becoming free. When a sequence runs reliably, attention is released for higher-order thinking. The person can focus on the quality of their craft rather than on whether they will show up at all. They can refine their sales approach rather than on whether they will muster the courage to contact someone. They can deepen their study rather than on whether they will start. Systems create the conditions for ambition to be expressed without constant self-negotiation.

A quiet motif threads through this chapter: rails. A stack is a set of rails laid down across the day's chaos. Rails do not remove agency; they channel it. They make movement more likely in the intended direction. A day without rails is not "more free". It is more vulnerable to whatever cue shouts loudest. A day with rails is still imperfect, still human, still subject to disruption, but it has shape. Shape is what makes consistency possible.

The momentum at the end is a kind of invitation disguised as a challenge. If the day is already a sequence—if your morning already stacks behaviours without your consent—then the only real question is whether you will continue to accept the sequence you have inherited, or whether you will begin to lay a few deliberate rails and discover how much of "discipline" is simply the art of making the next right action the easiest one to do.

What Habit Stacking Is

In August 1966 in Palo Alto, California, psychologist B. F. Skinner published *The Technology of Teaching*, arguing—controversially, and with characteristic confidence—that complex behaviours could be shaped through careful sequencing and reinforcement. The book sits at the intersection of education and behavioural science, and many of its claims have been debated for decades, but one idea remains stubbornly practical: behaviour is easier to produce when the path to it is structured into predictable steps. Not because humans are machines, but because humans become unreliable when every action requires fresh deliberation. A day is a chain anyway. Habit stacking is the act of choosing the links.

Chains run themselves.

A habit stack is a deliberately linked sequence of behaviours in which one action cues the next. The key word is *cues*. In earlier chapters we have treated habits as loops: cue, routine, reward. A habit stack takes that loop logic and extends it across time, building not one loop but a small chain of loops in which the "reward" of one action often becomes the cue for the next. Instead of relying on a single habit to emerge from willpower or memory, stacking makes the habit ride on the back of something that is already happening.

Show it with a small, familiar sequence. A person makes coffee in the morning. The smell is reliable; the kettle clicks; the mug is warm in the hand. That routine already exists. Now the person links a second routine to it: after the first sip, they open a short sales list and choose one contact. Then they send one message. The message itself can be minimum viable—one honest line that begins contact. The important thing is not the eloquence. It is the sequence. Coffee is the anchor. Coffee becomes the cue. The work becomes the follow-on behaviour. The reward is not necessarily pleasure; it may simply be completion and the mild relief of having done the rep. The implication is that outreach becomes less a heroic, separately scheduled event and more a small, reliable extension of something that already occurs.

This is habit stacking: "after X, I do Y." It sounds simple, and it is. It is also deceptively powerful because it shifts the burden of initiation. Most people do not struggle with executing a habit once they are already in motion. They struggle with *starting*. Stacks reduce the number of starts by turning new actions into continuations.

A five-word sentence belongs here. Start once, then glide.

This is why habit stacking is not multitasking. Multitasking is doing two cognitive tasks at once, which increases error, drains attention, and often degrades both tasks. Habit stacking is sequential. One behaviour ends; the next begins. The stack is not "write while checking messages". The stack is "after I check messages for a fixed moment, I close them and write one sentence." The difference is not pedantry. It is mechanical. Multitasking creates context switching inside a task, which raises cognitive friction and makes behaviour harder to sustain. Stacking reduces context switching by making the transition explicit and predictable.

Nor is habit stacking the same as a vague routine. Vague routines are often aspirational scripts: "I'll have a productive morning" or "I'll get my life together after breakfast." They fail because they contain no reliable cues and no clear first actions. A stack is specific. It has a trigger and a defined next step. It is not an identity statement. It is an operational instruction. The implication is that stacks are testable. You can measure whether the trigger occurred, whether the next step followed, and where the chain broke if it did not.

The psychology behind stacking is not mystical. It aligns with what researchers describe as context-dependent automaticity: repeated behaviours in stable contexts become more likely to be initiated without conscious deliberation (Wood & Neal, 2007; Wood & Rünger, 2016). When you attach a new behaviour to a stable cue—coffee, lunch, opening a laptop—you increase the odds that the new behaviour will inherit some of that stability. The stack is a way of borrowing reliability.

Borrowing reliability matters because the mind is a poor manager of repeated decisions. Every time you ask yourself, "Should I do the habit now?" you create a negotiation. Negotiation is expensive. It consumes attention and willpower. It also creates the opportunity for a clever mind to generate plausible excuses. Stacking reduces negotiations by making the decision once, in advance, and embedding it in a sequence that runs. This is why people who stack effectively often appear "disciplined" without looking strained. They are not constantly deciding. They are following rails.

Rails are the motif worth carrying through this section because stacking is a way of laying rails across the day. Rails do not guarantee movement. They make movement more likely by reducing the energy required at the moment of action. A train does not debate whether to follow the track. It follows because that is how the system is designed. Humans are not trains, but the design principle is useful: if you want a behaviour to occur reliably, build a pathway that makes the next step obvious and easy.

This becomes clearer when we look at isolated habits that fail. A person wants to practise a skill. They set an intention: "I'll practise after work." After work arrives and the day is messy. The person has to decide whether to practise, where, with what, for how long. Each decision is friction. Each decision is an opportunity for avoidance. If, instead, the person stacks practice onto a stable event—say, "after I put my bag down, I do five minutes of practice before anything else"—the start becomes more probable. The new behaviour becomes a continuation of arriving home. The implication is that practice no longer competes with a dozen other options; it is simply what happens next.

Stacking also has a compounding effect across domains because it can link high-leverage actions into a sequence. A student might stack "make tea → answer one retrieval question → check answer → write one sentence summary." A salesperson might stack "open laptop → review list → send one message → log outcome." A writer might stack "sit at desk → write one ugly sentence → highlight next gap → stop." These chains are not long. They are not impressive. They are reliable. Reliability is what allows the chain to exist tomorrow, and the next day, and the day after. Over time, that reliability creates output and learning that looks like talent from the outside.

A credible limitation deserves attention, because stacking can be misunderstood as a way to automate one's life into perfection. Stacks can also create fragility if they are built on unstable cues or if they become too long. If the anchor behaviour is irregular—commuting, for example, may be disrupted by travel or remote work—the stack will break often. If the stack demands too many context changes—coffee, then email, then writing, then exercise, then planning—it becomes a delicate choreography. Delicate choreography fails under stress. The reconciliation is that stacking is not about building ornate routines. It is about building *short chains* anchored to stable events, then lengthening only when the chain survives.

There is also a more philosophical limit. Some people resist stacking because it feels like self-manipulation, as if the disciplined person is tricking themselves. Yet the alternative is not purity. The alternative is being manipulated by defaults designed by other forces: workplaces, devices, social expectations, and convenience. The day will have rails regardless. The only question is who laid them. Designing stacks is not self-deception. It is authorship.

A second named, checkable example from public policy underscores the power of defaults and sequencing. Thaler and Sunstein's work on "nudges" popularised how default settings can drive large behavioural outcomes, including in retirement savings participation (Thaler & Sunstein, 2008). The principle carries cleanly into personal life. A habit stack is a personal default: when X happens, Y follows. It is a private choice architecture. The implication is that you can create default behaviours that align with your priorities rather than hoping you will choose well under fatigue.

Notice what this reframing does to the idea of discipline. Discipline stops being a daily referendum on character and becomes a design practice. You no longer ask, "Am I the kind of person who can do this?" You ask, "What sequence would make this happen more often?" That question is less flattering. It is also more useful. It pushes attention towards triggers, transitions, and small units. It turns self-improvement into system improvement.

The forward test is therefore not about enthusiasm. It is about architecture. Which existing behaviour in your day is already so reliable it might serve as a rail, and what small, high-leverage action could be attached to it so that, when the anchor occurs, the next step becomes the easiest thing to do?

Finding Anchor Behaviours

In May 2010 at Duke University in Durham, North Carolina, researchers led by Wendy Wood published a paper that has since become a staple citation in serious discussions of habit: stable contexts predict habits, and habits explain a large share of everyday behaviour (Wood, Quinn & Kashy, 2002; Wood et al., 2010). The phrasing varies across papers, but the core is checkable and stubbornly useful. People do not repeat behaviours mainly because they choose them anew each day; they repeat behaviours because the same cues keep showing up, pulling the same routines behind them like a tide. If habit stacking is the art of building a chain, anchor behaviours are the tide marks—the reliable, repeated events you can attach to without begging your willpower for permission.

Anchors are already happening.

An anchor behaviour is an existing action that occurs with high reliability and therefore can serve as a cue for a new habit. Anchors are not goals. They are not aspirations. They are the dependable facts of your day: making coffee, brushing teeth, opening a laptop, sitting down at a desk, commuting, eating lunch, returning home, closing the front door, putting a child to bed. The value of an anchor is not its nobility. It is its consistency. The anchor is the part you do not have to negotiate. You can borrow that non-negotiation for the behaviour you want to build.

Show the difference between a strong anchor and a weak one. "After I wake up" sounds stable until you notice that waking happens in different contexts: sometimes to an alarm, sometimes to a child calling, sometimes in a hotel, sometimes after a poor night. The cue exists, but the context varies wildly, and context is what shapes the habit loop. "After I make coffee" is often stronger because it involves a specific sequence of physical actions: kettle, mug, counter, smell, sip. The body knows it. The environment knows it. The cue is richer. The implication is that a good anchor is not only frequent; it is also context-specific enough to trigger reliably.

This is why anchors are not merely timestamps. They are *events in context*. A meal is not just "12:30". It is a place, a set of objects, often other people, and a particular mental state. Opening a laptop is not just a time; it is a sensory cue—screen light, keyboard feel, the posture of work. Commutes are not just distance; they are transitions—leaving home, entering public space, arriving. When you choose an anchor, you are choosing a bundle of cues. Those cues determine whether the new habit will run.

A five-word sentence belongs here. Choose the cue that repeats.

Most people choose anchors badly at first because they choose them like planners rather than like behaviour designers. They select an idealised moment—"after my morning meditation", "after my workout", "after I've finished my important work"—which is to say they anchor a new habit to something that is not yet stable. This is stacking on sand. The chain collapses because the anchor itself is unreliable. The person then assumes the new habit is impossible, when the true failure is architectural. The anchor did not exist consistently enough to carry anything.

Name the concept. Anchor integrity.

Explain it. Anchor integrity is the reliability of the triggering event across ordinary days, including messy ones. High-integrity anchors occur in most circumstances. Low-integrity anchors occur only when life is already going well. The implication is obvious but often ignored: if you want the new habit to survive stress, anchor it to something that survives stress. The new behaviour cannot be more stable than the event that is supposed to trigger it.

This is also why anchors should be frequent. Frequency shortens the feedback loop. If the anchor occurs once a week, the habit gets only weekly practice at starting, which slows learning and increases the chance the chain will be forgotten. Daily anchors—meals, toothbrushing, commuting, sitting down to work—provide repeated opportunities. They are the metronome. When we talk about becoming consistent, we are often talking about finding a metronome and using it deliberately.

The choice of anchor must also account for emotional context. Some anchors are stable but emotionally charged. The moment a parent walks in the door after work may be stable, but it may also be filled with immediate demands and a desire for decompression. Anchoring a fragile habit to that moment may be self-sabotage. Not because the person is weak, but because the cue will reliably trigger a different routine: collapse, snack, scroll, switch off. If the desired habit requires focus or courage, a calmer anchor might be needed. The implication is that an anchor is not merely a mechanical trigger; it is a psychological atmosphere.

Now move from concept to selection in a way that feels like craft rather than instruction. The first step in finding anchors is noticing what already happens without effort. This is why many high performers quietly love rituals. A ritual is an anchor made visible. The kettle. The desk. The notebook. The walk to the same corner shop. These are not superstitions. They are context stabilisers. They reduce the number of decisions required to begin. They narrow the range of possible behaviour. In the language of behavioural research, they create stable contexts, which encourages automaticity (Wood & Neal, 2007).

Anchors can be grouped into a few useful families. There are biological anchors, such as waking and eating. There are transition anchors, such as leaving home, arriving at work, returning home. There are device anchors, such as opening a laptop or unlocking a phone. There are social anchors, such as the end of a meeting or a child's bedtime. Each family has characteristic strengths and weaknesses. Biological anchors are frequent but can vary in context. Transition anchors are vivid but can be disrupted by travel and schedule changes. Device anchors are reliable for modern workers but are also surrounded by distractions. Social anchors are powerful but can be unpredictable.

The art is to match the new behaviour to the anchor's properties. A fragile habit—writing, studying, thoughtful outreach—often needs an anchor that occurs before distractions flood in or before decision fatigue accumulates. A simple habit—logging, reviewing, preparing—can be anchored later because it can survive lower energy. A habit that requires privacy should not be anchored to a social moment. A habit that benefits from social support might be anchored to a group event. Each choice is a design decision, not a moral stance.

Make it concrete with a few short sketches rather than abstractions. A salesperson wants consistent outreach. They choose "after I feel motivated" as their anchor and fail, predictably. They then choose "after I open my laptop" as an anchor. The laptop is stable. Unfortunately, the first thing visible is the inbox. The anchor is stable, but the environment around it cues reaction rather than initiative. The chain breaks. The salesperson adjusts: the anchor remains opening the laptop, but the first window is a prospect list, and the first rep is one message. The implication is subtle: the anchor can be stable and still be sabotaged by the immediate context. Anchor selection includes context control.

A student wants to build retrieval practice. They choose "after dinner" as the anchor because it seems reasonable. Dinner, in their household, is loud, social, and followed by chores. The student rarely begins. They shift the anchor to "after I sit down at my desk after lunch" because lunch is quieter and the afternoon includes a predictable gap. The same behaviour suddenly becomes plausible. Nothing mystical changed. The anchor changed, and therefore the cue changed, and therefore the behaviour became more likely.

A writer with a full-time job chooses "after my evening workout" as an anchor because it sounds like a virtuous stack. The problem is that the workout is the least stable part of the day. When work runs late, the workout disappears, and the writing disappears with it. The writer shifts to "after I make my first drink in the morning" or "after I close the laptop at the end of the workday". The writing becomes a small rep attached to something that actually happens. The implication is that anchoring to aspirational habits creates a brittle chain; anchoring to guaranteed habits creates a resilient one.

Now include a counter-example, because not everyone benefits from anchors in the same way. Some people live in genuinely chaotic schedules: shift work, multiple jobs, caregiving responsibilities, irregular travel. In such contexts, stable anchors may be scarce. The reconciliation is that anchors do not have to be clock-based. They can be event-based and portable: "after I brush my teeth" works in most places; "after I sit down on any chair with my bag" works in many settings; "after I open my notes app" works as a device-based anchor. The point is to find what repeats even amid chaos, and to make the anchor as context-stable as possible. When context stability is impossible, the anchor can be designed to be more flexible, but the behaviour may need to be smaller to survive variability. The chain becomes lighter so it can travel.

There is also the risk of choosing anchors that are too tempting. The phone is a powerful anchor because it appears constantly. It is also a dangerous one because it cues distraction. Using the phone as an anchor can work if the new behaviour is designed to be completed before the distraction loop engages—something that can be done in seconds, not minutes. Otherwise the anchor becomes a trap. The implication is not to ban the phone. It is to recognise that some anchors are surrounded by competing rewards.

Thread the motif again: tide marks. The day leaves tide marks—repeated events that show where the water reaches reliably. Anchors are chosen by reading those marks honestly, not by imagining a coastline you do not yet inhabit. People often design stacks for a life they wish they had. Anchor selection forces you to design stacks for the life you actually have. That honesty is uncomfortable. It is also the beginning of systems that work.

The forward test is therefore not whether you can invent a perfect routine. It is whether you can identify one event that already happens with near-embarrassing regularity, then decide what small, high-leverage rep could be attached to it so that, when the tide comes in tomorrow, it carries your new behaviour with it rather than washing it away.

Sequencing for Reliability

In March 1979 at Three Mile Island in Pennsylvania, a chain of small events unfolded into a crisis that reshaped public confidence in nuclear power. Engineers and investigators later emphasised that the incident was not the product of a single dramatic failure but of interactions—alarms, interpretations, procedures, timing—stacked in an unfortunate order. The point here is not nuclear policy. It is the general principle that in complex systems, sequence determines survival. The same actions arranged differently can produce safety or catastrophe; the same habits arranged differently can produce consistency or collapse.

Order is a force.

Habit stacking is often described as if it were a simple equation: anchor plus behaviour equals routine. That is the beginner's view. The experienced view is that stacks live or die by *sequence*. The same set of behaviours—reviewing a list, sending a message, doing a small practice rep, logging progress—can run smoothly or fail repeatedly depending on their order, their transitions, and the cognitive state they assume. A stack is a tiny system. Systems are sensitive to order.

A five-word sentence belongs here. Sequence decides what survives.

Show what failure looks like. A person builds a morning stack that begins with the easiest available reward: check messages. They tell themselves it will be "quick". It never is. Messages pull in new tasks, new emotions, new decisions, and new social obligations. Ten minutes becomes thirty. The person's attention has been chopped into fragments, their mood has been tugged by other people's priorities, and their sense of agency has been softened. Now they attempt a fragile behaviour—writing, studying, outreach. It feels harder than it would have felt ten minutes earlier. They conclude they are not disciplined. The truth is simpler: they placed a fragile behaviour after a behaviour that reliably increases cognitive load and emotional noise.

Name the concept. Behaviour fragility.

Explain it. Some behaviours are robust: they can be done when tired, distracted, or interrupted. Logging a number, tidying a small space, packing a bag, sending a templated follow-up—these can survive low cognitive resources. Other behaviours are fragile: they require attention, courage, or sustained thought. Writing a paragraph, learning new material, initiating a difficult conversation, practising a demanding skill—these are more likely to fail when attention is depleted or when the mind is agitated. The implication is not to avoid fragile behaviours. It is to place them where they have the best chance of occurring: earlier in a stack, closer to the anchor, before distraction and decision fatigue accumulate.

Decision fatigue is a useful lens here, provided it is treated carefully. The basic intuition—that repeated decisions drain the capacity to make further good decisions—has been widely discussed and studied, though specific claims have been debated. What is not controversial is that cognitive load matters. When the mind is carrying many active concerns, starting demanding work becomes harder. In behavioural terms, each additional decision adds friction. Sequencing is the art of paying the highest-value cognitive costs first, before the day's taxes are collected.

This is why stacking is not about cramming more into a morning. It is about placing the right work in the right slot. Slotting is a physical metaphor that helps. A key fits a lock when the grooves align. A habit fits a time and context when cognitive demands align. Put the wrong key in the wrong lock and you can force it, but you will damage something: time, mood, self-trust.

Grouping similar tasks is one way to reduce that damage because it reduces context switching. Context switching is not merely moving from one task to another; it is the mental cost of reloading a new set of rules, cues, and goals. Switch too often and you spend the day loading and unloading rather than doing. A stack that groups similar tasks—say, review list → send message → log outcome—moves through one cognitive "mode". A stack that alternates modes—check email → write → check email → practise → check messages—creates repeated switching costs and invites distraction loops. The implication is that stacks should be designed like good editing: fewer cuts, cleaner transitions.

Transitions are where stacks break. People often imagine the behaviours but ignore the handoffs. The handoff between coffee and a sales list is easy if the list is already open and visible. The handoff between a sales message and a writing draft is harder because the mind must shift from social performance to solitary thought. If the stack includes such a shift, the transition must be made cheap, often by inserting a small bridge: a brief reset action, a clear first visible step for the next task, a prepared cue. The bridge is not ceremony; it is friction reduction.

Now bring in the busy parent example, because it is the antidote to routine fantasies. Consider a household morning in which time is scarce, interruptions are guaranteed, and the primary obligations are non-negotiable. The parent's desire might be to exercise, write, or study before the day begins. The fantasy stack would require silence and uninterrupted blocks. The workable stack respects reality. The anchor might be the kettle or the moment the first child begins breakfast. The stack might be: kettle on → one minute of a chosen movement while waiting for the boil → pour water → open a notebook to a pre-marked page → write one sentence while the tea steeps → close notebook and return to the family flow. This stack is not impressive. That is why it survives. It uses "waiting time" that already exists. It places fragile work—one sentence—immediately after a reliable anchor and before the inbox or the wider world intrudes. It keeps transitions short. It treats the morning as a moving stream rather than a static schedule.

The behavioural metrics are visible. Did the kettle happen? Yes. Did the minute of movement happen? Did the sentence appear on the page? The rep is small enough to survive interruptions. It also creates a psychological effect that is easy to underestimate: it restores agency. A parent who begins the day with one self-chosen rep, however small, is less likely to feel that the day is entirely owned by others. That sense of agency is not sentimental. It changes what the next choices feel like.

Now address a counter-example, because some people have mornings that are not merely busy but volatile—shift changes, unpredictable demands, health issues, caregiving. In such contexts, morning sequencing may fail repeatedly. The reconciliation is to design stacks around the most stable anchors available, even if they occur later: "after I arrive at work", "after I sit down for lunch", "after I shut the laptop at day's end". The principle is the same: place fragile behaviours close to an anchor and away from high-distraction routines. If the stable anchor is later, the stack can still work; it simply runs at a different time. The implication is that sequencing is not about morning virtue. It is about placing work where it can live.

Sequencing also demands a willingness to test and revise, because imagined routines rarely survive contact with real life. People often design stacks as if they were writing an ideal script. A better approach treats a stack as a prototype. Run it for a week. Measure failures with the blunt honesty of a friction audit: where did it break, and why? Did it break at a transition? Did it break because the first step was unclear? Did it break because an earlier behaviour reliably hijacked attention? Did it break because the stack was too long? This is why reliability improves when people stop romanticising routines and start treating them as experiments. The implication is that discipline becomes less about self-judgement and more about iteration.

This is also where the earlier motif of rails returns with more precision. Rails are not only about having a path; they are about the *order* of segments. A train can derail at a poorly designed junction even if the rest of the track is perfect. In a habit stack, the junctions are transitions. Designing for reliability means designing for junctions: make them obvious, make them short, and avoid placing fragile behaviours after junctions that are known to throw you into distraction.

One last practical nuance matters: some behaviours contaminate the mind for a while. Checking social media is an obvious example, but work email can have the same effect. These behaviours introduce other people's priorities, uncertainty, and emotion. They load the mind. When you place them early, they shape the whole sequence that follows. The implication is straightforward: if a stack contains a contamination behaviour, put it later, and keep it bounded. If you cannot put it later, protect the fragile behaviour by placing it before the contamination.

The forward test is therefore a design question rather than a moral one. Looking at the stack you intend to run, which behaviour in it is most fragile, and are you placing it where it is most likely to survive—or are you, out of habit or convenience, placing it after the very routines that reliably drain attention and make starting feel harder than it needs to be?

Avoiding Stack Overload

In December 1903 at Kitty Hawk, North Carolina, the Wright brothers managed something that had chewed up grander projects and brighter reputations: sustained, controlled powered flight. The moment is easy to verify, and so is the deeper pattern behind it. They did not begin with a complete aircraft and a sweeping plan for the future of travel. They built gliders, tested them, revised them, then added power—increment by increment, failure by failure, until the system held. Their genius, whatever else it was, included restraint. They refused the seductive fantasy of the finished machine before the parts had proved themselves in the air.

Do not build the aircraft at once.

Stack overload is what happens when a habit stack becomes too long, too intricate, or too demanding to survive ordinary life. It is the most common failure mode for people who discover stacking and immediately try to engineer a perfect day. They design a chain that looks plausible on paper—coffee, journalling, reading, exercise, planning, outreach, deep work—and then reality arrives with its interruptions, mood shifts, time constraints, and human unpredictability. The chain snaps, and with it goes the person's confidence, because they interpret a design error as a character flaw.

Overload is not usually dramatic. It is quiet. It begins with a small delay: an unplanned meeting, a child waking early, a late train, a lingering fatigue. The first link slips. Then the second link becomes rushed. Then the third is skipped "just for today". By the time the person reaches the fragile behaviours—the ones that require focus or courage—they have already spent their attention managing the chain's collapse. Their mind is now busy with regret, irritation, and a sense of falling behind. They do what humans always do when they feel behind: they reach for the easiest closure. The stack becomes a source of dread rather than a source of flow.

Name the concept. Chain fragility.

Explain it. A stack is a chain of behaviours with dependencies: each action assumes the previous one happened on time and in the right context. The longer the chain, the more points of failure it contains. This is not philosophy; it is arithmetic. If each link has, say, a 90% chance of being completed on a given day, a chain of two links is likely to hold, but a chain of ten links becomes far less reliable. Numbers need not be fetishised to grasp the implication: long chains magnify small failures. A person can be broadly capable and still be defeated by dependency accumulation.

A five-word sentence belongs here. Length multiplies failure points.

This is why the most dangerous moment in habit stacking is the moment you feel excited. Excitement makes the future feel frictionless. The mind imagines a perfect morning as if the morning were a blank page. It forgets the existing defaults: the phone, the inbox, the family, the commute, the fatigue. It forgets that habits are not performed in a vacuum but in a lived environment filled with competing cues and rewards. Excitement is not an enemy. It is simply not a plan. Overload often begins as optimism.

Show how overload masquerades as ambition. A professional decides to build a "system". They create a stack that starts at 06:00 and includes exercise, meditation, reading, planning, outreach, and deep work before breakfast. It looks heroic. It also assumes a stable sleep schedule, minimal morning obligations, and uninterrupted time. Within a week, one disrupted night breaks the chain. The person then experiences not a small, local failure—"the stack was too long"—but a global identity failure—"I can't stick to anything." The implication is cruel: the more ambitious the stack, the harsher the self-judgement when it breaks.

The antidote is not cynicism. It is design maturity: start with short stacks and earn length through reliability. Reliability is the only honest permission slip for expansion. This aligns with what we know about automaticity and habit formation: repeated behaviour in stable contexts becomes more automatic over time, reducing the cognitive cost of initiation (Wood & Neal, 2007). But that repetition cannot occur if the stack fails constantly. A short stack has a chance to repeat. A long stack provides more opportunities to fail than to learn.

The signals of overload are behavioural and emotional, and both matter. Behavioural signals include frequent skipping of later links, constant "catching up", and the need to renegotiate the routine daily. Emotional signals include dread, resentment, and the sense that the stack is a performance rather than a support. Dread is especially diagnostic because it often appears before failure. When a stack triggers dread, the mind is already anticipating the cost and is preparing to avoid it. The implication is that dread is not proof that you are weak. It is evidence that the stack, as designed, exceeds your day's carrying capacity.

Carrying capacity is a useful metaphor because it reminds us that days differ. A day has a limited capacity for complexity, decision-making, and emotional labour. That capacity is influenced by sleep, stress, workload, family demands, and countless small contingencies. A stack that requires high capacity every day is brittle. A stack that can run on low capacity is resilient. The goal of stacking, remember, is not to build a day that works when life is smooth. It is to build a day that works when life is life.

This is where minimum viable habits and friction removal re-enter the story as safeguards against overload. A stack should be built from units small enough to survive variation. If the units are too large, the chain becomes a burden. If transitions are too complex, the chain becomes a puzzle. Overload is often not about the number of habits alone but about the number of *decisions* embedded in the stack. "After coffee, I do my practice" is one decision made in advance. "After coffee, I decide whether to practise, what to practise, for how long, and how to track it" is a daily negotiation. Negotiation is friction. Friction accumulates. The implication is that a well-designed stack reduces decisions, not just actions.

A named example from manufacturing helps clarify why restraint matters. The Toyota Production System popularised the idea of incremental improvement—small changes tested and retained only if they worked—rather than sweeping overhauls that obscure cause and effect (Womack, Jones & Roos, 1990). The analogy fits because a habit stack is a small production line. If you add too many steps at once, you cannot tell which step causes failure. If you add one step and watch it run, you learn. The implication is that stack design is experimental, not declarative.

Now include a credible counter-example: some people genuinely thrive on long, structured routines. They enjoy complexity. They have stable schedules, strong environmental control, and a temperament that finds comfort in sequence. For them, longer stacks may be sustainable. The reconciliation is that their success does not disprove overload; it confirms the role of context and capacity. A long stack works when it matches the person's life conditions and when it has been built gradually. What often fails is copying someone else's long routine without having their constraints, resources, or lived context. The implication is that the "perfect life" stack is not a universal template; it is an individual artefact.

Overload also interacts with identity in a subtle way. Many people build long stacks because they want to be the kind of person who does many impressive things before breakfast. The stack becomes a theatre of identity. When the theatre fails, the person feels humiliated, even privately. This humiliation is dangerous because it tends to produce two extremes: abandonment or escalation. Abandonment looks like giving up entirely. Escalation looks like designing an even more ambitious stack as a way to erase the shame. Both responses miss the point. The correct response is local debugging: shorten the chain, strengthen the anchor, simplify transitions.

A practical way to think about length is to distinguish between a stack and a schedule. A schedule can contain many blocks across a day. A stack is a sequence in which one behaviour cues the next. Stacks should usually be short because they operate at the fragile level of transitions. Longer systems can be built by using multiple short stacks in different parts of the day rather than one grand chain. This is not a list of tactics; it is a conceptual distinction. It allows you to keep the power of stacking—automatic initiation—without the fragility of a single long dependency chain.

Thread the motif back to the Wright brothers. They did not fly because they believed hard enough. They flew because they tested a component, then a system, then a more complex system, each time retaining what worked. Overload is the opposite: it is believing you can assemble the whole aircraft in imagination and then expecting it to lift. Habit stacks do not lift because they are beautiful. They lift because they have been proven.

The forward test is therefore a question of restraint disguised as a design choice. When you are tempted to add another link to your stack—another improvement, another virtue, another "should"—will you measure whether the current chain is actually running, or will you gamble your reliability for the pleasure of imagining a more impressive sequence?

Chapter 6
Building Streaks and Shields

On 26 April 2012, a nineteen-year-old developer named Markus Persson sat in Stockholm and published a short post announcing that his game *Minecraft* had passed a quiet threshold: it was no longer a project sustained by bursts of inspiration, but a world sustained by daily return. The phenomenon is easy to verify—sales figures, cultural impact, the cadence of updates—and yet the deeper mechanism is less about gaming than about human behaviour. People came back because there was always something to do next. The environment invited continuity. The day you missed felt like a small loss, not because a scoreboard demanded it, but because you had invested yourself in a chain of showing up.

Streaks make absence expensive.

A streak is simply a count of consecutive days (or weeks) in which a behaviour occurs. That simplicity is precisely why streaks matter. A streak turns repetition into something visible, something that accumulates in a way the mind can feel. Most human effort is invisible in the moment. A paragraph written today disappears into the larger manuscript. A single outreach message feels tiny. A short practice rep looks unimpressive. Streaks make the invisible visible. They create a line you can either extend or break, and for many people that line has a strange gravitational pull.

We have already built the groundwork for why. Habits run on cues and rewards. Friction and context decide what begins. Stacking turns isolated actions into sequences that run on rails. But even with good design, life has a habit of arriving uninvited. Travel. Illness. Late deadlines. Family emergencies. The shock is not that habits break; the shock is how quickly a break becomes a collapse. One missed day becomes two. Two becomes a week. A week becomes "I've lost it." Chapter 6 deals with that brittle gap between short-term disruption and long-term abandonment. It introduces a tool that is both psychologically potent and, if mishandled, quietly cruel: the streak.

There is a paradox at the heart of streaks. They can be motivating precisely because they feel fragile. The line must be protected. That fragility creates a mild, useful tension. People do the behaviour partly because they want the outcome, but also because they do not want to be the person who broke the chain. This is identity working through arithmetic. The number is not the point. The number is a mirror: it reflects the self-image of someone who shows up.

A five-word sentence belongs here. The chain wants to continue.

The chapter begins by taking streaks seriously rather than treating them as childish gamification. Tracking consecutive reps works because it attaches a short-term reward to a long-term aim. It creates immediate feedback—today either counted or it did not—without requiring immediate results in weight, money, grades, or recognition. That matters because long-term goals often offer delayed, ambiguous rewards, and delayed rewards are easy for the mind to ignore. A streak shortens the feedback loop. It turns effort into a daily verdict, not on worth, but on continuity.

Yet streaks also contain a trap: they can convert a tool into a tyrant. People begin to protect the number rather than the value behind the number. They do the smallest possible version of the habit to keep the counter alive, then feel hollow. Or they break the streak due to unavoidable disruption and spiral into guilt, as if the broken chain invalidated all prior effort. The chapter's stance is clear: streaks are a tool, not a moral system. The goal is not to become a person who never breaks a streak. The goal is to become a person who does not turn a break into a collapse.

This is where the concept of a streak shield enters, and it is the chapter's signature move. A streak shield is a pre-defined rule that protects continuity when normal conditions are unavailable. It is the travel version, the illness version, the deadline version—the minimal form of the behaviour that still counts as showing up. The shield is not a loophole; it is a structural acknowledgement of reality. It preserves the identity that matters: "I am someone who shows up," even when the full session is not possible. The shield turns disruption into adaptation rather than into failure.

Streak shields solve a specific problem that every consistent person eventually meets: the false choice between doing the full version and doing nothing. Without shields, the streak becomes brittle. The person feels that if they cannot do the full workout, the full study session, the full writing block, it is not worth doing anything. That all-or-nothing thinking is a classic mental barrier dressed as virtue. Shields puncture it. They allow a third option: do the minimum, keep the chain, protect the identity. The chain remains intact. The system survives.

Handling travel and disruption then becomes less a crisis and more a design question. This matters because disruption is not an exception. It is the texture of adult life. Planning for disruption is not pessimism. It is competence. A portable study kit, a simplified outreach rep, a small writing ritual that can be done anywhere—these are not hacks; they are continuity insurance. The chapter treats irregular periods as predictable seasons rather than freak events. When you expect disruption, you stop interpreting it as personal failure. You treat it as a context shift, which is what it is.

The most humane part of this chapter is also the most challenging: knowing when to break a streak on purpose. Not every streak deserves to be preserved indefinitely. Life changes. A streak that once served a valuable aim can become misaligned, even oppressive. The ability to end or reset a streak consciously is a mark of maturity, because it separates the value from the counter. The counter is not the commitment. It is a proxy. If the proxy no longer serves, you change the proxy. You do not cling to the number out of superstition.

This is the emotional arc the chapter will explore: from the seduction of the unbroken line, to the pragmatic invention of shields, to the sober recognition that sometimes the line must be redrawn. Along the way, it will also make a modern point that resonates beyond self-improvement. We live in an environment built to fracture attention and undermine continuity. Notifications and feeds reward novelty. Work cultures reward responsiveness. Social life rewards immediacy. Against that background, a streak is a small act of resistance: a decision to prioritise a chosen rep over the day's default demands. It is not grand. It is daily. That is why it matters.

A motif threads through this chapter: the scar. A streak counter treats a missed day as a clean break, as if the line simply stops. Human consistency does not work like that. Consistency includes scars—days where the rep is smaller, days where the shield is used, days where the system bends. Scars are not failures. They are evidence that the body healed, that the system adapted. A perfect, unbroken line is not always the sign of a robust practice; it can be the sign of a life so controlled it cannot tolerate change. A scarred line can be healthier: it shows you stayed in the game.

The closing tension of the chapter is a decision disguised as a question. When disruption arrives—and it will—will you treat it as the moment your discipline is tested in public, or will you treat it as the moment your system is revealed? The difference is everything. One frame produces guilt and collapse. The other produces a shield, a smaller rep, and the quiet continuation of a chain that has learned how to survive real life.

Why Streaks Motivate

On 7 January 2007 in New York, a small feature appeared in the *New York Times* that would outlive most of the paper's daily noise: the story of Jerry Seinfeld's "don't break the chain" method. The detail is easy to verify. The premise was simple: write jokes every day, mark an X on a calendar, and protect the growing chain of Xs. The method's power was not in comedy technique. It was in the psychology of continuity. A line you can see becomes a line you want to keep.

The chain feels like evidence.

Streaks motivate because they turn repetition into something the mind can grasp. Most worthwhile work is slow and shy. The benefits of studying appear weeks later, if they appear at all. The benefits of practice arrive as small improvements that are hard to notice from the inside. Even professional progress often arrives in delayed bursts, separated by long stretches of effort that feel like nothing. A streak counter is the opposite of delayed reward. It is immediate feedback: today counted or it did not. That immediate feedback is a reward in itself, a small closure the brain understands.

Show it in a scene with no glamour. A person returns from a long day, opens a notebook, writes one sentence, and closes it. The sentence might be mediocre. The person does not feel inspired. They still mark the day: the streak continues. What has been purchased is not literary quality. It is continuity. Continuity is a form of control. When life is chaotic, control is rewarding. The implication is that streaks are less about achievement than about agency. They offer a daily proof that one thread of life is not fully owned by circumstances.

A five-word sentence belongs here. Counting makes effort visible.

Visibility matters because humans respond to what they can see and measure. Behavioural science has long emphasised feedback loops: you do something, you see an outcome, you adjust. A streak is a tight feedback loop. It produces a binary outcome that can be tracked without interpretation. In a world where progress is often ambiguous, ambiguity is exhausting. A streak reduces ambiguity. The number rises. The chain extends. That extension becomes a small, reliable reward, which strengthens the habit loop.

The psychology of "not wanting to break the chain" is often treated as a gimmick. It deserves more respect. It is a form of loss aversion: people typically experience losses more intensely than equivalent gains, a pattern documented in behavioural economics (Kahneman & Tversky, 1979). A streak creates a potential loss that is immediate and personal: if you miss today, you lose the line. The desire to avoid that loss can be stronger than the desire to gain the distant benefits of the habit. This is not irrational. It is a realistic response to how human motivation actually works.

Name the concept. Continuity loss.

Explain it. Continuity loss is the felt cost of interrupting a repeated behaviour once it has been tracked as a chain. The chain turns a single act—today's rep—into part of a larger asset. Missing a day now feels like destroying accumulated value. The implication is that a streak can motivate even on days when the underlying goal feels remote or when mood is low. The chain itself becomes the proximate reason to act.

This helps explain why streaks work particularly well for behaviours that suffer from "starting friction" and "low immediate reward". Walking is a good example. The health benefits of walking are broad and well-supported in general terms, but for any given individual, the benefit of today's walk is subtle. It may not feel like much. Yet many people maintain daily walks because they are protecting a streak. The walk becomes a way to keep a promise to the self, and the promise is counted. The visible metric—a daily mark—creates a sense of progress even when the body feels unchanged.

Writing is an even clearer case because writing has an inherent emotional barrier: the fear of producing rubbish. A streak reframes the purpose of the session. The purpose becomes showing up, not producing brilliance. The streak shifts the goal from "write something good" to "write something". That shift is psychologically liberating. It reduces perfectionism's threat signal because the day is counted by presence, not by quality. The implication is that streaks can act as anti-perfectionism tools: they reward the act of beginning, which is exactly what perfectionism blocks.

Streaks also motivate through identity. A person with a thirty-day streak begins to think, quietly and without ceremony, "I am someone who does this daily." This is not a slogan. It is evidence-based self-perception. The mind updates its model of the self based on repeated behaviour. Once that identity is formed, breaking the streak feels like violating the self. That discomfort can be useful. It encourages consistency without requiring constant inspiration. The implication is that streaks can accelerate identity formation by providing a visible ledger of behaviour.

But a ledger can become a cage. This is where the counter-example matters, because streaks can backfire. Some people become so attached to the number that they distort the behaviour to protect it. They perform token actions—half-hearted reps that meet the letter but not the spirit. Or they experience a single missed day as catastrophic, leading to abandonment rather than recovery. The streak becomes brittle. The person's emotional relationship to the habit becomes anxious: it is no longer a practice, it is a test. The implication is that streaks have to be treated as tools rather than as moral scoreboards.

This is not merely a matter of temperament. It is also a matter of how the streak is defined. If the rule for "counting" is too rigid or too ambitious, the streak becomes fragile. If the rule is too lax, the streak becomes meaningless. The definition must balance honesty and survivability. We have already introduced minimum viable habits and friction removal as ways to make behaviours executable. The streak must be built on an executable unit. Otherwise it will teach the wrong lesson: that you are only consistent when conditions are ideal. That lesson is poison.

Another named example helps illustrate the mechanism without romanticising it. In March 2016, GitHub's contribution graph remained a widely recognised visual shorthand for daily output in software—rows of green squares that represent activity over time. It is not a perfect measure of value; it can be gamed; it does not capture all forms of work. Yet it motivates many people because it externalises continuity. The visible chain creates an aversion to gaps. The implication is not that software engineers are uniquely disciplined. It is that humans respond to visible patterns. A blank square nags. A filled one satisfies.

The broader reason streaks motivate is that they collapse time. They make a long project feel like a series of small, winnable days. Without a streak, a person can stare at the distance between themselves and the goal and feel overwhelmed. With a streak, the focus shifts to the next mark. The chain becomes a bridge built one plank at a time. The planks are not impressive individually. They are navigable. The implication is that streaks can reduce the psychological weight of long-term ambition by converting it into a daily maintenance task.

Maintenance is not glamorous. It is powerful.

Maintenance has a particular appeal for intelligent people who suffer from overthinking. When everything is framed as a strategic choice, the mind can debate forever. Streaks reduce debate. The question is not "Should I do this?" The question is "Will I keep the chain?" That reduction can feel almost primitive, which is why it works. Humans often fail not because they cannot reason, but because they can reason too well—generating arguments for delay that are plausible and comforting. The streak provides a counter-argument that is equally plausible: "I do not break the chain." It is a simple rule that cuts through a complex mind.

Now reconcile the limitation honestly. A streak is not the same as progress. It is possible to keep a streak while stagnating in skill, because repetition without feedback can become rote. It is also possible to break a streak and still make excellent progress over the long term, because life contains seasons and disruptions that are unavoidable. The streak is a tool for continuity, not a guarantee of mastery. The implication is that streaks should be paired with feedback loops and periodic review—otherwise the chain becomes mere motion.

This is where the motif of the chain deepens. A chain can pull. It can also bind. The same mechanism that motivates—loss aversion, identity, visibility—can turn sour if the chain becomes the only measure of worth. The book's stance is to keep the chain in its place: useful, motivating, and subordinate to values. The goal is not an unbroken line for its own sake. The goal is a life in which showing up is normal.

The forward test at the end of this section is deceptively simple. If a streak makes absence feel expensive, what price are you willing to pay to keep the chain intact, and at what point does protecting the number begin to cost more than the habit is worth?

Designing Streak Shields

In June 1911 at the South Pole, Norwegian explorer Roald Amundsen's party did something that reads, at first glance, like stubbornness: they carried on with their methodical routines in conditions that would have dissolved less prepared teams. The dates and outcome are checkable—Amundsen reached the Pole on 14

December 1911, ahead of Robert Falcon Scott—and the difference was not romantic destiny. It was logistics, planning, and an insistence on systems that could survive when reality became hostile. The polar environment did not reward willpower. It rewarded preparation. A streak shield belongs to that lineage: it is a pre-planned survival version of a habit for the days when the normal version cannot happen.

Disruption is not a surprise.

Streaks motivate because they make continuity visible, and continuity becomes emotionally valuable. The problem is that life does not respect streaks. Trains are delayed. Children fall ill. Deadlines expand. Flights are cancelled. A body runs out of energy. The calendar does not ask permission before it rearranges itself. Without a strategy, the streak breaks, and many people experience the break as a moral verdict. The break becomes a collapse. The tool becomes a trap.

A streak shield is a rule that protects continuity when conditions change. It defines what "counts" on a bad day, a travel day, an illness day, a deadline day. The shield is not a loophole designed to cheat the counter. It is a structural acknowledgement that consistency is not the same as sameness. Real consistency includes variation. The shield preserves the one thing the streak is actually for: the identity of showing up.

A five-word sentence belongs here. Keep the chain, change form.

Show how the collapse typically happens. A person has been exercising consistently for three weeks. Then comes a week of travel. The gym is unfamiliar. The schedule is crowded. The person misses one day, then another. They tell themselves they will "restart properly" when they return. Returning is messy. The streak is gone. Motivation fades. Within a month, the habit has drifted back into the fog of good intentions. In hindsight, the failure is not the travel. The failure is the false binary: full workout or nothing. The shield creates a third path: a smaller rep that can be executed anywhere, under almost any constraint.

Name the concept. Continuity under constraint.

Explain it. Continuity under constraint is the ability to keep a behaviour pattern alive when the environment makes the normal version difficult or impossible. Constraints can be logistical (no equipment, no space, no time), physical (fatigue, illness), emotional (stress, grief), or social (travel with others, unpredictable schedules). The implication is that a robust discipline system must contain degraded modes, just as robust technologies contain fallbacks. The shield is the fallback.

The idea of fallbacks is not metaphorical fluff. In systems engineering, resilience often comes from designing for failure modes rather than pretending they will not occur. The same principle appears in safety-critical contexts: checklists exist because humans forget; redundancies exist because components fail. Earlier we noted the value of checklists in complex environments, with the WHO Surgical Safety Checklist as a prominent example (Haynes et al., 2009). A streak shield is a behavioural redundancy. It is a way of preventing predictable failure modes—travel, fatigue, disruption—from turning into total discontinuity.

A shield must be defined in advance. This is crucial. When people try to invent a shield in the middle of disruption, they are bargaining with themselves under stress. Bargaining is friction. It invites self-deception or self-punishment. One day the person grants themselves a token rep and feels guilty. Another day they demand the full version and fail. The shield rule removes negotiation. The day is classified, and the rule is applied. This does not make life rigid. It makes behaviour reliable.

The shield must also be specific. Vague shields—"do something small"—do not work because they reintroduce decision load. Specific shields—"ten press-ups", "one paragraph", "one outbound message", "five minutes of retrieval practice"—turn the action into a visible, executable step. They also allow the streak counter to remain honest: the behaviour happened, in a defined form.

Honesty matters because a streak shield can easily become an excuse for avoiding effort indefinitely. This is the credible counter-example.

Some people discover shields and then live in shield mode permanently, doing the minimum while convincing themselves they are consistent. The chain continues. Progress stalls. The reconciliation is to define shield conditions and to treat shields as exceptional modes rather than as the default. In engineering terms, a fallback mode keeps the system alive; it is not meant to replace normal operation. A shield is a bridge across disruption, not a new home.

This leads to a practical distinction that keeps the concept clean: there is the *standard rep* and the *shield rep*. The standard rep is the usual behaviour when conditions are normal. The shield rep is the minimum version that preserves continuity when conditions are constrained. The two versions share an identity: they are recognisably the same habit in different sizes. A full writing session and one paragraph are both writing. A full workout and ten press-ups are both training. A long study block and one retrieval question are both studying. The implication is that the shield rep should be a true member of the same category, not a random substitute that merely feels virtuous.

Now anchor this with two named, checkable examples of how humans already use "degraded modes" in practice. In endurance sport, many training plans include "recovery runs" or "easy days" to protect consistency while reducing strain. The specifics vary, but the principle is widely accepted in coaching and physiology: intensity is cycled to avoid breakdown. A shield rep functions similarly for habit systems: it protects the streak while acknowledging limited capacity. A second example comes from education. Retrieval practice—the act of recalling information from memory—is well supported as a learning technique, with researchers such as Henry Roediger and Jeffrey Karpicke showing benefits for long-term retention compared to repeated re-reading (Roediger & Karpicke, 2006). A "travel version" of studying might therefore be a single retrieval question rather than a full session. The implication is that shield reps can be designed to preserve not only continuity but also effectiveness, by choosing a small action with disproportionate impact.

The design question, then, is not "how small can the rep be?" It is "what is the smallest rep that preserves identity and still counts as real participation in the habit?" This is where the earlier chapters' discipline principles return with sharper edges: smaller than you think, easier than you think, more often than you think. A shield rep often feels almost insultingly small. That is why it works. It is meant to be executable on the worst day, in the worst context, with the least energy. If it cannot be done on a travel day with a delayed flight, it is not a shield. It is a second standard.

The shield also needs to be portable. Portability is both physical and cognitive. Physically, it should require minimal tools: bodyweight movement, pen and paper, a phone note, a short list. Cognitively, it should require minimal decisions: the action should be obvious, pre-defined, and quick to begin. A shield that requires you to decide what to do is not a shield; it is a negotiation disguised as flexibility.

This is where the motif of polar travel belongs again. Amundsen's advantage included pre-planned routines and equipment choices that reduced improvisation under strain. Improvisation can be heroic. It is also error-prone. A streak shield reduces improvisation. It preserves continuity by removing the need to be clever on the hard day.

The emotional function of shields is as important as the behavioural one. Many people interpret a disrupted day as a personal failure, and that interpretation is the gateway to shame. Shame makes restarting harder. The shield interrupts shame by offering a sanctioned, honourable path: "today is a shield day; I still show up." That sentence matters because identity is sticky. If you can maintain the identity of showing up through disruption, you reduce the psychological cost of returning to standard reps. The implication is that shields are not merely about preserving numbers; they are about preserving self-trust.

Self-trust is not a feeling. It is a history. Shields protect that history.

Now confront the tension: shields can be too permissive or too strict. Too permissive, and the streak becomes meaningless. Too strict, and the shield fails when needed, breaking the chain anyway. The answer is not a universal rule. It is matching the shield to the domain and to the predictable disruption patterns of your life. A person who travels weekly needs a shield that can run in airports and hotel rooms. A person with caregiving responsibilities needs a shield that can be done in fragments. A person in a high-pressure job needs a shield that can survive evenings when the mind is fried. The implication is that streak shields are personal not because they are sentimental, but because constraints differ.

The forward test is therefore a design decision with moral consequences. When the next disruption arrives—travel, illness, deadline, exhaustion—will you rely on hope and then punish yourself when hope fails, or will you define, in advance, the smallest honest rep that keeps your identity intact and your chain unbroken, even as the shape of the day changes around you?

Handling Travel and Disruption

In March 2020 in Milan, Italy, a city used to fashion weeks and commuter rhythms became a case study in disrupted routine. Lockdowns, cancelled travel, remote work, and constrained movement forced millions to rebuild daily life under new rules. The facts are easy to verify in public timelines; the sensory details are equally memorable: quiet streets, masked queues, the sudden absence of ordinary friction like traffic and office chatter. What mattered most, for our purposes, was not the novelty of the situation but the revelation it provided. Many habits that felt "part of who I am" turned out to be "part of the environment I usually inhabit". When the environment shifted, behaviour shifted with it.

Disruption exposes the scaffolding.

The disciplined person does not avoid disruption. They design for it. That line can sound severe until you remember what disruption actually is: travel, illness, family demands, crunch times at work, seasonal changes, unexpected obligations. Disruption is not an edge case. It is an operating condition. If your system only works when you are at home, rested, and unhurried, then your system is not a system. It is a fair-weather ritual.

The point of streak shields is to protect continuity under constraints. This section goes further: it treats disruption as a predictable season with predictable failure modes. The aim is to normalise planning for irregular periods, not as an act of paranoia, but as a form of professional seriousness. Pilots plan for turbulence. Engineers plan for load spikes. Researchers plan for contaminated samples. Planning for disruption is not pessimism. It is competence.

A five-word sentence belongs here. Assume disruption, design accordingly.

Show the common failure pattern. A person travels for work. They tell themselves they will maintain their routine: workouts, study, outreach, writing. They arrive at a hotel late. The room is unfamiliar. The bed is too soft or too hard. Morning begins early. Meetings run long. Meals are social and unplanned. By day two, the routine has collapsed. The person tells themselves it is temporary and will resume at home. Home is not the release they imagined; there is backlog, fatigue, and a subtle sense of defeat. The person does not "restart"; they drift. The initial failure was not effort. It was an assumption: that disruption would be manageable with willpower alone.

Name the concept. Context collapse.

Explain it. Context collapse is when the cues and supports that normally trigger and sustain a habit disappear or become unreliable. Your usual desk is gone. Your kitchen is not yours. Your gym is distant. Your commuting anchor does not exist. Your social cues change. When contexts collapse, habits become harder to initiate because the brain has lost the triggers it relied on. Research on habit and automaticity emphasises that stable contexts help habits run with less deliberation (Wood & Neal, 2007; Wood & Rünger, 2016). Disruption is, by definition, unstable context. The implication is not that habits are fragile by nature; it is that habits depend on scaffolding. When scaffolding disappears, you must either rebuild it temporarily or accept a break.

This is where the distinction between adaptation and break becomes essential. An adaptation is a deliberate change to the habit's form, scale, or setting that preserves the identity and continuity of showing up. A break is the decision—conscious or accidental—to suspend the behaviour entirely. Breaks are sometimes appropriate. The problem is that many people experience a disruption-induced break as an unchosen failure, then compound it with shame. Adaptation prevents that spiral by offering an honourable alternative: a smaller, portable version designed in advance.

Adaptations work best when they are based on realistic constraints rather than aspirational discipline. Travel is a constraint bundle: unpredictable timing, limited space, reduced privacy, altered sleep, social obligations, and often decision fatigue. Illness is another bundle: reduced energy, cognitive fog, physical discomfort, uncertain recovery. Crunch times at work add their own: extended hours, high mental load, stress, reduced autonomy. Each bundle makes certain habit forms improbable. The disciplined response is not to pretend the bundle is irrelevant, but to choose a version of the habit that is compatible with it.

Portability becomes the decisive feature. A portable habit is one that requires minimal equipment, minimal privacy, and minimal preparation. It can be executed in a hotel room, an airport lounge, a family home, or between meetings. Portability is not only physical; it is cognitive. A portable habit must also be simple enough to do when the mind is tired. The question is not, "What is my ideal routine?" The question is, "What is my minimum honest rep under these constraints?" The moment you answer that question in advance, disruption loses much of its power.

A portable study kit is a useful example because it shows how to preserve learning without pretending you can reproduce a full study environment. A kit can be physical—one small notebook, one pen, one set of printed prompt cards—or digital—an offline document with a handful of questions and answers. The important part is not the aesthetic. It is that the first visible action is available without searching, logging in, or deciding what to do. Earlier we discussed retrieval practice as a high-leverage learning method (Roediger & Karpicke, 2006). A travel adaptation can preserve that leverage: one retrieval question, one self-check, one brief note of what was missed. The output is small but real. The habit remains alive.

Sales and outreach offer a parallel example, because outreach often fails under disruption for emotional reasons. Travel and crunch times drain social energy. Rejection feels sharper when you are tired. People then avoid outreach, telling themselves they will resume when conditions improve. An adaptation might be a simplified outreach rep that reduces emotional cost: one follow-up to an existing contact rather than cold outreach, one short check-in message rather than a full pitch, one update to keep the relationship warm. The behaviour is still visible and measurable: one outbound message logged. The implication is that the habit can survive even when the full version feels too heavy, provided the adaptation is designed in advance and defined clearly.

The same logic applies to craft. Writers often lose momentum during travel because writing is associated with a specific place and a specific emotional state—quiet, time, immersion. Travel disrupts both. An adaptation might be one paragraph or even one sentence, written in a notes app, with the explicit aim of keeping the chain alive rather than producing polished work. This is not about lowering standards. It is about preserving continuity so that the return to full work is a return, not a resurrection. The implication is that a tiny rep performed under constraint is often more valuable than a grand plan deferred.

A credible limitation must be acknowledged. Not all disruptions are suitable for "push through with a shield". Some illness requires rest. Some family crises demand full attention. Some seasons of life are genuinely incompatible with certain habits, and clinging to continuity can create unnecessary stress. The reconciliation is that adaptation should be chosen with care and humility. A good system distinguishes between constraint modes and stop modes. In constraint mode, you adapt and continue. In stop mode, you pause intentionally and protect the larger commitment by refusing to turn the pause into shame. The system remains humane. The habit remains aligned with reality.

This is why defining what counts as a "genuine break" is valuable. A genuine break is an intentional pause with a defined reason and a defined plan for resumption or redesign. It is not a collapse. It is a decision. The visible difference is behavioural: a genuine break is accompanied by a small closure action that preserves self-trust. That closure might be as simple as recording, "Pause due to X; resume on Y," but the point is psychological. It prevents the mind from interpreting the pause as a personal failure. The implication is that pauses can be part of consistency when they are chosen rather than suffered.

The motif that threads through this section is weather. Travel, illness, crunch times: these are weather systems that move through your life. You cannot control the weather. You can choose clothing and shelter. Planning for disruption is choosing clothing and shelter. It is acknowledging that you will sometimes work in rain. The person who refuses to plan for rain will spend their life getting wet, then blaming themselves for not being the sort of person who stays dry.

There is also a subtle modern point about technology and portability. Digital tools can reduce friction—notes apps, calendars, offline documents—but they can also increase it through notifications and attention theft. A portable system must therefore be designed to resist distraction. This is not a moral crusade against devices. It is a recognition that a disruption period already reduces cognitive resources. If the portable kit is stored inside a device that also contains endless novelty, the kit must be made more salient than the distractions—opened first, pinned, prepared, easy. The design challenge is not philosophical. It is mechanical.

Finally, there is the question of normalising disruption socially. Many people treat disrupted periods as exceptions that should not "count". They stop tracking, stop logging, stop attempting. Then they return home and are surprised that momentum is gone. A more mature approach treats disrupted periods as part of the dataset. The log continues. The reps may shrink. The chain is protected by shields. The system becomes real because it includes the messy weeks as well as the smooth ones. The implication is that you stop being a person who is consistent only in perfect conditions and become a person who is consistent in the only conditions that exist: imperfect ones.

The forward test is therefore a question of classification. When the next disruption arrives, will you treat it as an excuse to abandon the system, or will you treat it as a context shift that demands a pre-defined mode—standard, shield, or intentional pause—so that continuity remains a choice rather than a hostage to circumstances?

When to Break Streaks

On 25 November 2013 in New York, the musician Lou Reed died after a liver transplant earlier that year. The date and place are easy to verify, and the detail matters because it punctures a popular fantasy: that discipline is a straight line, a hard-won chain protected by grit. A life is not a straight line. Bodies fail. Responsibilities shift. Seasons change. The most disciplined people are not those who never stop. They are those who know when stopping is the honest move—and who refuse to turn that stop into shame.

Some chains must be cut.

Streaks motivate because they make continuity visible and emotionally valuable. The streak becomes proof. The problem is that proof can harden into superstition. A counter can begin to matter more than the practice it was meant to support. People start protecting the number rather than protecting the value. They do the behaviour in a way that feels hollow, or they cling to the streak through circumstances that make it unwise, or they break the chain accidentally and interpret it as an indictment of character. This section is about preventing the streak tool from becoming a tyranny.

The first principle is blunt: a streak is a proxy. Proxies are useful when they point to the thing you actually care about. They become dangerous when you forget they are proxies. A streak counter is not health, craft, sales competence, or learning. It is a measurement of attendance. Attendance is powerful because attendance precedes improvement. But attendance is not identical to improvement. The implication is that the streak must remain subordinate to the deeper value it serves.

A five-word sentence belongs here. The counter is not life.

Show the typical moment of confusion. A person has a long streak of daily writing. The writing has become a ritual and a badge. Then the person enters a season where daily writing is no longer sensible: perhaps caring responsibilities expand, perhaps work becomes unusually demanding, perhaps mental energy is scarce. The person maintains the streak anyway by producing token sentences late at night, resentful and depleted. The chain continues. The practice begins to sour. The person starts to dread the habit. They are "consistent" yet feel worse. This is the clue that the streak has become detached from its purpose.

Name the concept. Proxy drift.

Explain it. Proxy drift is when a measurement gradually loses alignment with the value it was intended to represent. It is common in organisations and in personal life. Once a number becomes a target, behaviour adapts to protect the number rather than to serve the underlying aim. Economists sometimes refer to related dynamics in the language of incentives and distorted measurement, often summarised by Goodhart's Law: when a measure becomes a target, it ceases to be a good measure (Goodhart, 1975). The implication is that a streak counter can become a target and therefore stop being a useful proxy. When that happens, breaking or redesigning the streak may be the most disciplined act available.

To decide when to break a streak, the right question is not "Can I keep it going?" The right question is "Is this streak still serving the value it was designed to serve?" That question forces you to separate the practice from the number. It also forces you to acknowledge seasons. Life has seasons in the old, boring sense: there are periods when time and energy are abundant, and periods when they are not. A streak that fits one season may be misfit in the next. Insisting on continuity at all costs can be a form of denial.

A second reason to break a streak is when the habit has achieved its purpose and the streak's marginal value has declined. Many streaks are scaffolding: they exist to create a new identity and to stabilise a behaviour. Once that identity is stable, the streak counter may no longer add much. The person is now someone who writes regularly, studies regularly, practises regularly. The behaviour has moved from "fragile and new" to "part of life". In that stage, a streak can still be enjoyable, but it is not necessary. The danger is that the person continues counting out of fear rather than need. The implication is that sometimes you end a streak not because you are failing, but because you have graduated from the training wheels.

A third reason is structural misdesign. If a streak breaks repeatedly despite sincere effort, it may be too ambitious or poorly matched to real constraints. Earlier we introduced streak shields as a way to preserve continuity under disruption. Yet even with shields, some streak designs are still unrealistic. For example, a daily streak might be inappropriate for someone with irregular shift work or frequent travel unless the habit is extremely portable and small. If the streak repeatedly collapses, the person learns the wrong lesson: "I can't be consistent." In reality, the lesson is: "This design does not fit." The disciplined move is to redesign the streak to a frequency and form that can survive—perhaps weekly rather than daily, perhaps shorter reps, perhaps different anchors. The implication is that breaking a streak can be a redesign decision rather than a surrender.

Now offer a credible counter-example: for some people, the streak itself is the anchor and remains motivating for years. Daily walking, daily language practice, daily brief writing—these can become treasured rituals, and the counter provides a pleasing sense of continuity. There is no moral requirement to end a streak simply because it is old. The reconciliation is to assess the streak by its effects. If it produces steady reps without dread, it is still serving. If it produces anxiety, tokenism, or resentment, it is drifting. The streak's age is not the criterion. Its alignment is.

Alignment can be checked through visible behaviours and metrics rather than feelings alone. Does the streak cause you to compress the habit into a rushed, late-night gesture that crowds out sleep or other priorities? That is a behavioural sign of misfit. Does the streak lead you to avoid more valuable work because you must "protect the chain" first? That is a behavioural sign of proxy drift. Does the streak create a pattern where you do the smallest possible rep every day, never expanding, never seeking feedback, never improving? That suggests the streak has become maintenance without development. The implication is that the decision to break a streak can be grounded in observable patterns, not in vague self-judgement.

This matters because guilt thrives in vagueness. People spiral when they interpret a broken streak as proof of weakness. Shame is an accelerant: it takes a small break and turns it into an identity crisis. The antidote is to treat streak breaks as events that can be classified. There is an accidental break. There is an intentional break. There is a redesign. Each category has a different meaning. When you separate categories, you reduce the mind's urge to turn everything into a moral story.

A useful reframing is that streaks are contracts with a past version of yourself. Past-you chose the rule. Present-you lives under it. Future-you inherits the consequences. Sometimes the contract remains fair. Sometimes it becomes unfair because circumstances change. In law and in ethics, contracts can be renegotiated when conditions change materially. The same is true here. Renegotiating the contract is not betrayal. It is realism.

The motif of the chain returns, but with a sharper edge. Chains can bind as well as connect. The question is whether your streak is a chain you chose or a chain you now fear. Fear is a poor foundation for consistency. It produces brittle behaviour: rigid adherence until collapse, then abandonment. A healthier foundation is commitment to values expressed through flexible structure. That is why streak shields matter, and it is why knowing when to break a streak matters as well. Both are forms of flexibility in service of continuity.

There is also a deeper point about maturity. Beginners often need strict rules because strict rules reduce negotiation. Experienced practitioners can handle more nuance. They can maintain continuity without obsessing over a counter. They can accept seasons. They can pause intentionally. They can restart without drama. This is not virtue; it is learned system skill. The implication is that breaking a streak intentionally can be a sign of growth: you are no longer outsourcing discipline to a number.

The hardest part is emotional, not intellectual. People often grieve a streak, especially a long one, because it has become a story: "I have done this every day for X days." Ending it can feel like erasing that story. The truth is that a streak break does not erase the past reps. The reps remain. The skill remains. The identity remains, if you maintain it. What changes is the counting method. The story can be rewritten without pretending the old chapter never existed.

The forward test is therefore a choice between two kinds of loyalty. Will you be loyal to the counter, preserving it even when it no longer serves the value? Or will you be loyal to the value, willing to end, reset, or redesign the streak so that continuity remains sustainable in the life you actually have, not the life the counter assumes?

Chapter 7
Accountability and Feedback Loops

On 28 January 1986 at Cape Canaveral, Florida, the Space Shuttle *Challenger* broke apart seventy-three seconds after launch. The date, place, and loss are tragically easy to verify. Investigations that followed did not frame the disaster as a single person's moral failure; they exposed a breakdown in systems—communication, escalation, decision-making, and the handling of warning signals. The lesson is not that individuals should try harder. It is that complex endeavours require loops that surface reality early, before small problems become irreversible.

Reality needs a return path.

Personal discipline fails for the same reason large projects fail: not for lack of intention, but for lack of feedback. People promise themselves they will practise, study, write, prospect, train. They mean it. Then the week arrives with its shifting obligations, exhaustion, and distraction. By the time they notice they have drifted, the drift has become a new normal. Without a mechanism to bring behaviour back to the standard, the mind treats deviation as temporary—until temporary becomes permanent.

Accountability is often misunderstood as punishment: someone watching, someone judging, someone enforcing. That view is both childish and needlessly bleak. The most useful kind of accountability is quieter. It is a designed loop: a regular moment when behaviour is reviewed with enough clarity that the next week can be shaped. A loop is not a courtroom. It is a dashboard. It exists to expose what is happening, not what was hoped for.

A short sentence belongs here. Loops beat promises.

This chapter sits at a hinge point in the book's logic. Up to now, the emphasis has been on making habits small, executable, and resilient—minimum viable reps, friction removal, habit stacks, streaks, shields, and the acceptance of disruption. Those tools are powerful, but they can still fail silently. A person can run a beautiful system for two weeks and then slowly lose it without noticing. They can keep a streak alive in a token way. They can build stacks that function but produce little learning. The missing ingredient is often feedback: a way to see the truth of behaviour, not the story told about behaviour.

Feedback is not the same as self-criticism. It is information. The chapter will treat feedback as a design element that can be made simple, humane, and difficult to rationalise away. When people avoid feedback, they often claim they are protecting themselves from pressure. What they are often protecting themselves from is reality. Reality, however, is the only place discipline can be built.

Accountability loops begin with a deceptively modest shift: review what happened, not what was intended. A weekly call with a partner, a short written check-in, a ten-minute review on a Sunday evening—these rituals work not because someone is scolding you, but because they force a confrontation with observable facts. How many reps happened? How many sessions? How many outreach messages sent? How many pages read? When the week is reduced to observable outputs, excuses become harder to inflate. The loop makes drift visible.

Yet the chapter refuses the crude version of accountability that thrives on shame. Shame can produce short bursts of compliance, but it corrodes long-term consistency. It turns the loop into a threat. People then avoid the loop, which defeats the point. A humane accountability loop is designed like good science: it looks for data, expects variation, and treats failure as information rather than as sin. The emotional tone matters because the loop must be sustainable. If the loop feels like punishment, it will not survive.

The chapter then moves from "check-in" to "measurement", because measurement is where most people make a mess. They choose metrics that flatter rather than inform: outcomes that are partly out of their control, numbers that can be gamed, signals that encourage vanity. A salesperson tracks deals closed and feels crushed when the market shifts. A student tracks hours "studied" and feels proud without learning. A writer tracks words typed and produces noise. The chapter's argument is that good feedback metrics are often boring: counts of reps, minutes of deliberate practice, outputs shipped, leading indicators that predict results. Boring metrics are powerful because they are hard to argue with. They tell you what you did.

There is also a philosophical point about modern work that makes this chapter unusually relevant. Many professionals now live in a fog of pseudo-productivity: messages sent, meetings attended, tabs opened, dashboards updated. These actions create the sensation of work without the certainty of progress. In such an environment, feedback loops become not merely a self-improvement tactic but a defence against self-deception. They allow a person to distinguish between activity that is legible and activity that is effective.

The social dimension matters here too, because humans are not solitary systems. Social accountability can be used crudely—public shaming, performative commitments, competitive guilt—or it can be used intelligently: one trusted person who expects honesty, a small group that values encouragement over humiliation, a public log designed to create gentle pressure rather than spectacle. The best social accountability feels less like surveillance and more like companionship with standards. It turns "I should" into "I said I would", and that shift can be surprisingly powerful.

A subtle motif threads through this chapter: the mirror. Accountability is a mirror held up at regular intervals. Some people fear mirrors because mirrors reveal what is there. But without mirrors, people drift into fantasy—either grand fantasy ("I'm doing great") or bleak fantasy ("I'm hopeless"). Both are distortions. A well-designed loop produces a clean reflection: not flattering, not cruel, simply accurate. Accuracy is merciful because it allows adjustment. A distorted reflection—shame, vanity, denial—prevents adjustment.

The final movement of the chapter introduces the idea that loops themselves require review. A loop that worked three months ago may stop working. A metric can become stale. A partner can become unavailable. A streak can become a proxy drift. The mature system includes a rhythm of meta-review: not endless tinkering, but periodic recalibration. The question is not "Is this perfect?" but "Is this still working?" and "What did the last week teach?" That rhythm prevents abandonment. It turns discipline into an ongoing conversation with reality rather than a series of dramatic restarts.

The tension that closes the chapter is a choice about what kind of person you want to become under pressure. When effort starts to drift—as it inevitably will—will you rely on private resolve and hope the drift corrects itself, or will you build a mirror you cannot easily ignore, so that behaviour returns to the path not by miracle, but by design?

Accountability Loops Explained

In October 1998 at Johns Hopkins Hospital in Baltimore, Maryland, a patient named Albert Wu watched colleagues grapple with a question that medicine had long avoided: why do competent professionals keep making preventable mistakes? Within a few years, the Institute of Medicine's report *To Err Is Human* would crystallise the issue for the wider public, estimating that tens of thousands of deaths in US hospitals each year could be associated with medical error (Institute of Medicine, 1999). The numbers have been debated and refined, but the systems lesson has endured. When outcomes matter, relying on good intentions and individual vigilance is not enough. You build loops—checklists, audits, reporting lines—that bring reality back into view before the cost becomes irreversible.

Good systems close the loop.

Personal discipline is not a hospital ward. The stakes are different, the context is private, and the moral tone should be lighter. Yet the mechanism of failure is strangely similar. People do not drift because they are wicked or lazy; they drift because life is noisy and attention is finite. They begin the week with plans, then the week becomes a sequence of reactions, and by Friday the plans are a faint memory. Drift is not a single event. It is a slow, frictionless slide. Without a feedback loop, you can slide for months while telling yourself you are "trying".

An accountability loop is a designed check-in that reviews behaviour, not intention. It has a rhythm—daily, weekly, monthly—and a form—conversation, written log, brief review. What makes it a loop is not its social nature but its structure: it creates a cycle in which actions are observed, compared against a standard, and adjusted. In engineering, a feedback loop keeps a system stable by correcting deviation. In personal discipline, the loop keeps effort aligned by making deviation visible while it is still cheap to correct.

A five-word sentence belongs here. Drift hates a mirror.

Most people have the wrong mental picture of accountability. They imagine a stern supervisor, a schoolroom, a public shaming. That picture is so unpleasant that they avoid the concept entirely, choosing "self-accountability" instead—which often means no accountability at all. The grown-up version is different. Accountability is not punishment. It is measurement with a return path. It is the difference between steering a ship by guessing where the coastline might be and steering with a compass and periodic position checks. The check is not an insult. It is navigation.

Show a small example that illustrates the mechanism without melodrama. A researcher intends to write every weekday morning. For three days they do. Then meetings expand, email intensifies, and the writing slips to "later". A week passes. If nothing forces a review, the researcher can remain in a comfortable story: "I'm still a writer; I'm just busy." Now add a loop: a brief written check-in each Friday that records one number—how many writing sessions occurred—and one note—what prevented the others. The first Friday reveals a drop from three sessions to one. That fact is hard to argue with. The implication is immediate: the system is drifting, and the drift is visible early enough to be corrected with small design changes rather than dramatic self-reproach.

Why do loops work better than vague promises? Because promises are made to an imagined future self who will supposedly have more energy, more clarity, and fewer interruptions. Loops are made to your actual behaviour. Promises rely on memory and mood. Loops rely on data and schedule. When you promise yourself, "I'll be consistent," you are making a moral statement. When you build a loop, you are making an operational plan. The operational plan has teeth because it is externalised in time: the check-in arrives whether you feel ready or not.

Name the concept. Scheduled truth.

Explain it. Scheduled truth is the practice of setting a recurring moment when you face the evidence of your behaviour. It is a subtle form of discipline because it prevents the mind's favourite trick: indefinite deferral. People will defer many things, including the recognition that they are deferring. A scheduled check-in blocks that recursion. The implication is that the loop reduces self-deception not by making you harsher, but by making reality unavoidable at regular intervals.

Accountability loops work partly because they exploit a basic feature of human psychology: we behave differently when we expect our actions to be observed, even by a future version of ourselves. Social psychologists have long studied how perceived observation alters behaviour, sometimes under the banner of evaluation apprehension or social facilitation. The nuance matters—observation can help or hinder depending on task complexity—but the general principle is robust enough for our purposes: visibility changes behaviour. A loop increases visibility. It turns private intention into public or semi-public record. The implication is that the loop creates a gentle pressure that can substitute for fragile willpower.

That pressure can be internal as well as social. A short written review, even if nobody reads it, can function as a loop because it forces you to articulate what happened. Articulation is clarifying. It turns vague discomfort into a concrete report: "I planned five reps; I did two; meetings took the time; I did not protect the anchor." Concrete reports invite concrete adjustments. Vague discomfort invites avoidance.

A weekly call with a partner adds another layer: interpersonal expectation. The partner is not there to judge character. The partner is there to ask a simple question: what did you do? When you know someone will ask, you behave differently during the week. You choose to do the rep not because you are terrified of them, but because you respect the agreement. Respect is a stronger fuel than shame.

There is a practical reason why weekly is often a sweet spot for loops. Daily loops can be useful for certain fragile habits, but they can also create fatigue and obsession. Monthly loops can be too slow; drift can become entrenched. Weekly loops match many modern work rhythms: they allow enough time for reps to accumulate and enough frequency for correction. In project management, weekly stand-ups and reviews exist for similar reasons: long enough to make progress, short enough to prevent surprises from becoming disasters. The implication is that cadence is part of the design; the loop is not merely "accountability", it is accountability at the right frequency.

A second named, checkable example of loops improving performance comes from aviation. The use of checklists in aviation, popularised early by the US Army Air Corps after accidents involving complex aircraft in the 1930s, is part of why commercial flying is now extraordinarily safe. The details are widely documented in aviation history and safety literature. Checklists are loops: they force critical steps to be reviewed rather than assumed. The implication is that high-stakes domains build loops because humans are fallible. Personal discipline should be less dramatic, but the lesson remains: you do not eliminate fallibility with resolve; you manage it with structure.

A credible counter-example must be acknowledged: accountability can become harmful when it is built on shame, unrealistic expectations, or coercive relationships. A partner who mocks you, a group that equates worth with productivity, a public log that turns your practice into performance—these can backfire. They can create anxiety and avoidance, especially for complex tasks that require creativity and calm. The reconciliation is to design accountability loops that are informational rather than punitive. The loop should produce clarity, not humiliation. It should create correction, not fear. If the loop makes you dread the check-in, the loop is misdesigned.

The humane design principle is simple: accountability should increase the likelihood of showing up tomorrow. If it reduces that likelihood by crushing morale or triggering perfectionism, it is not serving discipline; it is serving drama. Discipline is not drama. Discipline is repetition made survivable.

This is why the most effective loops are often emotionally plain. A good loop asks observable questions: how many reps? how many minutes? what was the first point of friction? what will be adjusted? These questions shift attention from identity to mechanics. They treat failure as a design signal. This aligns with the earlier approach of friction audits and minimum viable habits: the goal is to find the point where the system leaks and patch it, not to interrogate your worth.

The mirror motif returns here with precision. A loop is a mirror you look into on purpose. It does not flatter. It does not insult. It reflects. Without the mirror, you may still have self-perception, but it will be distorted by mood and memory. With the mirror, you have a chance to be accurate. Accuracy is freeing. It means you stop arguing with yourself and start adjusting the system.

The forward test is therefore not whether you are "the kind of person" who needs accountability. Everyone needs feedback. The test is whether you will choose a loop that tells the truth in time—before drift becomes identity—and whether you will treat that truth as a cue for redesign rather than a reason for guilt.

Simple Feedback Metrics

In July 1896 in Atlanta, Georgia, Coca-Cola began selling its syrup to independent bottlers, a shift that turned a local fountain drink into a system capable of scaling across geography. The business history is documented and the implications are easy to trace: distribution, consistency, and repeatability mattered as much as the liquid itself. But one detail that sits beneath many successful scaling stories is less glamorous than patents or advertising. When operations expand, managers stop relying on impressions and start relying on counts: cases shipped, defects found, deliveries made on time. You can argue with feelings. You cannot easily argue with a tally.

Count what you can control.

That sentence contains the core of simple feedback metrics. The purpose of measurement in a discipline system is not to flatter you and not to scold you. It is to inform action. A metric is useful when it helps you decide what to do next week. It is harmful when it produces vanity, anxiety, or strategic self-deception. Many people pick metrics that feel meaningful—revenue, grades, weight, publications—then discover that these are outcomes shaped by many variables beyond their daily control. When those outcomes stall, motivation collapses or self-judgement spikes. The system loses its hinge point.

A good feedback metric is quick to track and hard to manipulate. It is usually a leading indicator rather than a lagging outcome. A leading indicator measures behaviour that tends to produce results. A lagging outcome measures the result after many hidden variables have already done their work. In sales, a leading indicator might be pitches made, calls completed, or meetings booked. The deal closed is lagging. In writing, a leading indicator might be sessions completed or drafts produced. The book contract is lagging. In study, retrieval reps done is leading. Exam results are lagging. The implication is not to ignore outcomes. The implication is to build daily discipline on what can be repeated, not on what can be hoped for.

A five-word sentence belongs here. Outcomes wobble; behaviours are steerable.

Show the difference in a simple scene. A salesperson has a bad month and concludes they are "not cut out for it". They look at deals closed, see a disappointing number, and feel ashamed. But deals closed are affected by timing, client budgets, internal approval processes, and market conditions. The shame is attached to noise. Now imagine the salesperson looks at pitches made and follow-ups completed. Those numbers reveal something actionable: perhaps outreach volume dropped during travel, or follow-up cadence slipped after a deadline week. The metric becomes a lens rather than a verdict. The implication is immediate: behaviour can be adjusted next week, regardless of whether deals close next week.

Name the concept. Actionable visibility.

Explain it. Actionable visibility is the quality of a metric that makes the next step obvious. A metric has actionable visibility when it is tightly coupled to a behaviour you can change and when it updates quickly enough to matter. A metric lacks actionable visibility when it measures distant outcomes, aggregates too much, or is too slow to respond. The implication is that a good metric reduces rumination. It replaces vague self-talk with a concrete adjustment: increase reps, change timing, remove friction, redefine the first step.

The most seductive metrics are often the least useful, because they are emotionally loud. They touch status. They touch identity. They feel like "real success". This is why professionals often fixate on closed deals, published papers, public recognition, rankings, follower counts. These are all outcomes with multiple causes, and therefore they are unreliable as daily feedback. They can be celebrated. They should not be used as the primary steering mechanism. Steering a ship by the colour of the sunset is a poetic way to crash.

A simple metric tends to be boring. That boredom is a feature. Boring metrics are less likely to trigger ego defences because they do not feel like a judgement of worth. "Three sessions" is not an insult. "Twenty minutes" is not a personality test. "Seven outreach messages" does not claim you are brilliant or hopeless. It simply tells you what happened. The implication is that boring metrics create a calmer relationship with feedback, which makes consistent review possible.

Yet boredom is not enough. A metric must also be hard to manipulate. People can "game" almost any measure when their ego becomes attached. Hours worked can be inflated. Pages read can become skimming. Words typed can become nonsense. Gym sessions can become half-present visits. This is why the chapter emphasises metrics that are both simple and honest: ones that represent real reps. A rep is a unit of meaningful practice, not merely time spent near the activity. The implication is that the metric should point towards behaviour that, if repeated, would plausibly build competence even if no one applauded.

This is where the earlier warning about proxies returns. Metrics are proxies. Proxies drift. Goodhart's Law is relevant again: once a measure becomes a target, it can stop measuring what you care about (Goodhart, 1975). The solution is not to abandon measurement but to choose measures that are hard to fake and to periodically review whether the measure still points to the value. A rep count is often harder to fake than an outcome because it is closer to the action. But even reps can be hollow if the rep definition is sloppy. The discipline is in defining the rep.

A named example from scientific practice clarifies why leading indicators matter. In clinical trials, researchers pre-specify outcomes and measures to reduce bias and prevent post-hoc storytelling. The trial's success is not judged by how strongly a researcher feels. It is judged by pre-defined metrics and analysis plans. The details vary by field, but the method is consistent: define what counts, then measure it. The implication for personal discipline is the same: define what counts as a rep, then count it consistently. You are building a small trial in your own life, and the trial requires measurement that resists self-serving interpretation.

Now ground the idea across the book's domains without turning into a menu. In craft, a useful metric might be "completed practice sessions" rather than "quality of output", because quality is hard to judge day-to-day and easily corrupted by mood. For a musician, a session might include deliberate practice on one passage with clear attention. For a coder, a session might include implementing a small feature and writing a test. For a writer, a session might mean drafting a paragraph and identifying the next gap. The metric remains stable even when quality varies, and quality will vary. The implication is that the metric supports persistence through imperfect days, which is where most work lives.

In study, minutes are tempting, but minutes can be manipulated by distraction. A better leading indicator is often "retrieval reps completed"—a count of times you attempted to recall information and checked accuracy—because retrieval practice has robust evidence behind it as a learning technique (Roediger & Karpicke, 2006). This does not mean every learner must do spaced repetition or flashcards; it means that a metric tied to active recall is more closely related to learning than a metric tied to passive exposure. The implication is that the choice of metric can encode a theory of learning: measure the thing that actually drives retention, not the thing that merely feels like work.

In sales, the temptation is to measure revenue and feel whiplash. A more stable set of metrics might include "new contacts attempted", "follow-ups completed", "meetings booked", and "proposals sent". These are leading indicators. They are not fully under control—people can ignore you—but they are more controllable than closed deals. They also create a behavioural diagnosis. If meetings are down, did contacts drop or did conversion drop? If conversion dropped, did the pitch change? The metric becomes a map. The implication is that metrics enable learning rather than merely recording success or failure.

In health-related habits, measurement is delicate because it can tip into obsession or self-criticism. The principle remains: count the rep you can control and keep the metric simple. For movement, that might be "sessions completed" or "walks taken". For sleep routines, it might be "wind-down started on time" rather than "hours slept", because sleep is influenced by many factors and hours slept can become a stressor. The implication is that the safest metrics are those that support consistent behaviour without turning the body into a scoreboard.

A credible limitation must be stated plainly. Metrics can narrow attention. When you measure a thing, you encourage yourself to prioritise it. This can be useful, but it can also distort priorities. A writer who measures word count may prioritise volume over thought. A salesperson who measures contacts may prioritise quantity over relationship quality. A student who measures retrieval reps may neglect deeper understanding. The reconciliation is to pair simple metrics with periodic qualitative review. The metric drives daily behaviour; the review protects the larger aim. Daily is for repetition. Weekly or monthly is for meaning.

The motif that can unify this section is the dashboard. A dashboard is not the destination. It is the instrument panel that keeps you from drifting without noticing. A good dashboard has a few key dials, not a wall of numbers. Too many dials create noise; too few create blindness. The same applies here. Metrics should be few enough to track honestly and often, and meaningful enough to inform adjustment.

The last tension in this section is a choice about honesty. If a metric is to be useful, it must sometimes tell you something you do not want to hear. That is its job. The forward test is therefore simple and uncomfortable: will you choose metrics that make you look good, or metrics that make you better—even when the numbers are small, even when the week is messy, and even when the dashboard shows drift that would be easier to ignore?

Using Social Accountability

In July 1997 at Queen Elizabeth Hospital in Birmingham, England, a transplant surgeon named Sir Roy Calne reflected publicly on a truth that medicine learns the hard way: nobody performs reliably alone. Surgical teams rely on shared protocols, mutual checking, and the quiet permission to speak up when something looks wrong. The principle is older than modern hospitals, but its modern articulation is easy to verify in safety literature and in the spread of checklists across high-stakes work. The striking part is not that humans need help. It is that help works best when it is structured, expected, and ordinary.

Other people are mirrors.

Social accountability is the use of another person—or a small group, or a public log—to create a feedback loop that is harder to ignore than a private intention. It can be as simple as a weekly call with a friend, a brief message confirming that a rep happened, or a shared spreadsheet that records effort. It can also be misused: turned into humiliation, performance, or coercion. This section is about the difference. The aim is not to recruit a judge. It is to recruit a witness.

A five-word sentence belongs here. Witnesses change what we do.

The psychology is straightforward. Humans are social animals with reputations, and reputation is not merely public status; it is the sense of being seen accurately by someone who matters. When you commit privately, you can revise the story later. "I meant to, but…" is a comfortable sentence when no-one is listening. When you commit socially, you are making an agreement that lives outside your head. Breaking it has a cost that is not financial but relational: a small dent in trust, a small discomfort in how you are perceived. For many people, that discomfort is just enough to tip the decision towards action on a dull day.

Show it with a simple example rather than grand claims. Two colleagues agree to do a twenty-minute practice session each weekday and send each other a message afterwards: "done". The message is bland. That is why it works. It is not a motivational speech and not a performance. It is a receipt. On day six, one person feels tired and considers skipping. The thought of sending "missed" makes them uncomfortable. Not because the other colleague will punish them, but because they do not want to be unreliable. They do the session. The implication is subtle: social accountability does not require inspiring friendship; it requires a reliable mechanism for visibility.

Name the concept. Relational friction.

Explain it. Relational friction is the small cost you experience when you anticipate disappointing someone whose opinion you value. It can be a useful force when it is mild, respectful, and aligned with your own goals. It becomes harmful when it is intense, shame-based, or tied to coercion. The implication is that the goal is not to maximise pressure. The goal is to create *just enough* relational friction to counteract inertia without creating dread.

This is why social accountability should be designed, not improvised. People often attempt it informally—"keep me accountable"—and then discover that the phrase contains no structure. It gives no cadence, no definition of success, no agreed response to failure. Without structure, the other person does not know what to do, and the arrangement dissolves into awkwardness. A well-designed social loop makes expectations explicit: what will be observed, how often, in what form, and what the response will be. It turns interpersonal goodwill into a system.

The form matters because different forms of social accountability create different psychological dynamics. A trusted friend is often ideal for many professionals because the relationship contains care as well as expectation. Care matters because it keeps the loop humane. Small groups add a different force: not the fear of disappointing one person, but the desire to belong. Belonging is powerful. It can also be dangerous if the group's norms are toxic. Public logs add a third force: reputation at a distance. The benefit is reach and visibility. The risk is performance and vanity. The system has to be matched to the person and to the domain.

The domain matters because accountability interacts differently with different kinds of work. For sales outreach, social accountability can be straightforward because outputs are visible: messages sent, calls made, meetings booked. A peer or group can ask for counts and a brief note about what was learned. For study, accountability works best when it asks for observable reps rather than for claims of understanding. For craft, especially creative craft, accountability can be tricky because visibility can alter the work's texture. The presence of an audience can raise anxiety and reduce experimentation. The implication is that creative accountability often works best when it focuses on attendance—sessions completed—rather than on evaluation of quality.

This is where shame enters the conversation, because shame is the thing most people fear when they hear "accountability". Shame is not merely discomfort; it is the experience of being judged as defective. Shame tends to produce concealment. People hide, they lie, they avoid check-ins. In other words, shame breaks loops. The irony is that the accountability arrangement, designed to create consistency, becomes the reason consistency collapses. The implication is that the emotional tone is not an optional kindness; it is an operational requirement. If the loop produces shame, the loop will not last.

A named, checkable example of social accountability done well in a group setting comes from Alcoholics Anonymous, founded in 1935 in Akron, Ohio, where mutual support and regular meetings created a structure for sustained behaviour change. The model is not for everyone and has been debated and studied extensively, but the core mechanism is undeniable: regular social contact, shared language, and accountability to a community can help people sustain difficult changes over time. The implication is not to import AA wholesale into every life domain. It is to notice that social structures can carry behaviour when individual resolve is exhausted.

A second named example, from a very different domain, is the use of "stand-ups" and regular check-ins in software teams, popularised in agile methods from the late 1990s onwards. The details vary by organisation, but the principle is consistent: short, regular moments of visibility reduce drift and increase follow-through. A person is more likely to finish a task when they will report progress to a team. The implication is that social accountability is not merely self-help folklore; it is embedded in professional practices that value reliable execution.

Now address the credible limitation: social accountability can lead to performative behaviour. People may optimise for looking consistent rather than being consistent. They may pick easy tasks that produce easy check-ins. They may avoid ambitious work that risks failure, because failure would be visible. Public logs can intensify this dynamic, turning reps into content and discipline into branding. The reconciliation is to design accountability around specific, observable commitments that are aligned with values and to maintain privacy where necessary. A witness does not have to be a crowd. Often one person is enough.

Specificity is the key to avoiding both shame and performance. A vague commitment—"I'll work on my project"—invites storytelling and argument. A specific commitment—"three practice sessions logged" or "five outreach messages sent" or "two retrieval reps completed each weekday"—reduces ambiguity. The witness can verify without interpreting. The person can report without defending. The loop stays clean. The implication is that social accountability works best when it resembles a receipt rather than a confession.

Another subtle design choice is the response to failure. If the witness responds with judgement, the system corrodes. If the witness responds with indifference, the system loses friction. The best response is usually curiosity and adjustment: what blocked the rep, what can be changed, what will be attempted next. This aligns with the book's overall ethic: treat failure as information. Social accountability should amplify that ethic, not replace it with moral drama.

The motif of the mirror can now sharpen. A mirror is useful because it reflects without opinion. Human mirrors, of course, have opinions. The art of social accountability is to borrow the mirror's clarity without importing the mirror-holder's ego. This is why trusted friends matter. Trust reduces the fear that feedback will become judgement. Trust also increases the cost of breaking commitments, because you do not want to erode a relationship that matters.

The forward test for this section is a choice about where you will place your discipline—inside your own fluctuating mood, or partly inside a relationship and a rhythm that can hold you steady. If social accountability is a tool and not a tribunal, what kind of witness would strengthen your reps: a single person who expects a simple check-in, a small group with shared standards, or a public log that offers visibility without turning your practice into performance?

Reviewing and Adjusting Loops

On 15 April 1912 in the North Atlantic, the RMS *Titanic* sank after striking an iceberg. The date is fixed in public memory; the investigations that followed are likewise well documented. Among their lasting impacts was not a single clever improvement, but a suite of systemic changes: more lifeboats, new standards for radio watches, the creation of the International Ice Patrol in 1914, and a new seriousness about drills and oversight. The catastrophe did not teach the world to "try harder". It taught the world to review assumptions, redesign systems, and keep reviewing—because conditions change, confidence drifts, and safety depends on feedback.

Systems decay without review.

Habit systems decay too. Not because people are weak, but because life is dynamic and discipline structures are static unless you update them. A streak that once motivated becomes a burden. A metric that once clarified becomes noise. An accountability partner changes jobs. A routine that fit winter mornings fails in summer evenings. The danger is not change; the danger is pretending that what worked last month must work this month. When people fail to review, they interpret misfit as personal failure. They abandon the system entirely and then begin again with a new system, repeating the same cycle of enthusiasm, drift, and collapse. Review breaks that cycle by turning failure into adjustment rather than into drama.

A five-word sentence belongs here. Review turns drift into data.

The point of reviewing loops is not endless optimisation. People who love systems can fall into a different trap: tinkering as procrastination. They redesign weekly, adjust metrics daily, switch tools obsessively, and call it "being intentional". That behaviour is not discipline. It is avoidance wearing a smart outfit. A good review rhythm is therefore periodic and contained. It happens often enough to correct drift, rarely enough to allow the system to run. It is more like an aircraft's scheduled maintenance than a mechanic hovering over the engine mid-flight.

Show the difference between abandonment and adjustment in a familiar scene. A professional begins a weekly accountability call with a friend. For a month, it works. Then work becomes intense. The calls are missed. The person feels awkward about resuming. The loop collapses. In the absence of review, the person tells a story: "accountability doesn't work for me." But the story hides the real issue: the loop's cadence and format did not fit the new constraint. A review would reveal this quickly and suggest a small adjustment: a shorter check-in, a different day, a written update instead of a call. The implication is that many "failed systems" are merely outdated systems.

Name the concept. Loop maintenance.

Explain it. Loop maintenance is the practice of periodically reviewing both the behaviour being tracked and the tracking structure itself. It asks whether the loop still produces the intended effect—clarity, follow-through, learning—and whether its cost remains acceptable—time, emotional strain, logistical friction. The implication is that accountability is not a set-and-forget gadget. It is a living mechanism that must be tuned as circumstances change.

The review process begins with a distinction that matters: behaviour review and system review are not the same. Behaviour review looks at what happened: reps completed, sessions missed, outputs produced, streaks maintained or broken. System review looks at why it happened: triggers, friction, timing, environment, social support, and the loop's own design. Without the second, the first becomes self-judgement. Without the first, the second becomes fantasy. The two together create a feedback cycle that is both honest and useful.

A review must therefore surface evidence quickly. Evidence can be simple: counts of reps, minutes, outputs, the presence or absence of check-ins. The aim is not to build a database. The aim is to establish a clear picture of what the system is actually producing. The emotional advantage of evidence is that it reduces argument. Instead of debating whether you were "consistent", you can look at a number. Instead of debating whether the loop is "helpful", you can look at whether it increased reps or reduced drift.

Then come the questions that do the real work. "Is this still working?" is a diagnostic question because it forces the mind to confront the possibility that the system has changed from helpful to burdensome. "What did I learn from last week?" is an even better question because it reframes failure as information rather than as shame. It also forces specificity. Learning requires detail: what blocked the rep, what increased friction, what reduced energy, what made starting easier. Vague answers—"I was busy"—are comforting but useless. Useful answers identify a lever: "I attempted to do writing after email, and email derailed me," or "my travel week required shield reps, but I had not defined them," or "the check-in was too long and became a chore." Each answer points towards an adjustment.

A named example from professional practice illustrates why such questions matter. In aviation, near-miss reporting systems and routine debriefs exist not because pilots are incompetent but because safety depends on learning from deviations before they become disasters. NASA's own approach to safety reviews and post-mission debriefs, refined over decades, reflects the same logic: complex systems require structured reflection. The implication is that a review is not a confession; it is an operational ritual.

This chapter's insistence on review also aligns with what we know about behaviour change: the act of monitoring itself can influence behaviour, a phenomenon often discussed in research on self-regulation. People change what they notice. A review increases noticing. But noticing without adjustment can create frustration. Adjustment is the point.

Adjustment should be small. That deserves emphasis because intelligent people often reach for dramatic redesign. They change everything at once: new habits, new tools, new schedules, new partners, new metrics. Then they cannot tell what worked. They also increase cognitive load and therefore reduce consistency. Small adjustments preserve continuity. They keep the chain alive while improving its fit. The implication is that review should produce the smallest change that plausibly improves the next week, not a new identity project.

Small does not mean timid. Small can be decisive. Moving a habit earlier in the day can be decisive. Removing one friction point can be decisive. Changing a metric from an outcome to a leading indicator can be decisive. Shortening a check-in from thirty minutes to five can be decisive. The scale of the change is not the measure of its impact. Its effect on reliability is.

Now include a credible limitation, because review can itself become harmful. Some people turn review into rumination. They relive failures, intensify guilt, and mistake self-criticism for seriousness. Others turn review into perfectionism: endless tweaks, constant dissatisfaction, a refusal to let the system settle. The reconciliation is to limit review by time and by scope. Time limits prevent spirals. Scope limits prevent overfitting. A review should be long enough to see clearly and short enough to remain repeatable. Repeatability is the whole ethic of this book.

A monthly review adds a different layer from weekly review. Weekly review tends to focus on immediate execution: did reps happen, what blocked them, what will change next week. Monthly review can examine patterns and fit: is the habit still aligned with current priorities, is the streak still serving, is the accountability relationship still healthy, are the metrics still honest. Month-scale review is where you ask whether you are measuring the right things, not merely whether you are meeting them.

The "script" of a review is not about theatricality; it is about reducing cognitive load. A pre-defined sequence of prompts prevents you from turning the review into a mood-driven performance. It also makes reviews comparable across time. If you ask yourself the same core questions each month, you can detect shifts: rising friction, emerging dread, declining usefulness of a metric. The implication is that a review script is a stability device: it keeps reflection from becoming improvisation.

A simple script can be expressed in prose without turning into a list. The review begins by looking at the evidence: the counts, the streaks, the check-ins. Then it names what worked: which behaviours felt easy, which structures held under pressure. Then it names what failed without melodrama: where the loop broke, what pattern repeated. Then it identifies one lesson: a single sentence that captures the most useful insight from the month. Then it chooses one adjustment: a small change that will be tested next month. Finally, it reaffirms the deeper value: why the reps matter, not in sentimental language but in concrete terms—what the habit supports in your work, health, craft, or study.

The motif from *Titanic* returns here in a quieter form: the iceberg is not the unexpected event. The iceberg is the unreviewed assumption. People assume their systems will keep working because they have worked for a while. That assumption is comforting and often false. Review is how you spot the iceberg earlier. It does not prevent all collisions. It reduces the likelihood that one collision becomes a sinking.

The forward test is therefore not whether you can build a loop once. It is whether you can maintain it. When your accountability structures start to feel stale or oppressive—when the check-ins slip, the metrics lose meaning, the streak becomes a burden—will you abandon the system and call it a failure, or will you perform the quieter, more demanding act of review: seeing clearly, learning honestly, and adjusting just enough to keep the system alive?

Chapter 8
Cadence Calendars and Planning

In September 1905 in Bern, Switzerland, a young patent clerk named Albert Einstein tried to live two lives at once: the daylight life of a civil servant and the night-time life of a theorist. The dates and place are checkable; so is the outcome. Within that year he produced papers that altered physics. What is rarely romanticised is the mundane constraint behind the myth: time had to be carved out, protected, repeated. Genius did not float above the calendar. It hid inside it. A schedule, however imperfect, became the vessel that carried thinking forward.

Time is the real material.

Discipline is often spoken about as if it were made of willpower, character, or grit. In practice, discipline is made of days. Days arrive with fixed constraints: bodies need sleep, work consumes hours, obligations multiply, attention fragments. The question is not whether a person has ambition. Most people do. The question is whether ambition has a rhythm it can survive. When rhythm is absent, discipline becomes a series of heroic rescues: late-night sprints, frantic catch-up weekends, bursts of intensity followed by collapse. The person feels busy and still feels behind. They blame themselves. The real problem is often structural.

A short sentence belongs here. Rhythm beats intensity.

This chapter introduces a different way of relating to the calendar. Many people treat their calendar as an enemy: a hostile ledger of meetings, deadlines, and obligations that "steal" time from what matters. They look at it with resentment, as if their real life lives elsewhere. That attitude is understandable and also unhelpful. The calendar is not a judge. It is a map. If discipline is repetition made survivable, then the calendar is where survivability is negotiated.

A cadence calendar is a planned pattern of recurring behaviour over time. It is not merely a to-do list. A to-do list is a pile. A cadence calendar is a rhythm: certain actions occur daily, others weekly, others monthly. Some weeks carry heavy sessions; other days are deliberately light. Some seasons emphasise one skill; other seasons emphasise consolidation. The essence is recurrence. Recurrence turns aspiration into a pattern that can be lived.

The chapter's argument will feel quietly radical to anyone who is used to motivational approaches. The most disciplined people do not win by squeezing more into each day. They win by deciding what repeats, how often, and at what intensity—and by planning rest as aggressively as effort. They treat time as a finite resource that must be allocated, not a moral arena where they must prove themselves.

There is also a modern relevance that makes cadence calendars more urgent now than in the age of paper diaries. Digital work has blurred boundaries. Messages arrive at all hours. Tasks proliferate. Most knowledge work is never "done"; it simply stops when you stop. Without a cadence, life becomes reactive. You do what shouts the loudest. You mistake urgency for importance. You spend your best attention on the day's noise and leave your long-term skills starving. A cadence calendar is a defence against this drift: it ensures that certain non-urgent actions still happen because the rhythm requires them.

Cadence calendars begin at the smallest scale: the daily repetition. A daily rep is not necessarily a daily *session*. Some reps are too heavy for daily execution and become brittle if treated as such. This chapter will treat daily repetitions as the skeleton, but not as the entire body. The idea is not to create a life of relentless daily effort. The idea is to decide which small actions belong in the daily category because they are light, high-leverage, and identity-building.

Then comes the weekly scale, which is where most adults actually live. Weeks contain variability: meetings, travel, family needs, deadlines. A weekly cadence allows you to distribute effort across days rather than attempting to do everything every day. It invites a more mature design question: minimum effective frequency versus ideal frequency. Many people design for the ideal and then feel guilty when they cannot meet it. A better approach is to design for the minimum that keeps the habit alive and the skill moving forward, then treat anything beyond that as optional reinforcement rather than as a moral requirement.

A sample week can make this tangible without turning into a timetable. Imagine someone balancing sales outreach, exercise, and creative work. If they attempt all three daily, they may end up doing shallow versions of each, constantly switching context, constantly feeling behind. A weekly cadence might instead assign outreach to certain days, deep creative work to others, and movement to a rhythm that alternates strain and recovery. The trade-offs become visible. Instead of pretending a "perfect" week is possible, the person designs a *good enough* week that fits the constraints of their actual life. The payoff is not optimisation. It is consistency.

This is where planned rest enters, because rest is not the absence of discipline. Rest is part of discipline when it is deliberate. People often treat rest as a reward: "If I do well, I earn rest." That framing is childish and dangerous. The more accurate framing is mechanical. Bodies and minds have recovery needs. Skills consolidate during rest. Burnout is not a moral weakness; it is the predictable outcome of sustained overload. A cadence calendar that refuses to schedule rest is a calendar that is planning failure.

The chapter will therefore treat intensity as something to be cycled. Hard sessions require light sessions around them. Deep work requires shallow days for admin. Sales outreach requires recovery from rejection and cognitive fatigue. Study requires review days to consolidate learning. This cycling is not a concession to laziness. It is a design principle. It makes discipline survivable over months rather than impressive for a fortnight.

Then the chapter zooms out to the longer horizons that many people neglect: quarterly and annual cadence. Most individuals have goals that cannot be achieved through weekly repetition alone. Skills develop in seasons. Projects require phases: learning, building, refining, shipping. The quarterly view allows you to choose a theme: a quarter focused on improving sales skill, a term devoted to a qualification, a season of deep craft practice. Themes prevent diffusion. They reduce the temptation to chase everything at once. They also allow you to adjust your weekly cadence to match the season. A heavy learning season might reduce other commitments. A busy family season might shift habits into shield mode. The year becomes a set of rhythms rather than a blur.

A subtle motif will thread through this chapter: the tide. Tides rise and fall. They are predictable at scale and variable in the moment. A cadence calendar is a tidal plan for your effort: high tide days of intensity, low tide days of consolidation, and an awareness that fighting the tide is exhausting. The disciplined person learns to work with tides rather than insisting every day must feel the same.

The emotional payoff of this approach is not merely productivity. It is relief. When a calendar contains a cadence that reflects your values, you stop relying on guilt to force action. You stop making daily decisions about whether to practise, write, study, or prospect. The decision is already made by the rhythm. Your job becomes execution and small adjustment, not constant negotiation.

The closing tension of this chapter is therefore a diagnostic question. When you look at your calendar, do you see a record of what life did to you, or do you see a pattern you designed—one that makes your chosen reps inevitable enough to survive ordinary chaos, yet flexible enough to adapt when the tide changes?

Cadence Calendars Overview

In April 2019 in London, the UK Parliament was forced to acknowledge a mundane truth about human attention: time expands to fill the noise you allow into it. The period around the Brexit debates is notorious for procedural repetition, late sittings, and calendar churn; it was political theatre, yes, but also a demonstration of how a schedule can be consumed by urgency until it contains nothing else. Anyone who has watched their own week disappear into meetings and messages recognises the pattern. The calendar becomes a battlefield, and the important work becomes the casualty.

The diary is not neutral.

A cadence calendar is the practice of deliberately shaping the diary into recurring rhythms that protect the reps you actually care about. It is not a new app, a colour-coded aesthetic, or an attempt to dominate life with spreadsheets. It is a design choice: deciding which behaviours repeat daily, which repeat weekly, which repeat monthly, and how those repetitions interact with the constraints of real life. A cadence calendar turns discipline from a mood into a timetable. Not rigid. Repeatable.

A five-word sentence belongs here. Rhythm makes effort survivable.

Most people already have a cadence calendar; they simply did not choose it. Work meetings recur weekly. Bills recur monthly. School runs recur daily. Deadlines recur in cycles that feel suspiciously similar every quarter. The unchosen cadence calendar is usually built by other people's needs, your own avoidance, and the blunt force of inertia. It produces a life that feels busy and strangely unproductive: you are always doing something, yet the actions that would compound over years—practice, study, outreach, deep work—get squeezed to the edges.

The cadence calendar proposes a different relationship with time. Instead of treating the calendar as a record of what happened to you, you treat it as an instrument you play. The point is not to control everything. The point is to control the repetitions. Repetitions are where compounding lives. If you can make the right repetitions recur, the long-term outcomes begin to move almost without drama. If you cannot, you will keep relying on heroic bursts of effort, and heroic bursts are expensive.

Show how cadence changes the texture of a week. Consider outreach in sales or research. Without cadence, outreach is squeezed between urgent tasks. It becomes sporadic. It becomes emotionally heavy because each attempt feels like starting again. With cadence, outreach has a recurring slot: certain days contain it, and the rest of the week is not haunted by it. The behaviour becomes ordinary. The mood required to begin shrinks. The implication is that a cadence calendar reduces initiation friction by making the start time predictable.

Name the concept. Temporal scaffolding.

Explain it. Temporal scaffolding is the use of recurring time blocks and rhythms to support behaviours that otherwise collapse under competing demands. Scaffolding is not the building; it is what allows the building to be constructed reliably. The implication is that many people do not fail because they lack discipline; they fail because they expect discipline to float without scaffolding. When you provide scaffolding, the same person can become consistent with surprising ease.

Cadence calendars work because the human mind is poor at holding long-term priorities in working memory while navigating daily chaos. This is not a moral weakness. It is a cognitive constraint. Cognitive psychologists have long described the limited capacity of working memory and the costs of constant task switching. When the day is full of interruptions, the brain defaults to what is salient. The calendar is a way to externalise priority so the brain does not have to remember it. The diary becomes a second brain that does not get tired.

Daily, weekly, and monthly rhythms each serve a different role. Daily rhythms keep identity alive. They are the small reps that anchor the day: a short practice session, a brief review, a single outreach message, a small piece of craft. Daily does not mean heavy. Daily means frequent enough that the identity "I am someone who shows up" remains intact even when the day is messy. In earlier chapters, the minimum viable habit and streak shields made this logic explicit. Cadence calendars put it into time.

Weekly rhythms are where real adults build consistency. Weeks contain variability and therefore require distribution. Heavy behaviours are often best placed weekly: long runs, deep study blocks, concentrated creative sessions, longer prospecting sessions. Weekly rhythms also allow you to cluster similar work and reduce context switching. If deep work is scattered in ten-minute fragments across the week, it will feel constantly interrupted and may never reach depth. If deep work has protected weekly slots, it can actually become deep. The implication is that weekly cadence is a tool for quality as well as consistency.

Monthly rhythms create a different kind of power: perspective. Monthly blocks allow you to do what daily and weekly cannot do well: review, plan, adjust, and reset. They also accommodate tasks that are important but not urgent: skill audits, pipeline reviews, curriculum planning, financial admin, longer reflective sessions. When these tasks are not given a monthly rhythm, they either never happen or happen in frantic bursts. The implication is that a monthly cadence protects the system itself, not just the reps.

A second named, checkable example clarifies why calendars change behaviour. In professional sport, training is rarely an improvisation. Runners follow periodised plans that vary intensity across weeks and months; weightlifters cycle volume and load; teams schedule training, recovery, and competition phases. The specifics differ, but the principle is consistent and well documented in coaching literature: progress requires planned repetition and planned variation. The implication is that cadence calendars are not bureaucratic. They are how serious practitioners protect their bodies and skills from chaos.

Now include the counter-example honestly. Some people find calendars oppressive. They have chaotic jobs, caregiving responsibilities, or unpredictable health. They may hear "cadence calendar" and feel the tightening in the chest: another system that will fail, another plan that will mock them. The reconciliation is that cadence calendars are not about filling every hour. They are about choosing a small number of repetitions that can survive unpredictability. If unpredictability is high, the cadence becomes lighter and more flexible. The rhythm remains; the blocks shrink. A tide still has a pattern even when waves are rough.

The calendar becomes a support for discipline precisely when it stops pretending to be a fantasy. A fantasy calendar is full of perfect mornings and uninterrupted afternoons. A useful cadence calendar is full of realistic slots: small daily reps, a few weekly anchors, a monthly review. It contains buffer. It assumes disruption. It includes lighter days. It does not rely on your best self. It accommodates your average self.

A quiet motif runs through this chapter: the tide. Tides are not constant, but they are patterned. If you plan to swim, you check the tide. If you plan to build consistency, you plan with your energy and obligations rather than against them. A cadence calendar is a tide chart for your work and life. It does not eliminate storms. It helps you stop being surprised by them.

There is also a moral dimension to this, though it should not be sentimental. When you refuse to plan your cadence, someone else's cadence will plan you. Employers plan cadence through meetings. Platforms plan cadence through notifications. Social expectations plan cadence through availability. You can drift into a life where your only regular behaviour is responsiveness. Responsiveness feels productive. It rarely compounds. The implication is that protecting cadence is a form of autonomy. It is how you keep your life from being entirely defined by other people's urgency.

The forward test is therefore a simple but uncomfortable diagnostic. When you look at the next week in your calendar, can you point to the repetitions that will build the future you want—daily, weekly, monthly—or does the calendar only show what will happen *to* you, with your most important reps left to the mercy of spare time that rarely arrives?

Mapping Weekly Repetitions

In January 1970 at the University of Oregon in Eugene, the psychologist Walter Mischel ran a set of experiments that would later be popularised as the "marshmallow test". The public often remembers it as a morality play about self-control. The more useful reading is structural: children did better when the situation was redesigned—when temptation was moved, attention was redirected, cues changed. The lesson is not that willpower is magical. The lesson is that behaviour follows arrangements. A week is an arrangement. If you want reps, you arrange them.

Weeks don't happen by accident.

Most adults do not fail because they lack goals. They fail because their weeks are overcommitted, underdesigned, and filled with invisible trade-offs. A week is the smallest unit of life that contains real complexity: work obligations, social commitments, fatigue, errands, interruptions, and the small crises that never make it onto the calendar. Planning at the day level can feel precise and still be fragile. Planning at the month level can feel inspiring and still be vague. The week is the proper battlefield for consistency because it is where repetition meets reality.

Mapping weekly repetitions means deciding how often a given behaviour should occur across seven days and then placing those occurrences so they survive. This sounds simple until you try it. People tend to overestimate capacity, underestimate disruption, and design weeks that require them to be at their best every day. Then a normal Thursday arrives—tired, interrupted, socially complicated—and the plan collapses. The collapse is then interpreted as a character flaw. It is more often a frequency error.

A five-word sentence belongs here. Too often means never happens.

The core distinction is between ideal frequency and minimum effective frequency. Ideal frequency is what you would do if time and energy were abundant: five workouts, daily deep work, daily outreach, daily study. Ideal frequency is useful as an aspiration and dangerous as a plan. Minimum effective frequency is what keeps the habit alive and the skill moving forward under ordinary constraints: perhaps two or three sessions a week, perhaps a handful of outreach days, perhaps one long study block and one review block. Minimum effective frequency is not laziness. It is a strategic floor that protects consistency when life is unromantic.

Show why the difference matters with a common scenario. A professional wants to improve in three domains at once: sales activity, physical training, and creative craft. The ideal plan is simple in the mind: do all three daily. It feels disciplined. It is also a recipe for chronic context switching and fatigue. Within two weeks, one domain becomes neglected, then another, and soon the person is doing shallow versions of all three while feeling guilty. Now redesign the week around minimum effective frequency. Sales might occur on three days, training on three days with one lighter day, creative work on two deep sessions plus smaller daily reps. The week becomes survivable. The implication is that frequency design is not about ambition; it is about sustainability.

Name the concept. Frequency budgeting.

Explain it. Frequency budgeting is the allocation of limited weekly slots to behaviours based on their leverage, recovery cost, and fragility. It treats time and energy like a finite budget rather than an infinite moral resource. The implication is that you stop asking, "How much can I cram in?" and start asking, "What pattern can I reliably repeat?" Reliable repetition is the entire point.

Frequency budgeting requires you to see trade-offs clearly. Every repetition has a cost: time, attention, preparation, recovery. Some repetitions are light and can be daily without harm: a short review, a single outreach message, a brief practice rep. Some repetitions are heavy and become counterproductive if forced daily: long runs, deep creative work, intense study. The heavy repetitions need space around them. They also need protection from the week's noise. The implication is that mapping repetitions is not simply adding more; it is spacing intelligently.

Spacing has a relationship to learning that is worth noting. Cognitive psychology has long supported the "spacing effect": distributed practice tends to improve long-term retention compared with massed practice (Ebbinghaus's early work and a large body of later research have explored this, though specifics depend on task and context). The relevance here is not a slogan about flashcards. It is that weekly planning can exploit spacing by distributing study and review across the week rather than crushing it into one heroic night. The same logic applies to skill practice and sales: frequent touches can beat occasional marathons because they keep the behaviour and the identity alive.

Now bring in a second named, checkable example that illustrates weekly rhythm as a design principle. In distance running, many training approaches structure the week around one long run, one faster session, and several easier runs or recovery days. The details vary by coach and athlete, but the pattern is widely recognisable. It works because it respects recovery and distributes stress. The implication is that frequency is always tied to intensity. You cannot decide how often without deciding how hard.

This leads to a crucial point that most ambitious people resist: a "good enough" week is often the highest-performing week over the long run. A good enough week is one you can execute repeatedly without needing perfect conditions. It tolerates disruption. It contains buffers. It includes lighter days. It acknowledges that some weeks will be messy. The alternative is the "perfect week" that only exists on paper. Perfect weeks are seductive because they flatter the planner. They betray the doer.

A quiet motif can unify this: the metronome. A metronome does not demand passion; it demands time. It keeps the musician honest. A weekly cadence is a metronome for your life. It does not guarantee artistry. It guarantees rhythm. Rhythm is what lets artistry show up repeatedly rather than by accident.

Consider the three-domain sample week more closely, not as a timetable but as a set of decisions. Sales activity is often emotionally tiring because it involves rejection and uncertainty. If you schedule it every day, you may start avoiding it. If you schedule it on two or three days with clear reps—outreach blocks, follow-up blocks—you may actually do it. Training is physically tiring and requires recovery. If you schedule intense training daily, you may break down or burn out. If you schedule two harder sessions and one lighter session, you may improve steadily. Creative work is cognitively demanding and often requires warm-up time. If you try to do it in ten-minute fragments between meetings, you may feel constantly blocked. If you schedule two protected sessions, the work has room to deepen. The implication is that weekly repetition design is about matching the behaviour to the kind of energy it requires.

Now address the limitation honestly. Some weeks are not stable. Shift work, caregiving, travel, and unpredictable deadlines can make weekly planning feel futile. The reconciliation is to plan with flexible slots rather than fixed times, and to plan with minimum effective frequencies that can survive variability. If the week cannot promise

Tuesday at 7 a.m., it can still promise "three sessions somewhere in the week", supported by pre-decided shield reps and cues. The week becomes a container rather than a script.

The key is to remove the need for constant recalculation. People often waste energy re-deciding the same questions every day: Should I work out today? Should I study tonight? Should I do outreach now? Weekly mapping answers those questions in advance. Not with rigid enforcement, but with a default. Defaults are powerful because they reduce decision load. They also reduce bargaining. If you know that Wednesday is an outreach day, you do not spend Wednesday negotiating with yourself about whether outreach matters.

You also learn faster. When a behaviour is scheduled weekly, you can compare weeks. You can observe patterns: outreach on Monday works better than outreach on Friday; deep work in the morning produces more output than deep work at night; training after a late meeting leads to skipped sessions. These are not motivational insights. They are operational. You cannot learn them if the behaviour is random.

A credible counter-example must be included: some people thrive on daily rituals and find weekly planning too loose. They prefer daily reps that are small and predictable. That can work, especially when the reps are truly minimum viable and the calendar permits consistency. The reconciliation is to distinguish daily identity reps from weekly heavy reps. Daily can hold the identity—small, portable, shield-friendly. Weekly can hold the heavy lifts—deep work, long sessions, concentrated effort. The week becomes layered. The metronome ticks, and occasionally it strikes a louder beat.

The forward test for this subchapter is therefore a design choice that cannot be dodged. When you look at the next seven days, will you design for the week you wish you had—ideal frequency, perfect energy, no disruption—or will you design for the week you are likely to get, with minimum effective frequencies that you can actually repeat, so that progress becomes a property of your calendar rather than a miracle of mood?

Balancing Intensity and Rest

In October 1954 at the Commonwealth Games in Vancouver, Canada, Roger Bannister watched a rival, John Landy, lose a race he should have won. Landy looked over his left shoulder too early; Bannister passed on the right and took gold. The dates, place, and athletes are easy to verify. The point is not the melodrama of a glance. It is that Landy's race was decided by a moment of mismanaged attention under strain. He had trained hard. He was fit. But strain does peculiar things: it narrows perception, distorts judgement, and makes small errors decisive.

Fatigue is not moral.

That sentence is the hinge of this section. Many people treat fatigue as if it were a failure of character, a sign that they are not "disciplined enough". They try to bulldoze through it with more intensity, more effort, more self-talk. This works briefly. Then the system collapses. Burnout is often described as mysterious. It is usually predictable. It arrives when intensity is scheduled as if the body and mind were machines that do not need recovery.

Balancing intensity and rest is the practice of designing a cadence where harder sessions are deliberately paired with lighter sessions, and where rest is planned rather than begged for after the damage is done. The aim is not comfort. The aim is continuity. Rest is not a reward for perfection. Rest is a tool for consistency.

A five-word sentence belongs here. Rest protects tomorrow's reps.

Show the common failure pattern. A professional commits to a new discipline: heavy workouts, deep study, daily outreach, ambitious creative work. The first week feels exhilarating because novelty provides energy. The second week feels harder. By the third week, the person is negotiating every session. They begin to skip. They feel guilty. They respond by trying to "make up for it" with even harder sessions. This is a classic oscillation: intensity spikes, fatigue accumulates, collapse follows, then a compensatory spike. The habit becomes a drama cycle rather than a stable rhythm. The implication is that many people do not fail because their goals are too hard; they fail because their cadence is too aggressive.

Name the concept. Load cycling.

Explain it. Load cycling is the deliberate alternation of high-demand sessions and low-demand sessions so that recovery can occur and performance can be sustained. The language comes from training, but the principle applies across domains: cognitive work, social work, sales work, study, and craft all have loads that accumulate. The implication is that "more" is not the same as "better". Better is what can be repeated without breaking you.

The underlying physiology and psychology are complex, but the practical consequences are simple. Intense physical training creates micro-damage that requires recovery to adapt. Intense cognitive work consumes attention and increases decision fatigue. Sales outreach can drain social energy and resilience because rejection is a real stressor. Study at high intensity without review can produce diminishing returns and frustration. Rest is when systems repair and consolidate. In learning, consolidation is literally a concept: memory traces stabilise over time and with sleep. In training, adaptation happens between sessions. In work, insight often arrives after a pause. The implication is that intensity without rest is not discipline; it is a countdown.

A second named, checkable example illustrates the danger of ignoring recovery. In January 1912, the British expedition led by Robert Falcon Scott reached the South Pole and then died on the return journey. The causes are debated—weather, planning, logistics—but the broader lesson is that endurance systems fail when they do not respect limits. Polar expeditions are extreme. Ordinary lives are not. Yet the psychological pattern is similar: people overextend, then discover that the environment does not care about their resolve. The implication is not to dramatise personal habits as heroic suffering. The implication is to recognise that limits are not negotiable, and good planning respects them.

Now bring the argument down to the weekly cadence, where it belongs. A sustainable week is not a uniform week. It is a week with texture. Texture means variation in intensity. Hard days are followed by easier days. Deep work is followed by admin or recovery. Heavy study sessions are followed by review sessions. The alternation does not require elaborate tracking. It requires the willingness to treat rest as part of the plan rather than as a guilty indulgence.

Consider exercise, because it makes the pattern visible. If a person schedules three heavy workouts back-to-back and then collapses for four days, the net weekly consistency is poor. If the person alternates one harder session with a walk or a lighter movement day, they may accrue more total reps and maintain motivation. The metric that matters is not the intensity of any one day; it is the ability to show up repeatedly. The implication is that "light days" can be the scaffolding that keeps heavy days possible.

Consider study, which often suffers from the same intensity trap. People schedule long, intense study blocks and then avoid them because they are psychologically heavy. They attempt to cram, then feel confused, then conclude they are "not good at it". A load-cycled approach might alternate focused study with review, retrieval, or lighter consolidation work. The alternation reduces dread and increases frequency. The implication is that rest in cognitive work is not idleness; it can be a different kind of work that allows learning to settle.

In craft, intensity often looks like long sessions of creative effort, and rest is mistaken for procrastination. But creative work has its own recovery needs: the mind needs space to connect ideas, to notice flaws, to generate alternatives. Many writers, designers, and engineers report that solutions appear while walking or doing something unrelated, a phenomenon often linked to incubation in creativity research. The implication is that a cadence that includes lighter days can increase creative yield by allowing the subconscious to work.

In sales, rest is emotionally relevant. Prospecting and pitching can be draining, especially when rejection is frequent. If the schedule demands high-intensity outreach every day, many people begin to avoid it, not because they are weak, but because the emotional cost becomes too high. A cadence that alternates outreach days with follow-up or preparation days can maintain pipeline activity without exhausting the person. The implication is that managing intensity is also managing emotional sustainability.

A credible limitation must be acknowledged: some people use "rest" as a sophisticated excuse to avoid discomfort. They label avoidance as recovery. They create a soft life that feels sustainable because it contains little challenge, then wonder why progress is slow. The reconciliation is to define rest and light days clearly. A light day is not an empty day. It is a day with a lower load that still preserves identity and continuity. It might include a minimum viable rep, a review session, a walk, or a short practice. The key is that the day supports the system rather than abandoning it. Rest that protects tomorrow is useful. Rest that becomes permanent avoidance is not.

This is why the calendar matters. If rest is left to "when I feel like it", it will either never happen or happen as collapse. If rest is scheduled, it becomes legitimate and predictable. Scheduling rest also reduces guilt. You can stop arguing with yourself. The rest day is not a failure; it is the plan. The implication is that planned rest is a psychological intervention as much as a practical one.

The tide motif returns naturally here. High tide is effort. Low tide is recovery. The mistake is to treat every day as high tide and then act surprised when the shoreline erodes. A sustainable cadence respects tides. It uses high tide for heavy work and low tide for consolidation. It does not demand the sea stand still.

The forward test is therefore a design choice disguised as a moral question. Will you treat rest as something you must earn by suffering—thus making it rare, guilt-soaked, and reactive—or will you treat rest as a deliberate instrument of consistency, placed into the week with the same seriousness as effort, so that intensity can recur without eventually sabotaging itself?

Quarterly and Annual Cadence

In January 1843 in London, Charles Dickens published *A Christmas Carol* after writing it in a concentrated burst that followed months of mounting frustration and financial pressure. The date and place are checkable; so is the outcome. The novella appeared in time for Christmas, sold quickly, and became part of cultural memory. What is easy to forget is that Dickens did not simply "write when inspired". He worked inside seasons: serial deadlines, annual publishing cycles, and the economic reality of Victorian print culture. His output was not a daily miracle. It was a rhythm across months and years.

Lives have seasons.

Daily reps build identity. Weekly reps build reliability. Quarterly and annual cadence builds direction. Without the longer horizons, a person can be impressively consistent and still feel strangely static: always busy, always practising, always "working on it", yet never quite moving into new territory. The missing ingredient is theme. Theme gives a season a purpose. It tells the weekly calendar what to privilege and what to temporarily de-emphasise. It reduces diffusion—the quiet killer of adult ambition.

A five-word sentence belongs here. Themes prevent discipline from scattering.

Quarterly cadence is a practical compromise between grand annual resolutions and the short-term tunnel vision of weekly planning. A quarter is long enough to produce meaningful change in skill, output, or system design. It is short enough to feel urgent and to allow correction. It also maps onto many institutional rhythms: academic terms, business quarters, project cycles. When you choose a quarterly theme, you are not predicting the future. You are selecting a direction for effort and deciding what the calendar will repeatedly feed.

Show the difference between a themed quarter and an untethered one. Consider someone who wants to improve in sales, craft, and study simultaneously. Without a theme, they allocate small amounts of energy to each every week, then complain that progress is slow. The effort is sincere. The dispersion is fatal. Now choose a theme: "this quarter, deepen sales skill." The week shifts. Outreach is protected. Practice includes role-play, script refinement, and review of calls. Craft and study remain alive through minimum viable reps, but they are not the primary focus. At the end of the quarter, the person has actually moved. The implication is that theme allows depth without requiring the abandonment of everything else.

Name the concept. Seasonal primacy.

Explain it. Seasonal primacy is the deliberate elevation of one domain or project to first priority for a fixed period, while keeping other domains on maintenance cadence. It is not obsession. It is sequencing. The implication is that you can pursue multiple long-term aims across a year without attempting to pursue all of them at full intensity at once.

This is where many intelligent professionals stumble, because they are capable of many things and therefore try to do many things. Capability becomes a curse when it produces constant simultaneous partial effort. The mind likes novelty and variety. It feels sophisticated to juggle. Yet compounding requires concentration. A quarterly theme is a disciplined refusal of excessive variety. It is a choice to accept that trade-offs exist and that progress requires saying "not now" to some worthy things.

A second named, checkable example can anchor this in a system outside individual self-management. In higher education, terms exist for a reason. A student does not attempt to master an entire discipline in a week. They work within a syllabus across a term, with sequences of topics and assessments. The term creates a contained horizon: long enough for learning, short enough for deadlines. The implication is that quarter-scale planning is not an invention of productivity culture; it mirrors how institutions structure sustained effort.

Quarterly cadence also supports projects that are too large for weekly planning alone. Many projects have phases: exploration, building, refining, shipping. If you attempt to do every phase every week, you create cognitive churn and lose coherence. A themed quarter can align phases with time. One quarter might emphasise building; another might emphasise refinement. This is not rigid project management. It is simply an acknowledgement that different phases demand different kinds of attention.

To make this concrete, consider how habits shift under a theme. In a sales-focused quarter, the weekly repetitions might emphasise outbound activity, pipeline review, and skills practice. In a craft-focused quarter, the weekly repetitions might emphasise deep sessions and deliberate practice, with metrics tied to outputs and feedback. In a study-focused term, the weekly repetitions might emphasise learning blocks, retrieval, and review. The daily reps remain small and consistent; the weekly heavy sessions reconfigure; the monthly review checks alignment. The implication is that habits are not static virtues; they are adjustable tools.

Annual cadence is the next horizon. It is where you stop thinking in weeks and start thinking in chapters of life: seasons of high energy and seasons of constraint, peaks of workload and troughs, predictable cycles like academic years, fiscal years, school terms, or even climate. Annual cadence is not about producing an annual plan that will be perfectly executed. It is about recognising that your capacity and priorities are not constant across twelve months and designing with that reality rather than against it.

A credible limitation must be acknowledged: annual planning can become fantasy. People create beautifully ambitious yearly maps, then reality arrives with illness, family events, job changes, and unexpected demands. The reconciliation is to treat annual cadence as a set of hypotheses rather than promises. You can plan in seasons and still allow revision. The annual view is for direction and sequencing, not for rigid prediction.

This is where the tide motif from earlier sections becomes useful again. Over a year, tides are more obvious. Energy rises and falls. Motivation fluctuates. Work cycles intensify and ease. Even daylight patterns can affect behaviour for some people. Annual cadence respects tides by placing heavier themes in seasons where capacity is higher and maintenance themes in seasons where life is busy. The implication is that discipline becomes kinder and more realistic without becoming soft.

Annual cadence also allows you to build in deliberate periods of consolidation. Many people try to stack new habits and projects continuously, quarter after quarter, year after year. They become perpetually in "build mode". Build mode is exhilarating and exhausting. Consolidation is where systems become automatic, where skills stabilise, where you stop needing novelty to continue. A year that contains no consolidation becomes brittle. The implication is that sustainable ambition requires seasons of deepening, not just seasons of adding.

This is also where identity shifts become visible. A person who chooses quarterly themes and maintains daily reps is effectively writing a story about who they are becoming. The story is not told through affirmations. It is told through repeated allocation of time. Time allocation is the most honest autobiography. The calendar does not lie. If a year's calendar repeatedly prioritises study, you become a learner. If it repeatedly prioritises craft, you become a practitioner. If it repeatedly prioritises outreach and skill-building, you become someone who can sell and persuade. The implication is that annual cadence is identity design through scheduling.

It is important to keep this grounded in metrics and decisions rather than abstractions. A quarterly theme is not a mood board. It is a decision that changes the weekly repetition count of a behaviour. If "sales skill" is the theme, then the calendar must show more reps of outreach or practice than it did last quarter. If "qualification" is the theme, then the calendar must show regular study blocks and review blocks. If "health" is the theme, then the calendar must show regular movement sessions and recovery days. The theme is proved by the reps.

A final limitation deserves attention: some roles and life situations resist long-horizon planning. People in crisis, in caregiving overload, or in unstable work may not be able to commit to quarterly themes. The reconciliation is that seasonal primacy can shrink. A "quarter" can become a "month theme". An "annual cadence" can become a "seasonal intention". The structure remains. The horizon adapts. The aim is not to impose a corporate rhythm on a human life; it is to provide just enough horizon to prevent drift.

The forward test in this section is a question about courage disguised as a scheduling question. If you were to choose one domain to hold primacy for the next quarter, what would it be—and what would you be willing to place on maintenance cadence without guilt, so that the year becomes a sequence of deepening themes rather than a blur of simultaneous, shallow striving?

Chapter 9
Managing Boredom and Motivation

On 3 July 2016 in Paris, France, Andy Murray played a fourth-round match at Wimbledon that lasted three hours and sixteen minutes, then spoke afterwards about the monotony of training: the endless drills, the repeated movements, the day-after-day sameness that makes champions look almost ordinary in the making. The tournament was in London, but the point travelled. Elite performance is built on repetitions so familiar they stop feeling heroic. The crowd sees the highlight reel. The athlete lives in the loop: same court sounds, same ball thwack, same footwork patterns ground into muscle and mind.

Boredom is the price of mastery.

This chapter begins with the problem most discipline books politely sidestep. The hard part is not knowing what to do. The hard part is doing the same useful thing again, and again, and again, long after the first flush of enthusiasm has evaporated. Boredom is not a nuisance that occasionally interrupts discipline. Boredom is the central climate of discipline. It is the weather you live in when you decide to become consistent.

A short sentence belongs here. The brain wants novelty.

There is nothing wrong with that. Novelty is a feature of human cognition, not a defect. The brain is attuned to change because change might mean opportunity or danger. It notices the unusual. It habituates to the familiar. This is why the first week of a new habit feels vivid and the fourth week feels grey. The task did not change. Your perception did. And because modern life is saturated with engineered novelty—notifications, feeds, endless content—the contrast becomes sharper. Repetition feels flatter than ever. The disciplined person is not someone who never feels bored. The disciplined person is someone who can work with boredom without letting it steer the wheel.

The chapter's stakes are larger than personal productivity. Boredom is where talented people quietly quit. A gifted musician stops practising scales because scales feel beneath them. A promising coder abandons a project because the middle is repetitive and unglamorous. A capable salesperson stops prospecting because rejection and routine feel numbing. A strong student stops revising because the material is "already known", then discovers at exam time that familiarity was not mastery. In each case, the person is not defeated by difficulty; they are defeated by dullness. Dullness is what separates the brief burst from the long arc.

This is also why boredom is misunderstood. People interpret it as a signal: "this is not for me," "I'm not motivated," "I've lost my passion." That interpretation feels sophisticated because it frames quitting as self-knowledge. Sometimes it is. Often it is simply the brain doing what brains do: craving stimulation. The chapter's aim is not to shame that craving, nor to romanticise suffering. It is to make boredom legible, so that it becomes a manageable variable rather than a mysterious verdict.

A useful way to see boredom is as a tax on repetition. Every rep has an upfront cost: time, effort, attention. Some reps have an additional cost: emotional dullness. The dullness can be so strong that it masks progress. Deep progress is often slow and subtle; it does not announce itself daily. Boredom fills the gap between effort and visible payoff. This is why so many people chase intensity: intensity feels exciting. Intensity also burns out. The challenge is to build a relationship with repetition where excitement is not required for action.

This chapter therefore explores three complementary moves. The first is to name boredom accurately and refuse to treat it as a moral or existential crisis. Boredom is not proof that the rep is worthless. It is often proof that the rep is familiar. Familiar reps are where skill consolidates. Athletes run drills. Musicians practise passages. Programmers write tests, refactor, and debug. None of this is glamorous. All of it is foundational. The chapter will show that boredom is not the opposite of progress; it is often the texture of progress.

The second move is to make reps *slightly* more interesting without destroying their recognisability. This is a delicate art. Change too little and boredom wins. Change too much and the habit dissolves into novelty-chasing. The sweet spot is small variation: a different running route, a timing experiment, a new constraint, a tweak in sequence, a different opening line in a sales call, a slightly altered practice piece. The goal is not entertainment. The goal is freshness—just enough to keep attention engaged while keeping the rep fundamentally the same. Variation becomes seasoning, not a different meal.

The third move is to use challenges and games as scaffolding. Gamification has a bad reputation because it is often applied with plastic rewards and shallow optimism. Used well, it is simply a way to make progress visible and to introduce playful pressure. A points system can turn study into a measurable series of wins. A self-competition can make a boring task feel like a structured experiment. A "boss level" day can create a controlled spike of intensity when the system is stable enough to handle it. The chapter treats games as tools, not as identity. They are crutches you can use without pretending you were born limping.

Running through all of this is the most important skill: separating feelings from actions. Many people believe they act because they feel motivated. In reality, motivation is often a consequence of starting, not a prerequisite. You begin cold, you warm up, the work becomes easier once you are in motion. This is as true for workouts as for prospecting calls as for writing. The chapter will treat boredom and low motivation as weather: real, influential, but not authoritative. Weather can be acknowledged and still not obeyed. A person can notice a feeling, name it, and then do the next small rep anyway.

This is not stoicism as theatre. It is mechanics. Habits run on cues, environment, and loops. Systems survive through cadence calendars, streak shields, and honest review. Social accountability and metrics provide visibility. All of those structures reduce reliance on mood. This chapter adds a missing piece: what to do when the structures are in place and the day still feels dull. Because it will. A calendar block can still feel boring. A streak can still feel pointless. A system can be perfectly designed and still require you to sit down and do the rep. The human mind is not a machine. It is a restless animal with a taste for novelty.

The modern relevance is plain. The culture sells instant dopamine. It sells constant stimulation. It sells the idea that if you are bored, you are doing life wrong. That message is commercially convenient and psychologically corrosive. It makes disciplined work feel like deprivation. It encourages people to abandon slow-building skills in favour of quick hits of novelty. The long-term cost is not merely personal underachievement. It is a society full of people who can start things but cannot finish them, who can dream but cannot endure the quiet middle where dreams become real.

And yet boredom is not purely an enemy. Boredom is also a diagnostic. It can reveal when a rep is too easy and needs gentle progression. It can reveal when a system has become mindless and needs attention. It can reveal when variation has been neglected. It can even reveal when a goal no longer matters. The chapter does not treat boredom as a dragon to be slain. It treats boredom as information to be interpreted. The trick is to interpret it accurately rather than melodramatically.

A quiet motif will thread through the chapter: the metronome again, now heard in a different register. The metronome is indifferent. It does not care whether you are inspired. It marks time. Boredom is often the sound of the metronome in your head: tick, tick, tick, the rep repeating. The disciplined person learns to hear that sound without panicking, to let it become a steady background rather than an alarm. Once the metronome becomes tolerable, the work becomes possible.

The closing tension of this chapter is a choice about what you believe motivation is. Is motivation the engine that must arrive before you move, or is it the warmth that often comes *after* motion begins? If boredom is unavoidable, will you treat it as a stop sign, or as the ordinary texture of a life built on reps—a texture you can soften with small variations, sharpen with games, and ultimately outlast by acting even when you do not feel like it?

Why Discipline Feels Boring

On 9 August 2016 in Rio de Janeiro, Brazil, Katie Ledecky swam the 800 metres freestyle at the Olympic Games and finished in 8:04.79, a world-record time reported widely and easy to verify. The moment on television looked like dominance made effortless. Underneath it sat years of repetitions so repetitive they would be unwatchable: length after length, turns drilled until they blurred into instinct, the same water smell, the same muted roar of a pool hall, the same clock watching. A performance that changes a record is built from practice that rarely changes at all.

Boredom is not a flaw.

A five-word sentence belongs here. It's the cost of repetition.

Most conversations about discipline treat boredom as an irritant—something to push through, something to ignore, something to "beat". That framing misses the central truth: boredom is the default emotional climate of consistent effort. It is not a side issue that occasionally appears; it is the thing that appears when you are doing the right work often enough for it to become familiar. If you expect discipline to feel thrilling, you are effectively planning to quit once the novelty fades.

Show what this looks like in ordinary life. Someone starts studying a language. The first week feels vivid: new words, new sounds, a quick sense of progress. By week four, the same person is staring at verb endings with a mild sense of resentment. The content has not become harder. It has become less novel. The brain, which once rewarded the person with excitement for beginning, has moved on. It is now asking: what's new? The implication is uncomfortable but liberating: the emotional drop is not evidence of failure. It is evidence of normal cognition.

Name the concept. Novelty hunger.

Explain it. Novelty hunger is the brain's tendency to prioritise new stimuli over familiar stimuli because new stimuli might carry information. The nervous system evolved to notice changes in the environment—movement in the grass, an unfamiliar sound, an unexpected pattern—because change can matter for survival. Familiar stimuli are filtered out to conserve attention. This filtering is not a moral judgement. It is an efficiency mechanism. The implication is that boredom arises precisely because the brain is doing its job: deprioritising what it has already seen.

Once you see novelty hunger clearly, several other puzzles become easier to understand. One is why people confuse boredom with lack of motivation. Motivation is often experienced as interest, and interest is often a by-product of novelty. When novelty declines, interest declines, and people conclude they have lost "motivation". But motivation is not a single substance that drains away. It is a shifting set of incentives, emotions, and expectations. In many cases, boredom is simply interest withdrawing because the brain no longer treats the task as urgent information. The implication is that you can remain committed even while feeling bored; commitment does not require constant interest.

Another puzzle is why deep progress often feels slow. Early progress is frequently visible because the gap between ignorance and basic competence is dramatic. The first improvements in fitness, writing, sales, or study can be obvious: you can run further, write more cleanly, make fewer errors, remember more. Later progress becomes subtler. Improvements are measured in marginal gains: a slightly cleaner turn in the pool, a slightly more persuasive opening line, a slightly faster recall, a slightly more stable form. The brain prefers big changes because big changes are easier to detect. When changes become small, the brain marks the work as "same". Boredom fills the perceptual gap between effort and obvious payoff. The implication is that boredom is often a sign that you are no longer a beginner—and that you have entered the phase where progress is real but less theatrical.

This is why people who rely on excitement tend to cycle through pursuits. They are brilliant starters. They mistake beginning for talent. They get the dopamine of novelty, collect early wins, then feel bored and move on, leaving a trail of half-built skills. This pattern is socially reinforced. Modern culture celebrates the launch, the announcement, the "new". It is less interested in the quiet months of improvement that follow. The disciplined person, by contrast, is willing to live in the unmarketable middle: the unsexy, repeated actions that do not make for good stories but do make for competence.

A second named, checkable example shows boredom's relationship to excellence in a different domain. In the early 1990s, the violinist Itzhak Perlman spoke publicly about practice as a long-term commitment to fundamentals—scales, tone, precision—rather than a daily pursuit of inspiration. The dates of particular interviews vary, but the broader point is widely recorded in profiles of classical musicians: virtuosity is not built by constantly playing only the exciting pieces. It is built by returning to the boring ones until they cease to be boring in the hands and become expressive. The implication is that boredom is often the doorway to depth. The work becomes interesting again not by changing the task but by changing the level at which you can perceive it.

The same is true in coding. Many people are attracted to programming because it promises creation—building apps, solving puzzles, making something run. In practice, professional programming contains a great deal of repetition: writing tests, reading other people's code, refactoring, documenting, fixing the same class of bugs in slightly different clothes. Much of it feels tedious. And yet those repetitive tasks are where reliability is built. A system does not become robust because a coder had a burst of brilliance. It becomes reliable because someone repeatedly did the unglamorous work that prevents failures. The visible behaviour is not "creativity". It is checking. It is review. It is testing. The implication is that boredom is not only a psychological obstacle; it is a professional environment. A person who cannot tolerate it will struggle to ship stable work.

At this point, it is worth naming the emotional trap boredom creates: the search for meaning. When people feel bored, they often interpret it as existential: "This isn't meaningful," "I'm wasting my life," "This is not what I'm meant to do." Sometimes that interpretation is accurate. Plenty of work is pointless. But boredom does not reliably distinguish pointless work from foundational work. Foundational work is often boring because it is repeated. The brain's boredom signal is not a meaning detector. It is an attention detector. The implication is that boredom should not be granted moral authority. It is information about stimulation, not a verdict on value.

Still, boredom can also tell the truth in one specific way: it can reveal that a habit has become mindless. Mindless repetition can produce stagnation. A musician can play scales with no attention and improve little. A salesperson can make calls with no reflection and learn slowly. A student can reread notes passively and mistake familiarity for mastery. When boredom arises from mindlessness, it is a sign that attention has decoupled from the rep. The reconciliation is not to abandon repetition but to reintroduce deliberate attention: a small focus point, a metric, a constraint, a feedback loop. The rep becomes informative again. The implication is that there are two kinds of boredom: boredom that signals familiarity, and boredom that signals disengagement. Both are manageable. Neither requires quitting.

Now address the limitation that a sceptical reader might raise. Some people appear to be immune to boredom. They claim to love the grind. They thrive on repetition. They feel calm in routine. Is boredom therefore a personal weakness? No. Temperament varies, and some people do find repetition soothing. Some people derive satisfaction from predictability and from incremental improvement. But even these people experience boredom in some domains. More importantly, the existence of boredom-resistant people does not make boredom a defect; it makes it a common variable with individual differences. The reconciliation is simple: design systems that assume boredom will appear and provide ways to keep acting when it does.

This design perspective matters because boredom has predictable behavioural consequences. It increases the attractiveness of distraction. It makes short-term rewards seem more valuable. It encourages avoidance and procrastination. It also encourages "optimisation" as a substitute for doing the rep: reorganising the workspace, researching new methods, shopping for new tools, building elaborate plans. These behaviours feel productive because they are novel. They are often a way to flee the dullness of execution. The implication is that boredom does not simply feel unpleasant; it changes your decision-making, making you more likely to trade compounding actions for immediate stimulation.

Here the motif from earlier chapters—the metronome—can do useful work. A metronome ticks with indifference. When you begin practising with one, it can feel irritating, even oppressive. You want the freedom to speed up and slow down according to mood. Yet the metronome's boredom is precisely its power: it reveals drift. It reveals inconsistency. It asks you to respect time. Discipline feels boring partly because it functions like a metronome: it asks you to show up at a regular beat, regardless of emotional weather. The implication is that boredom is the sound of rhythm demanding to be maintained.

One more concrete example clarifies the relationship between boredom and compounding. Imagine two people learning the same skill. Person A practises only when it feels exciting. Person B practises on a schedule, including on dull days. Person A's practice is intense but sporadic. Person B's practice is modest but consistent. Over months, Person B accrues more total reps. Over years, the difference becomes enormous. The invisible metric is not talent. It is hours spent in boredom without quitting. The implication is sharp: boredom tolerance is a competitive advantage disguised as a personality trait.

The forward test at the end of this section is not a motivational slogan. It is a diagnostic question about interpretation. The next time boredom arrives—during a workout, a study session, a sales block, a craft practice—will you treat it as evidence that something is wrong, or will you treat it as the predictable signal of familiarity, the metronome ticking, the tide going out and promising it will come back again, provided you keep showing up long enough to let the reps compound?

Making Reps More Interesting

In March 2020 in the United Kingdom, a strange and verifiable experiment in daily behaviour began at national scale: millions of people, confined by COVID-19 restrictions, started walking the same routes again and again. Parks became circuits. Streets became loops. At first, the repetition brought comfort. Then it brought irritation. People began taking detours, swapping pavements, counting steps, choosing different times of day—small changes made not for fitness science but for sanity. The sensory details were ordinary: the squeak of trainers on wet tarmac, the same dog barking behind the same gate, the metallic click of a garden latch. The actions were tiny. The effect was real.

The rep stayed. The wrapper changed.

That is the core problem this section addresses. Boredom is not defeated by abandoning repetition; it is managed by designing repetition so it remains tolerable. The objective is not to turn disciplined work into entertainment. The objective is to add just enough novelty to keep attention engaged without dissolving the habit into constant change. Too little variation and the mind drifts. Too much variation and you stop building the specific skill you came to build. The art is to vary the *surface* while preserving the *structure.*

A five-word sentence belongs here. Novelty must be rationed carefully.

Show the most common failure mode. A person begins running. They repeat a simple route and steadily improve. Then boredom arrives. They respond by swapping running for a completely different activity, or by constantly changing plans—different workouts, different apps, different routines. The result is a sense of activity without the compounding effect of consistent practice. Another person, equally bored, stays within running but adds micro-variations: a different route on one day, a slight pace experiment on another, a playlist reserved for longer runs. They keep the base rep intact. The implication is that variation can protect consistency when it is constrained.

Name the concept. Constrained variety.

Explain it. Constrained variety is the deliberate introduction of small, bounded changes within a stable habit so that the habit remains recognisable and therefore repeatable. The constraints matter. They limit variation to elements that do not break the core behaviour: route rather than distance, order rather than content, prompt rather than practice time, opening line rather than entire sales process. The implication is that you can refresh attention without abandoning the compounding engine.

Constrained variety works because boredom often arises from predictability rather than from difficulty. Predictability reduces the brain's alertness. The rep becomes automatic. Automaticity is useful—it reduces friction—but it can also reduce engagement. When engagement drops too far, avoidance becomes tempting. A small change can pull attention back into the present. It makes the rep feel slightly new, enough to reduce the urge to flee.

This is not a theory reserved for athletes. Musicians often practise the same passage with deliberate constraints to keep attention alive: different dynamics, different articulations, different tempos. The notes remain; the angle changes. Coders do something similar when they practise with small constraints—solving the same type of problem with a different approach, refactoring the same function with a different style, writing tests first rather than last. The core skill remains; the experience shifts. The implication is that boredom is not an argument against repetition. It is an argument for *intentional* repetition.

Timing experiments are one of the simplest forms of constrained variety. The same rep at a different time can feel like a different rep because your cognitive and physical state changes. A writing session at 6 a.m. differs from one at 9 p.m. in attention quality, emotional tone, and resistance. A workout at lunchtime differs from one after work. Prospecting calls in the morning can feel more assertive; calls late afternoon can feel more cautious. The visible behaviour here is simple: run the same rep in a different slot and observe the effect. The implication is that you can sometimes reduce boredom without changing the rep at all, merely by changing the temporal context.

A second named, checkable example anchors this in a domain where repetition is unavoidable: sales. In June 2012, the Obama re-election campaign's analytics team was widely reported to have used A/B testing on fundraising emails, changing subject lines and small wording choices to improve response rates. The details of specific tests vary by report, but the practice itself is documented and emblematic: keep the goal constant, vary one element, measure the result. The implication is not about politics; it is about method. Micro-variation turns monotony into an experiment. Instead of "I have to send another email", the thought becomes "I am testing a variable". The rep gains curiosity.

That is a broader principle worth naming: boredom shrinks when a rep becomes informational. If the rep feels like mere labour, it becomes emotionally heavy. If the rep feels like data collection—an experiment in technique, timing, or sequence—it becomes lighter. The rep remains effortful, but it becomes meaningful in a concrete way because it produces feedback.

Micro-challenges operate on the same mechanism. They create a local objective inside a repetitive task. The task stays the same; the focus shifts. A runner might aim to keep pace steady for a particular segment, or to finish the final kilometre slightly faster than the first. A student might aim to retrieve information without looking at notes for five minutes, then check accuracy. A writer might aim to draft a paragraph without editing, then revise in a second pass. A salesperson might aim to ask one extra question on each call. The behaviour is visible, measurable, and small. The implication is that micro-challenges can make reps feel alive by giving them a narrow edge.

There is a risk here, and it must be acknowledged: micro-challenges can become a way to avoid the boring core by endlessly inventing new games. If every session becomes a new gimmick, attention fragments and mastery slows. The reconciliation is to keep micro-challenges subordinate to the habit. They are seasoning, not the meal. The habit is the meal. A useful micro-challenge should be easy to repeat, easy to track, and easy to drop without breaking the overall cadence.

Another practical form of variety is sequence variation: changing the order of sub-steps while keeping the total work the same. For study, this might mean doing review first and new material second on one day, then reversing it on another, noticing which produces better retention. For creative work, it might mean drafting before outlining sometimes, outlining before drafting at other times. For training, it might mean doing mobility before strength on one day, and after on another. For sales, it might mean prospecting first then admin, rather than admin first then prospecting. The visible metric is not a feeling; it is the completion rate. Which sequence survives a tired Thursday? The implication is that boredom is sometimes a symptom of friction hidden in sequence, and sequence experiments can reduce both.

Environment variation is a subtler tool. People often assume they must practise in the same place for consistency. Sometimes that helps, particularly when cues matter. But environment can also be used as a controlled variable. Writing at a desk versus writing in a library can change attention quality. Studying in a quiet room versus a slightly noisier café can change endurance. Walking meetings can change energy. The aim is not to chase ambience. The aim is to refresh attention while keeping the behaviour intact. The implication is that place can be a gentle novelty lever when used intentionally.

Social variation can help too, when used sparingly and safely. Doing a rep in the presence of another person—working alongside someone, practising in a group, joining a study session—can reduce boredom by adding mild accountability and shared energy. The risk is that social context can turn practice into performance, which often increases anxiety and reduces learning. The reconciliation is to use social variation for consistency rather than for validation. The rep remains the unit of progress. The audience is incidental.

Another powerful lever is constraint-based practice, which is common in skill acquisition. Instead of making the rep bigger, you make it narrower. A musician plays a passage at half speed, focusing only on tone. A coder limits themselves to a particular method to learn its trade-offs. A writer drafts with a strict word limit to force clarity. A salesperson focuses on listening rather than persuading for a week, counting how many times they summarise the other person's needs. These constraints create novelty by narrowing attention. The rep becomes a laboratory. The implication is that boredom often dissolves when you turn the rep into deliberate practice rather than mere repetition.

Now bring back the motif: the metronome. The metronome does not change. The player changes around it. Making reps more interesting is not about silencing the metronome. It is about learning to play with it—adding dynamics, phrasing, small shifts—while the beat remains steady. The beat is the habit. The variations are your tools for staying present.

Still, a limitation must be handled with honesty. Some reps are intrinsically dull, and no amount of variation will make them delightful. Filing admin, doing basic drills, revising foundational material—much of it will never feel thrilling. The aim is not joy. The aim is tolerability. If variation helps you complete the rep reliably, it has done its job. If variation becomes another demand, another planning burden, it has failed. The reconciliation is to prefer variations that are simple, repeatable, and cheap in attention.

The deeper payoff of this approach is psychological. When you can make reps slightly more interesting, boredom loses its power to dictate behaviour. You stop treating boredom as a signal to quit. You treat it as a design prompt: adjust the wrapper, keep the rep. This is not self-deception. It is respect for how attention works.

The forward test for this subchapter is deliberately practical. When the next rep feels flat—when the run route feels stale, the study session feels grey, the outreach block feels numb—will you abandon the rep in search of novelty, or will you introduce one constrained variation, measure what happens, and keep the metronome ticking while your attention learns to stay in the room?

Using Challenges and Games

In June 1776 in Philadelphia, the Continental Congress appointed a committee to draft what would become the United States Declaration of Independence. The dates and place are easy to check. Less often discussed is the mundane machinery around it: committees, drafts, revisions, votes, and the slow conversion of messy deliberation into a finished text. One way to understand the achievement is not as a thunderbolt of inspiration but as a sequence of constraints: deadlines, roles, and rules that made progress unavoidable. When humans do hard things together, they often invent games without calling them games—structures that turn intention into action.

Rules create movement.

A five-word sentence belongs here. Games make effort feel lighter.

"Gamification" has become a slightly embarrassing word, like a motivational poster that wandered into a laboratory. It is associated with shiny apps, badges, and the faintly patronising idea that adults need gold stars. That caricature misses the point. A game is not a toy. A game is a system of rules that transforms effort into feedback. The appeal is not childishness; it is clarity. When the work is repetitive and the payoff is delayed, games pull the future into the present by making progress visible now.

Show the typical moment when games become relevant. A person sits down to study, or to write, or to make outreach calls. The task is clear enough. The resistance is not confusion. The resistance is emotional flatness. The mind wanders. Distractions become seductive. The person begins negotiating: maybe later, maybe tomorrow, maybe after a "quick check" of something else. A well-designed game short-circuits this negotiation by giving the rep a more immediate objective than "become better at this over months". The implication is that games can act as a bridge between long-term value and short-term behaviour.

Name the concept. Playful pressure.

Explain it. Playful pressure is the use of light, voluntary constraints—scores, streaks, levels, time limits—to create urgency and focus without relying on mood or external coercion. It differs from punishment because it is chosen. It differs from mere tracking because it adds a small stake: a goal to hit, a record to beat, a "level" to unlock. The implication is that you can harness the psychology of competition and progress in a humane way, using it to support discipline rather than to replace it.

Point systems are the simplest form of playful pressure because they translate messy effort into a clean count. Counting is not glamorous, but it is honest. If a behaviour can be counted, it can be repeated; if it can be repeated, it can compound. The point system does not need sophistication. It needs consistency. A point system is simply a rule that assigns points to actions you want more of, not to outcomes you cannot fully control. This is critical. If you score outcomes, you invite distortion. If you score reps, you build reliability.

A short, concrete example shows how a points game can transform study without becoming a gimmick. Imagine a student preparing for an exam or a professional learning a new body of knowledge. The work feels amorphous: "study more" is not a behaviour. The game makes it a set of observable actions. One set of rules might award points for retrieval practice—attempting to recall information without looking—because retrieval is effortful and informative. Another might award points for writing a brief explanation in one's own words, because that reveals understanding or lack of it. Another might award points for reviewing errors, because error review is the rep most people avoid. The exact numbers are not sacred. The behaviour is. The implication is that the points game shifts attention from vague time spent to concrete reps completed.

This is where evidence matters, but without overloading the page. Cognitive psychologists have repeatedly found that retrieval practice tends to strengthen long-term memory more than passive review, a finding summarised in influential work by Henry Roediger and Jeffrey Karpicke in 2006. The point is not to turn study into a clinical protocol. The point is to select reps that are likely to produce learning and then reward yourself for doing them. The implication is that games can be aligned with how learning actually works rather than with what feels comfortable.

Streak competitions with yourself operate differently. A streak is a simple narrative: "I have shown up X days in a row." The power comes from identity and loss aversion. Losing a streak feels like losing evidence of who you are. That can be motivating. It can also be brittle if the streak is designed without shields, as earlier chapters explained. When used well, a streak competition is not a fragile idol;

it is a metronome. It keeps time. It makes drift visible. It helps you return quickly after disruption.

The metronome motif belongs here. A streak is the beat.

Now consider "boss levels", the term borrowed from video games for a harder challenge that appears periodically. Boss levels are useful precisely because they are not daily. A daily boss level is just a miserable routine. A periodic boss level is a spike: a deliberate, contained increase in intensity that tests capacity and reveals progress. In training, a boss level might be a longer run or a slightly heavier session. In sales, it might be a high-volume outreach day, executed with preparation and review. In craft, it might be a longer deep-work session or a public deadline. In study, it might be a full practice exam or a timed recall session. The implication is that boss levels can keep monotony from becoming stagnation while preserving the core cadence.

A second named, checkable example grounds boss levels in a well-known tradition of challenge. In April 2013 in Boston, Massachusetts, thousands of runners competed in the Boston Marathon, a race with a course and qualifying standards that make it a symbolic test for many. The marathon functions as a boss level in training plans: a focal point that structures months of easier and harder sessions around a single day. The implication is not that everyone needs a marathon. The implication is that periodic challenges can give structure and meaning to long-term repetition, turning the year into a sequence of build, test, and recover.

However, games can backfire, and this must be handled with intellectual honesty. The most common failure is score obsession. People begin chasing points rather than progress. They choose actions that earn points easily, not actions that matter. They "game the game". This is not a sign of moral weakness. It is predictable human behaviour. If you create a measurement, people will optimise for it. The reconciliation is to design the score so it is hard to manipulate and closely tied to the behaviour you genuinely value. This echoes the earlier discussion of feedback metrics: count what you can control, count what predicts outcomes, and keep the metric simple enough that it remains honest.

A second failure mode is emotional dependence. Some people begin relying on the game for motivation, and when the game loses novelty, they stop. The reconciliation is to treat games as scaffolding rather than as identity. Scaffolding supports building. It is not the building. When a game becomes stale, you adjust it or replace it without panic. The underlying commitment remains to the reps.

A third failure mode is shame. A missed day becomes a moral event; a broken streak becomes self-condemnation. This is especially dangerous because shame tends to produce avoidance, and avoidance destroys consistency. The reconciliation is to keep games playful. Playful does not mean unserious; it means voluntary and forgiving. A game that punishes you for being human will not last. It will turn discipline into dread. Dread is brittle.

Now return to the practical mechanism that makes games work: immediate feedback. Long-term goals are abstract. A points tally is concrete. A streak count is concrete. A boss level completed is concrete. The brain responds to concrete signals. That response is not a flaw; it is an opportunity. When you provide immediate feedback for the behaviours that matter, you make it easier to keep doing them in the absence of excitement.

Games also have a social dimension even when played alone. The mind is surprisingly responsive to imagined audiences and internal narratives. "I am on a streak" is a story. "I hit my points target" is a story. "I beat my record" is a story. Stories create identity. Identity stabilises behaviour. The implication is that games are not merely behavioural hacks; they are narrative engines. They give the disciplined person a way to experience progress in the present tense.

There is also a deeper philosophical benefit. Games remind you that discipline can contain joy without requiring constant pleasure. Joy here is not euphoria. It is the quiet satisfaction of completion, the small spark of "I did the rep." In a world that treats work as either grim obligation or passionate calling, games offer a third path: earnest play. Earnest play is serious enough to matter and light enough to repeat.

The final tension is therefore a question of control. When motivation is low and boredom is high, will you wait for inspiration to descend like weather, or will you design a small game—a point system, a streak, a periodic boss level—that creates playful pressure and keeps the metronome beating, even when the rep itself feels plain?

Separating Feelings from Actions

On 28 April 1789 in the South Pacific, HMS *Bounty* was seized by mutineers led by Fletcher Christian. The names, date, and location are verifiable through naval history. It is remembered as a story of rebellion, but it is equally a story of mood as a decision-making system. Months of hardship, resentment, and longing for ease on Tahiti did not merely colour perceptions; they altered behaviour. A disciplined structure broke when feelings became the governing authority. The ship did not mutiny because the crew lacked information about what was expected. The ship mutinied because emotion became the pilot.

Feelings are persuasive liars.

A five-word sentence belongs here. They are not the boss.

This subchapter addresses the skill that sits beneath every other tool in this book. Habits, friction audits, stacking, streak shields, cadence calendars—these structures do crucial work, but they cannot fully remove the moment when a person does not feel like doing the rep. That moment is universal. It arrives on tired evenings, on grey mornings, after rejection, after boredom has dulled the work's edge. What matters then is not whether you can manufacture motivation. What matters is whether you can separate what you feel from what you do.

Show the everyday scene that makes this relevant. A professional blocks an hour for deep work. The calendar arrives. The desk is ready. The next step is clear. Yet the body feels heavy, the mind feels scattered, and a small internal voice suggests postponement. A student sits down to revise and feels a mild nausea of avoidance. A salesperson opens a list of prospects and feels an anticipatory pinch of rejection. These are not exotic experiences. They are normal responses to effort, uncertainty, and repetition. The implication is that if behaviour requires a matching feeling, behaviour will be rare.

Name the concept. Action independence.

Explain it. Action independence is the capacity to execute a pre-committed behaviour regardless of transient internal states such as boredom, reluctance, anxiety, or low enthusiasm. It is not emotional suppression. It is not denial. It is simply the refusal to treat feelings as instructions. The implication is profound: once you can act without waiting to feel ready, you gain access to consistency in conditions that would otherwise defeat you.

The idea can sound harsh, as if the inner world is being dismissed. It is not. Feelings contain information. Anxiety can signal risk. Fatigue can signal the need for rest. Boredom can signal familiarity or disengagement. But information is not governance. Weather informs travel; it does not decide whether you are the kind of person who keeps promises. Treating feelings as commands is an abdication of agency. Treating feelings as data is adult life.

The "feel like it" trap becomes clearer when you look at how the mind predicts effort. The brain attempts to conserve energy. It anticipates discomfort and inflates it. It imagines the rep will be worse than it often is. This is why starting feels harder than continuing. Many people have experienced this in exercise: the first minutes feel stiff and unwilling, then the body warms and the session becomes tolerable. The same pattern appears in writing: the first sentences feel clumsy, then rhythm returns. The same in sales calls: the first call feels daunting, the second less so. The implication is that feelings at the start of a rep are unreliable forecasts of feelings mid-rep.

A modest, checkable piece of evidence can be named without turning the page into a methods lecture. Behavioural psychology and clinical practice have long used the principle sometimes called behavioural activation, developed and studied in the context of depression and low mood: action can precede and influence emotion rather than the other way round. The implication in a discipline context is not clinical advice; it is a general human observation. Movement changes state. Starting changes state. The nervous system is not a static pond; it is a flowing river. You can step into it and change its direction.

The mechanism of "warming up" deserves respect because it is not mystical. In physical movement, temperature rises, joints lubricate, heart rate adjusts, breathing settles. In cognitive work, attention narrows, working memory loads the relevant material, distractions lose their grip. In social work like prospecting, the first interaction reduces anticipatory anxiety and restores a sense of competence. The visible behaviour is the same across domains: begin with a small step, and the system often follows. The implication is that action independence is not heroism; it is an understanding of state change.

This is where earlier concepts reappear in sharper form. Minimum viable habits lower the start-up cost. Friction audits remove obstacles. Streak shields protect identity under disruption. Cadence calendars reduce decision fatigue. All of these make action independence easier because they reduce the number of moments where you must negotiate with your feelings. But negotiation still happens. The crucial skill is to notice the negotiation, label it, and move anyway.

The weather metaphor is useful, and not merely poetic. Feelings rise and fall. They have patterns. They can be intense without being accurate. You can be drenched in reluctance and still walk to the desk. You can be buffeted by anxiety and still dial the number. You can be fogged by boredom and still do the next rep. Weather affects the journey; it does not change the destination. The implication is that the disciplined person learns to travel in varied weather rather than waiting for perfect skies.

A second named, checkable example can illustrate action independence as a deliberate practice rather than a personality trait. In February 1910 in Paris, France, the composer Igor Stravinsky premiered *The Firebird* with Sergei Diaghilev's Ballets Russes. Stravinsky's later career became emblematic of a working artist who produced under constraints, deadlines, and the unevenness of inspiration. Artistic myths suggest that creation arrives only when the muse appears. Working artists know otherwise. They show up, draft, revise, and endure imperfect sessions. The implication is that action independence is not anti-art. It is what makes sustained art possible.

At this point a credible limitation must be acknowledged, because the idea can be misused. There are times when feelings should influence action. Severe exhaustion is not a test of character; it can be a signal that rest is needed. Persistent dread may indicate that the system is misdesigned or that the task is unsafe or ethically wrong. Chronic anxiety might indicate a workload that is not sustainable. The reconciliation is not to obey every feeling but to create a distinction between transient resistance and legitimate signals. Transient resistance is common at the start of effort. Legitimate signals are patterns that persist and correlate with clear costs. The implication is that action independence requires judgement, not stubbornness.

That judgement can be made more reliable by pairing abstractions with visible metrics. If a person claims they are "too tired" to do a rep, what does "too tired" look like in behaviour? Are they unable to complete any minimum viable version, or are they unwilling to begin? If they skip often, is the skip followed by recovery or by further drift? If anxiety is cited, does anxiety decrease after beginning, or does it amplify? These are observable patterns. The implication is that you can measure whether feelings are acting as excuses or as warnings by looking at what happens when you take the first small step.

A key move is naming. Naming is not therapy language; it is precision. When you name a feeling—boredom, reluctance, anxiety—you turn a vague cloud into a specific object. Specific objects can be handled. Vague clouds cannot. The act of naming creates a small distance between the feeling and the self. It produces a gap in which choice can occur. The implication is that naming is a behavioural tool: it makes room for action.

The next move is shrinkage. Not because the rep is unimportant, but because the start is the main barrier. When feelings are heavy, the first action must be light. The brain's resistance is often directed at the imagined full session: the hour-long workout, the full prospecting block, the entire chapter of revision. But you do not need to begin with the full session. You need to begin with the first small step. Put on the shoes. Open the document. Dial one number. Read one paragraph. The implication is that action independence is often won by choosing a start that is too small to justify refusal.

This is why action independence does not require emotional numbness. It requires a commitment to process. People sometimes imagine the disciplined person as a cold machine, immune to feeling. That image is both false and undesirable. A more accurate image is a person who feels fully and still acts. They feel boredom and still practise. They feel reluctance and still begin. They feel anxiety and still take the first step. Their feelings are not weaker. Their relationship to feelings is different. The implication is that discipline is not a reduction of humanity; it is a cultivation of freedom.

The metronome returns again, quietly. The metronome does not speed up because you are excited. It does not slow down because you are tired. It keeps time. Action independence is choosing to keep time with it, even when your internal tempo wants to drift. This is not self-violence. It is self-governance. It is deciding that your commitments are sturdier than your moods.

The most practical proof of this skill is not a grand act. It is a small one repeated. A person who separates feelings from actions does not wait to feel like writing before writing; they write and then sometimes feel like it. They do not wait to feel confident before calling; they call and then sometimes feel confident. They do not wait to feel energised before moving; they move and then sometimes feel energised. The direction of causality flips. The implication is that life becomes less hostage to internal weather.

The forward test is stark because it must be. The next time you do not feel like doing the rep—and you will not—will you interpret that feeling as a veto, or will you name it, shrink the start, take the first small step, and discover, in the only way discovery is possible, whether the weather changes once you begin?

Chapter 10
Resetting After Relapse

On 16 January 2009 in the Hudson River, Captain Chesley "Sully" Sullenberger brought US Airways Flight 1549 down onto freezing water and kept every person alive. The date, place, and names are easy to verify; the sensory detail is not hard to imagine: the hard, wet slap of river spray against metal and glass, the sharp cold that turns breath into urgency. What matters for our purposes is not the drama but the principle. Aviation is built on the assumption that systems fail and humans drift. It is not a culture that waits for perfection. It is a culture of checklists, redundancies, and recovery—of treating error as expected and designing the response in advance.

Relapse is a kind of failure too, but the ordinary kind: a missed workout, a lost week of study, a quiet month where the outreach list goes untouched, a habit stack that collapses under a new season of life. The surprise is not that it happens. The surprise is how often people interpret it as a moral verdict. They miss a day and hear a sentence inside their head: you are the sort of person who quits. They miss a week and the sentence hardens: you always do this. They miss a month and the sentence becomes a story: you cannot be trusted. That story is the real damage. The lost reps matter, but the collapse of self-trust matters more, because it changes what feels possible next.

The modern world is particularly good at manufacturing relapse. Work arrives in bursts and then lingers; attention is constantly auctioned; sleep is negotiated rather than protected; screens provide instant relief from discomfort; schedules fracture and reassemble. Under such conditions, consistency is not only a skill, it is a design problem. And design problems do not yield to shame. Shame is a blunt tool. It can produce a short jolt of compliance, then it rots the will from the inside by making the task emotionally toxic. The person begins to avoid the work not because the work is hard, but because it has become associated with self-disgust. That is how a slip becomes a spiral.

The first move in recovery is therefore conceptual. It is not to "try harder". It is to distinguish types of failure with the cold clarity of someone who wants to learn. A slip is a miss inside an otherwise stable pattern: one day off, one session skipped, one set of calls avoided. A break is a more sustained interruption, usually driven by life events, exhaustion, travel, illness, or a season where the system no longer fits. A regression is the deeper drift where identity is rewritten and the habit becomes an old story rather than a current one. These are not labels for judging yourself. They are categories for choosing a response. The same intervention does not work for all three, because the problem is not the same.

A slip is often a matter of friction and attention. A break is often a matter of fit. A regression is often a matter of confidence and narrative. The stakes are practical. If you treat a slip like a regression, you overreact; you turn a small miss into a crisis. If you treat a regression like a slip, you underreact; you promise yourself you will "get back on it tomorrow" and then watch tomorrow become next month. Recovery requires calibration. The person who becomes consistent is not the one who never fails; it is the one who fails in small ways and recovers quickly.

This is why relapse should be treated as part of the learning curve, not as proof of failure. The learning curve is not a smooth graph. It is a jagged line with plateaus, spikes, and dips. Anyone who has built competence in anything recognises this. Athletes get injured. Writers go quiet. Students have chaotic terms. Salespeople lose rhythm after a string of rejections. The question is never whether disruption will occur. The question is whether disruption will be allowed to redefine the identity of the person doing the work.

A second principle follows: recovery is easier when it is designed before it is needed. People design their best systems while they are calm, optimistic, and in control. Relapse happens when they are tired, busy, emotionally flattened, or already disappointed. That is a bad moment to improvise. The human brain is not brilliant under discouragement. It reaches for familiar relief. It tells comforting lies. It exaggerates costs. It reduces options. A pre-planned reset is a way of borrowing your own competence from a better day and making it available when you most need it.

The chapter's centrepiece is therefore not grit but scripting: relapse resets. A reset is not a grand recommitment speech. It is a short sequence that creates traction. It begins with a minimum viable restart step—something small enough to do even with low confidence. It includes a brief reflection that does not become a trial—two or three honest observations about what changed. It ends with a small win that restores momentum, because momentum is not an emotion; it is a pattern of movement. When you see recovery as a script, relapse becomes less dramatic. The rep returns to being a rep. The metronome finds the beat again.

The elegance of a reset is that it respects human psychology without flattering it. People often imagine that the right way back is to punish themselves with intensity: to "make up" for lost time by doing twice as much, to prove they still have it. Sometimes that works for a day. More often it sets a trap. Intensity without stability produces another relapse, and the second relapse is heavier because it is accompanied by the story of failure returning. A reset, by contrast, is designed to be survivable. It assumes low motivation. It assumes imperfect conditions. It assumes the need for gentleness without indulgence. Gentleness here is not softness. It is precision about what actually restores consistency.

There is also a more philosophical payoff. Resetting after relapse is an apprenticeship in self-governance. Most people are familiar with two modes: strictness that collapses under pressure, and permissiveness that drifts without direction. A reset offers a third mode: adaptive discipline. Adaptive discipline is the capacity to keep a commitment while adjusting the method. It is not the rigidity of a machine. It is the resilience of a good system—one that bends and returns rather than snapping.

This is where learning enters. A relapse is not merely an interruption; it is a dataset. It tells you where the system failed. It reveals hidden friction. It exposes unrealistic assumptions. It shows where identity was too dependent on mood. It reveals which anchors were weak. The worst outcome of relapse is not that you missed the reps; it is that you missed the lesson. A gentle post-mortem is how you harvest information instead of collecting regrets. You look for patterns—time of day, social context, workload, sleep disruption, emotional triggers—without putting your character on trial. You revise the habit the way an engineer revises a design: by changing inputs and constraints, not by insulting the machine.

Still, honesty is required. Some habits fail because they were never truly chosen. They were borrowed ideals—someone else's routine, someone else's aesthetic, someone else's version of a good life. Those habits tend to relapse because they are built on obligation rather than value. The answer is not to force them to stick. The answer is to redesign around what is actually wanted, what is actually feasible, and what the current season permits. A system that does not fit will break. That is not a personal tragedy. It is feedback.

The most delicate work in relapse recovery is rebuilding confidence. Confidence is often treated as a feeling that must be restored through pep talks or affirmations. In practice, confidence is more like a ledger. It is built by evidence: small promises kept, small actions completed, small recoveries executed. When relapse has happened repeatedly, the ledger looks bleak. The person becomes cautious about committing because they have been burned by their own overpromising. The temptation is to swing to the opposite extreme: to stop promising anything at all. That solves the pain of disappointment by removing the possibility of progress. A better approach is to rebuild trust through behaviour—by shrinking commitments, stacking easy wins, and limiting promises to what can be delivered under ordinary conditions.

Modern relevance sharpens this point. Many people are not relapsing because they lack desire. They are relapsing because they are overloaded, fragmented, and operating without slack. Slack is not laziness; it is breathing room in a system. Without slack, any disturbance causes collapse. A single sick day, a delayed train, an unexpected meeting, a child's sleepless night—these are not rare events. They are normal life. A discipline system that cannot absorb normal life is not a discipline system; it is a fantasy. Resetting after relapse is how you make discipline realistic.

The closing question of this chapter is not whether you can avoid relapse. That is not the interesting question. The interesting question is what you do the day after. When the streak breaks, when the calendar goes messy, when the old boredom returns with teeth, will you interpret the lapse as a verdict on who you are, or will you treat it as a signal to execute a reset—small, precise, almost boring in its reliability—and learn whether the person you are becoming is defined not by uninterrupted performance but by how quickly you regain the beat?

Normalising Slips and Relapse

In 1978 in Wiltshire, England, James Dyson began building what became the bagless vacuum cleaner that would later carry his name. The outcome is not controversial; the process is the part most people miss. Dyson has described producing thousands of prototypes before one finally worked, a detail he later recorded in *Against the Odds* (1997). The scene is almost aggressively unromantic: a workshop, a growing pile of discarded plastic and metal, the repetitive noise of testing, the grit that gets under fingernails and into the seams of attention. This is not a tale of uninterrupted momentum. It is a tale of repeated re-starting.

The beat can return tomorrow.

That sentence is not consolation. It is a model. Dyson's work is a clean example of a truth that personal discipline often tries to deny: progress is rarely a single, continuous line. It is a series of attempts separated by misfires, pauses, wrong turns, and adjustments. When people speak of "relapse" in habits—falling off the plan, losing the streak, drifting back into old defaults—they often smuggle in a moral judgement. The underlying assumption is that a lapse reveals something essential about character. Dyson's workshop suggests a different assumption: lapses reveal something about the system.

Consider the ordinary form of relapse most professionals recognise. A person keeps a small practice for weeks—daily writing, regular study, consistent outreach, morning movement—then misses a day. The day is not missed because the person suddenly becomes a different person. The day is missed because something changes: a deadline expands, a night runs short, the commute breaks, the child gets ill, the mind catches a cold of boredom. The evidence is behavioural. The diary entry is absent. The workout is skipped. The call list is untouched. The implication is that the first question after a miss is not "what is wrong with me?" but "what changed in the conditions?"

This is the pivot from shame to curiosity. Shame tends to ask global questions—*why am I like this?* Curiosity asks local questions—*what happened on Tuesday?* Local questions have answers. Global questions breed stories. Stories harden into identity. Identity drives behaviour. That is how a single missed rep becomes a months-long regression.

A useful way to understand relapse is to treat it as a category problem rather than a moral one. Not all lapses are equal. A single missed session inside a stable pattern behaves differently from a week-long interruption, and both differ from the deeper drift where a habit stops feeling like "what one does" and returns to being "something one once tried". These differences matter because they determine what kind of repair is possible. A small tear needs a stitch. A larger tear needs a patch. A torn garment that no longer fits needs redesign.

The motif of stitching is not decorative. It is accurate. Human routines are stitched into days by cues, environments, social rhythms, and small rewards. When those stitches hold, behaviour feels almost automatic. When they tear, behaviour becomes effortful and emotionally loaded. The implication is that relapse should be analysed like a tear: where did it begin, how far did it spread, and what tension caused it?

A slip is the smallest tear: one or two misses that occur without changing the underlying pattern. The show is familiar. A person who usually writes after coffee gets pulled into an early meeting and the morning vanishes. The pattern remains. The next day, the coffee returns and so does the writing. The name—*slip*—matters because it frames the event as local and repairable. The explanation is mechanical: a cue was interrupted, a sequence was broken, and the day carried on without the rep. The implication is that the slip is not destiny. It is a signal about vulnerability in the system.

A break is a larger tear: a sustained interruption where the old cues stop firing and the habit loses its place in the day. The show looks different. A person travels, changes jobs, enters a crunch period, loses sleep, or carries an unexpected burden. The environment changes. The calendar changes. The habit is not merely missed; it becomes inconvenient. The name—*break*—acknowledges that the pattern has been disrupted rather than merely skipped. The explanation is structural: the routine was bound to a context that no longer exists. The implication is that returning requires re-binding the habit to new anchors, not merely "trying again".

A regression is the deepest tear: the habit collapses into the past tense. The show is not only behavioural but narrative. The person stops saying "I write" and starts saying "I should write". The person stops being "someone who trains" and becomes "someone who used to be fit". The name—*regression*—is not an insult; it is a description of distance. The explanation is psychological as well as structural: repeated misses degrade trust in one's own promises, and degraded trust makes the next attempt feel risky. The implication is that recovery must rebuild evidence of reliability, because motivation alone will not repair a damaged ledger of self-trust.

These distinctions are not academic. They shape what you expect of yourself, and expectations shape behaviour. When a slip is treated as a regression, people overreact. They make dramatic vows, intensify the plan, and raise the stakes in a way that makes the next miss catastrophic. When a regression is treated as a slip, people underreact. They assume tomorrow will restore the old pattern without changing anything about the conditions that caused the collapse. In both cases, the error is the same: misdiagnosis.

A second checkable example, far from self-help folklore, shows the same logic under pressure. Between March 2006 and August 2008, SpaceX attempted to reach orbit with its Falcon 1 rocket and failed in its first three launches—on 24 March 2006, 21 March 2007, and 3 August 2008 at Omelek Island in the Kwajalein Atoll (dates and location are part of the public record of launches). Those failures were not treated as proof that the organisation was fundamentally incapable. They were treated as information: each failure produced a post-mortem, design changes, and another attempt. On 28 September 2008, Falcon 1 reached orbit from the same site. The show is concrete—launch attempts, outcomes, iterations. The name is familiar in engineering: *iteration under constraint*. The explanation is that complex systems rarely work perfectly on first assembly. The implication for personal discipline is not that life should be treated like a rocket programme, but that relapse becomes less frightening when it is framed as expected data rather than as a verdict.

The analogy has limits, and those limits matter. Organisations can fund repeated attempts; individuals have finite time, energy, and social obligations. A rocket company can run a formal failure review. A student working nights cannot always do that. The reconciliation is to keep the principle while changing the scale. The principle is not "fail fast" as a slogan. The principle is "learn locally". Even a small, private review—what changed, what cue broke, what friction rose—can convert relapse from shame into information. The implication is that the burden of learning need not be heavy for learning to occur.

The emotional obstacle to this approach is the desire for a clean self-image. People want to believe that discipline is the behaviour of a "good" person and relapse is the behaviour of a "bad" one. This binary thinking is psychologically seductive because it simplifies the world. It is also false. Most disciplined people relapse. The difference is that they relapse differently. They relapse with smaller damage, shorter duration, and less moral drama. They have fewer catastrophic stories and more practical adjustments. The implication is that the mark of discipline is not uninterrupted performance; it is the speed and quality of recovery.

Psychology offers a lens for why shame is such a poor recovery tool. When setbacks are interpreted as stable personal traits—*I always quit*—people are more likely to disengage. When setbacks are interpreted as specific, changeable causes—*I lost the cue; the day shifted*—people are more likely to re-engage. This distinction is consistent with research on attribution and mindsets, synthesised for a general audience by Carol Dweck in *Mindset* (2006). The point is not to adopt a cheerful slogan. The point is to notice what kind of explanation you reach for after a miss, because the explanation often predicts the next behaviour.

The invitation here is not to be sentimental about relapse. It is to be exacting about it. A slip costs a rep. A break costs rhythm. A regression costs identity. Those are real costs. Yet the costs become far worse when the mind adds a second penalty: shame. Shame makes the missed rep feel like a contaminated object. It turns the habit into a reminder of inadequacy. That is how people begin avoiding the very activities they value, not because they have stopped valuing them, but because the activity has become emotionally charged. The implication is stark: shame multiplies the cost of relapse by making return psychologically expensive.

Curiosity, by contrast, reduces the cost by keeping return neutral. Curiosity asks for details. It wants a timeline. It wants conditions. It wants the smallest true explanation. It does not need drama. Consider how a researcher treats a failed experiment. The experiment is not a confession. It is a result. The researcher records what happened and adjusts the variables. That posture—cool, attentive, unsentimental—is available in personal discipline too, even if the subject is your own behaviour. The implication is that you can treat yourself as a system worth understanding rather than as a person to be punished.

A credible counter-example is necessary, because normalising relapse can become an excuse for endless cycling. Some people relapse not because the system is imperfect but because the commitment is not real; the habit is adopted as a temporary self-image rather than as a value. In such cases, normalising relapse without confronting the underlying mismatch produces churn: repeated enthusiastic starts, repeated quiet endings, repeated disappointment. The reconciliation is to separate normalising from indulging. Normalising means removing moral drama so learning can occur. It does not mean treating all goals as optional or all patterns as harmless. A pattern of repeated regression is still information. It may indicate that the habit is poorly chosen, poorly anchored, or incompatible with the current season. It may indicate that the social and environmental load is too high to support the design. The implication is that normalising relapse should sharpen diagnosis, not blunt it.

The modern pressure to display perfection intensifies the problem. Social media posts show streaks, not resets. People share before-and-after photographs, not the middle months where progress wobbled. Professional culture rewards polished narratives: the promotion, the publication, the acquisition. It rarely displays the messy recovery work—the missed weeks, the lost confidence, the re-starts made quietly with low enthusiasm. This creates a false baseline. People compare their private relapse to someone else's public highlight and conclude they are uniquely flawed. The implication is that many relapses are not personal failings but collisions between real life and an unrealistic imagined standard.

There is a more grounded baseline. Most long-term competence is built by those who have restarted many times before stabilising. The musician who returns after gaps. The researcher who regains momentum after a rejected paper. The salesperson who finds rhythm again after a slump. The student who learns, late, how to study consistently. These are not rare characters. They are the population of serious achievement. They are simply less visible because their progress is made of reps, not of announcements.

The stitching motif returns at the right moment. Each restart is a stitch. A stitch is small. It does not look heroic. Yet enough stitches hold a life together. Enough stitches make the routine wearable again. The forward tension, then, is not whether relapse will happen. It will. The tension is diagnostic: when the next tear appears, will it be treated as a moral wound, or as a practical signal—slip, break, or regression—calling for the kind of repair that keeps the fabric intact and the beat, however faint, still audible?

Designing Relapse Resets

On 15 January 2009 at 3:31 p.m. local time, US Airways Flight 1549 struck birds after take-off from LaGuardia Airport in New York and lost thrust in both engines. Minutes later it was in the Hudson River, and everyone survived. The event is well documented, and the sensory details are easy to picture: the abrupt change in engine sound, the cabin's sudden attentiveness, the cold insistence of winter light on water. What keeps this incident from becoming a simple miracle story is that it was not solved by inspiration. It was solved by a trained response under stress—actions selected in advance, rehearsed until they were available when the mind was least interested in deliberation.

Rehearsal beats improvisation.

A relapse reset is the civilian version of that principle. Not the drama, obviously. The structure. When routines break, most people improvise their return. Improvisation feels free, but under discouragement it becomes unreliable. The brain in a relapse state is busy doing two expensive things at once: justifying the lapse and negotiating the comeback. It replays what should have happened, then invents a grand plan to compensate, then quietly avoids starting because the plan is too heavy. A reset removes that negotiation. It is a pre-planned script that answers the only question that matters after a lapse: what happens next?

The appeal of a reset is not motivational. It is mechanical. A reset is designed to work when motivation is low, confidence is thin, and the day is already crowded. It assumes that you will not feel ready. It assumes that you will feel slightly guilty, slightly behind, slightly annoyed with yourself. The point is not to soothe those feelings. The point is to make them irrelevant to behaviour. A reset, properly designed, turns the return into a small sequence that can be executed without a heroic mood.

The first element is a minimum viable restart step. The phrase matters because relapse tends to inflate the perceived size of the restart. If you miss three workouts, the mind demands a "proper" session to make up for it. If you skip a week of studying, the mind insists on a full evening of focus to restore dignity. If you ignore your outreach list for a fortnight, the mind imagines an exhausting day of catch-up calls. This is the relapse trap: the more behind you feel, the bigger the comeback you demand, and the bigger the comeback you demand, the less likely you are to begin. The minimum viable restart step breaks the trap by shrinking the start until it is too small to frighten you.

Start small. Start now.

That sentence is not a slogan; it is a design constraint. The restart step must be concrete and countable. "Get back into it" does not count. "Try harder" does not count. A restart step is something you can do in a few minutes and tick as complete. It is also something you can do even if the day is compromised. The visible behaviour is the point: you are not trying to feel like the disciplined person again; you are acting like them, briefly, and letting the identity follow.

The second element is a quick reflection. Reflection is often misunderstood as either self-therapy or self-flagellation. A reset uses it differently. It treats reflection as a short diagnostic, limited in scope and duration, designed to extract information and prevent repeat failure. The reflection is not meant to be profound. It is meant to be useful. You identify what changed, where friction increased, what cue broke, and what assumption was false. The output is not self-judgement. The output is a small adjustment to the system.

A third element is a small win. The small win is not childish reward-seeking. It is reinforcement. A relapse depletes confidence because confidence is evidence-based. When you do not do what you said you would do, you accumulate evidence against your own reliability. The way back is to accumulate evidence in the other direction. A small win is a deliberately chosen action that restores a sense of traction. It should be observable and relatively easy, but meaningful enough to feel like genuine progress rather than theatre. The implication is that your brain begins to update its prediction: return is possible; the story is not over.

These three elements—restart step, reflection, small win form a script that can be executed in order. The order matters. The restart step comes first because action changes state. Reflection comes second because you can diagnose more accurately after movement than before it. The small win comes third because it locks in momentum and reduces the temptation to overcompensate with intensity. The sequence is a stitch in the fabric, and the motif is deliberate: a reset is not a reinvention; it is a repair.

Show how this works in a human context. A professional returns from travel with a disrupted routine. The suitcase is still half-packed. Sleep is irregular. Email has metastasised. The person looks at the old habit and feels a familiar dread: the gap between what they did last month and what they did this week. Without a reset, dread becomes delay. With a reset, dread becomes a cue: run the script.

The restart step is performed. The reflection is brief. The small win is collected. The day is not "fixed". But the direction is restored.

A named, checkable example helps to anchor the logic in reality rather than in aspiration. In the early 1980s, the British cycling system was not a model of world dominance. By 2002, UK Sport funding had increased significantly as Britain prepared for the London 2012 Olympics; in the decade that followed, British Cycling and Team GB became internationally dominant in track cycling, culminating in standout medal performances at Beijing 2008 and London 2012. The public record shows medals and funding; what is less glamorous is the operational culture that supports repeated performance: review, adjust, repeat. High-performance sport is a laboratory for relapse resets because training is never perfect. Sessions are missed. Bodies get ill. Travel disrupts rhythm. The response is not a crisis each time; it is a set of planned modifications. The implication for ordinary discipline is not to imitate elite sport's volume but to imitate its attitude: missing is expected; recovery is designed.

And yet a counter-example is necessary. Some people are allergic to scripts. They fear that scripting their comeback will make life rigid, joyless, or overly controlled. There is also a legitimate risk: a reset can become a ritual of self-punishment if it is packed with too many steps, too much reflection, or an excessive demand to "make up" for lost time. The reconciliation is to remember what the reset is for. It is not a ceremony. It is a bridge. It exists to move you from non-action to action with minimal drama. If the reset becomes dramatic, it has already failed its purpose.

The design principles are therefore strict. Keep the reset short. Keep it concrete. Keep it kind without being soft. The restart step must be embarrassingly doable. The reflection must be time-boxed and factual. The small win must be meaningful but not strenuous. If any element begins to require a "good day", it will not be there when you need it most.

The practical question becomes: how small is "minimum viable" after a relapse? Smaller than you think. After a break, confidence is often brittle. People treat brittle confidence with grand promises, then wonder why it shatters. A better approach is to treat brittle confidence like a healing bone: apply light load, repeatedly, and increase only when the structure holds. That is not medical advice; it is a metaphor for system design. The visible behaviour is restraint. You do not prove your seriousness with intensity. You prove it with return.

A concrete exercise reset can illustrate the pieces without turning into a prescriptive programme. Imagine someone whose baseline habit is regular movement. After a relapse—say, a fortnight of inconsistency—the reset step might be a short, defined action that requires minimal setup. Shoes on and a ten-minute walk counts. A single set of a familiar movement counts. The reflection might ask: what broke the cue—time, location, social disruption, fatigue? The small win might be one extra supportive action that makes tomorrow easier: laying out clothes, putting a note on the calendar, preparing the space. The point is not physiological optimisation. The point is behavioural restart.

A study reset can do the same. Imagine a student or researcher whose rhythm collapses under deadlines or fatigue. The restart step might be a small block of review—fifteen minutes with one source, one page of notes, one problem set question completed to the point of understanding. The reflection might identify the friction: unclear next task, an environment that invites distraction, an over-ambitious session length. The small win might be a friction reduction: setting the desk, opening the correct document, writing the next visible action at the top of the page. The point is not academic technique; it is the restoration of a reliable loop.

Notice how the small win often involves environment. That is not accidental. After relapse, people try to repair behaviour with emotion. They attempt to "feel motivated" again. Environment is usually a better lever because it does not require the right mood. A reset that ends with an environmental adjustment is quietly powerful because it makes the next restart step cheaper. It is recovery that compounds.

The deeper benefit of relapse resets is that they protect identity. Without a reset, relapse creates a narrative gap, and the mind fills gaps with stories. The stories are rarely kind. With a reset, the gap is filled with action. Action is evidence. Evidence edits identity. This is how you become the sort of person who returns quickly rather than the sort of person who disappears for months after a miss. The story changes from "I always fall off" to "I sometimes fall off and I have a way back". That is not an affirmation. It is a description built from observed behaviour.

The language of "script" can feel too theatrical for some readers, so it may help to think in terms of protocols. A protocol is not a performance. It is a sequence selected ahead of time because you know that in the moment you may not trust your judgement. Pilots use protocols. Surgeons use protocols. Researchers use protocols when bias is likely. The relapse state is a bias-rich state. It biases you towards self-criticism and overcorrection. A reset protocol protects you from yourself at precisely the moment you are least reliable as an interpreter of your own state.

If this sounds like control, it is. But it is a particular kind of control: control that reduces suffering rather than increasing it. Improvised comebacks often come with emotional violence—grand vows, harsh self-talk, punishing sessions, unrealistic schedules. They produce another relapse and then more shame. A designed reset is more humane because it assumes imperfection and builds around it. It is also more ambitious in the long run because it keeps you in the game. The person who can reset reliably will accumulate far more reps across a year than the person who alternates between heroic sprints and long disappearances.

The stitching motif returns for the second time because it earns its place. A relapse tears the fabric. A reset is a stitch, tight enough to hold, small enough to do quickly, placed where the tear began. Too many people respond to a tear by throwing out the garment. Too many respond by sewing an elaborate patch they never finish. A reset is simpler: stitch first, then decide what else is needed. The forward tension is not sentimental; it is diagnostic. When the next lapse arrives—and it will arrive—will you demand a dramatic comeback that flatters your pride, or will you run the small, pre-planned script that restores motion and asks, with quiet seriousness, what this particular tear is trying to tell you?

Learning from Failed Habits

On 23 September 1999 at NASA's Jet Propulsion Laboratory in Pasadena, California, a spacecraft called the Mars Climate Orbiter was declared lost after a navigation error. The failure was not treated as a cosmic moral lesson about hubris; it was treated as an operational problem, written up in a mishap report and translated into process changes. The image that lingers is not Martian romance but the quiet fluorescent reality of engineers reading logs, tracing assumptions, and discovering that small mismatches can become irreversible outcomes. In that room, blame is a tempting shortcut. It is also useless.

Data beats self-judgement every time.

A failed habit deserves the same posture. Not because a missed week of studying is equivalent to a lost spacecraft, but because the structure of failure is often the same: the gap between intention and execution is explained too quickly, with too little specificity, and with too much character language. People say they "just didn't have discipline", as if discipline were a personality trait, like eye colour, rather than a set of conditions that make certain behaviours more likely. That explanation feels honest because it is painful. It is also lazy. A gentle post-mortem is an antidote to lazy pain.

"Gentle" does not mean indulgent. It means precise. The goal is not to protect the ego; the goal is to protect the learning. If a habit did not stick—daily writing, consistent outreach, regular study sessions—there is information in that outcome. The information is usually about friction, fit, and season. Friction is what made the habit harder than it looked in imagination. Fit is whether the habit matched the person's actual constraints and values rather than their aspirational self-image. Season is the neglected truth that a behaviour can be good and still wrong for *now*.

Start with friction, because friction is visible when you know where to look. The show is always concrete: the running shoes are upstairs, the study materials are scattered, the prospect list is out of date, the workspace is shared, the time block is vague, the first step is unclear.

The name for this is not weakness; it is *start-up cost.* Human beings are exquisitely sensitive to start-up cost. A behaviour with high start-up cost tends to be delayed, and delayed behaviours tend to die, not because they are unimportant, but because they are inconvenient in the exact moment that matters: the moment of beginning. The implication is that a failed habit should be examined at the point of initiation, not only at the point of collapse.

The most common post-mortem mistake is to analyse the habit at its peak: the person remembers the best day, the strong day, the day when the full routine happened, and then concludes that the habit failed because they could not sustain that ideal. This is like judging a bridge by the day the weather was perfect. The system does not fail on perfect days. It fails on ordinary days—days with interruptions, tiredness, awkward meetings, emotional residue. A useful post-mortem therefore reconstructs the ordinary day. When did the habit usually happen? What usually preceded it? What usually derailed it? The metric is behavioural: how often did the habit begin, and what did "begin" actually mean in practice?

Here, it helps to borrow a discipline from aviation without borrowing the melodrama. When incidents occur, investigators look for chains: not a single cause, but a sequence of contributing factors. A habit lapse is rarely one thing. It is a chain. Sleep runs short, the morning starts late, the commute is tense, the first meeting is awkward, the lunch break is swallowed, the brain seeks relief, the easy behaviour wins. The point is not to narrate your day like a tragic novel. The point is to see the chain so you can break it at a weak link. The implication is hopeful: small changes can have outsized effect when they interrupt predictable sequences.

Fit is the second lens, and it is harsher than people expect—harsh on the plan, not on the person. Many habits fail because they were designed for a fictional citizen who has stable energy, uninterrupted time, a quiet home, and a clean calendar. That citizen exists mainly in the imagination of high-performing people who are temporarily forgetting their own lives. Fit asks an uncomfortable question: was the habit designed to impress you, or to be done by you? The visible behaviour here is telling. If the habit repeatedly failed at the same point—always on evenings, always during travel, always during social weeks—it may not be a discipline problem. It may be a design problem. The implication is that ambition is not the enemy; fantasy is.

Season is the third lens, and it introduces dignity into what people often interpret as personal inconsistency. A new job, a new child, an exam period, an intense project phase, a family obligation, a move—these are not mere "excuses". They are real shifts in the physics of the day. A habit that fit in one season can fail in another because the available time, privacy, and mental bandwidth have changed. The error is to treat the old habit as a moral obligation even when the season makes it structurally improbable. The implication is that mature discipline includes seasonal redesign rather than stubborn insistence.

A gentle post-mortem works because it changes the emotional climate around failure. Shame collapses the field of vision. Curiosity expands it. Yet curiosity must be directed. Otherwise it becomes rumination dressed up as analysis. The post-mortem should therefore resemble opening a black box: not a dramatic excavation, but a focused retrieval of the few signals that matter. That motif—black box—earns its keep because it captures the ideal mood. The black box does not tell you who you are. It tells you what happened.

A checkable historical example makes the method clearer. On 28 January 1986, the Space Shuttle *Challenger* broke apart shortly after launch from Kennedy Space Center in Florida. The Rogers Commission (formally, the Presidential Commission on the Space Shuttle Challenger Accident) reported its findings in 1986, with attention not only to technical causes but also to organisational decision-making. Without dwelling on tragedy, the lesson relevant here is structural: complex failures often arise from normalised deviance, where small compromises become routine, and routine becomes invisible. In habit terms, this looks like the small erosion that people stop noticing. "Just for this week" becomes "most weeks". "I'll do it later" becomes "I don't do it". The implication is that the post-mortem must notice normalised deviance early, when it still looks small enough to excuse.

Now bring the lens back down to the human scale, because that is where the work lives. Imagine a habit that failed: a daily study block that lasted twenty minutes, planned for 7:00 a.m. It worked for ten days, then dissolved. The temptation is to conclude that twenty minutes was too hard, or that mornings are impossible, or that the person lacks willpower. A post-mortem would instead reconstruct the chain. On the days it worked, perhaps the night ended on time, materials were ready, and the first task was obvious. On the days it failed, perhaps the phone was checked first, or the desk was shared, or the task was ambiguous, or a meeting shifted earlier. Name the concept: start-up cost and cue reliability. Explain why it matters: the brain avoids uncertain starts because uncertainty feels like risk. Implication: make the first action visible and the cue stable, or move the habit to a context with lower volatility.

Revision is where the post-mortem earns its keep. If the study habit failed at 7:00 a.m. because mornings were unstable, the redesign might relocate the habit to a different anchor: the first ten minutes after opening the laptop at work, or the first ten minutes after lunch, or the final ten minutes before shutting down for the night. If the habit failed because the first task was unclear, the redesign might include a pre-commitment made earlier—choosing the next item while energy is higher, so the start does not require thinking. If the habit failed because the environment was noisy, the redesign might involve a consistent physical location, even a particular chair, where the mind learns what happens there. No mysticism is required. The mind responds to cues.

The point is not that these particular revisions are universally correct; it is that revisions should be derived from observed failure rather than from renewed enthusiasm. Enthusiasm is a poor engineer. It loves grand designs. Evidence is a better engineer. It works with constraints. That is why the post-mortem must be anchored in what happened, not what you wish had happened. Behavioural evidence is the only honest material.

A second checkable example, less dramatic and more directly relevant to personal iteration, comes from manufacturing culture. Toyota's production system, associated with continuous improvement practices that became widely discussed in the late twentieth century, is often summarised as *kaizen*: incremental change driven by observation. The history is complex, but the central idea is simple enough to verify in the public record of industrial practice: improvements are made by repeatedly noticing small problems and adjusting processes, not by issuing heroic speeches. Translate that into habit design and the implication becomes sharp. A failed habit is not a referendum on your character. It is a small process failure asking for a small process change.

Still, there are limits to what a post-mortem can solve. Some habits fail because the underlying goal is poorly chosen or not truly valued. A person may adopt a habit because it signals virtue—reading difficult books, practising an instrument, building a side project—yet the lived experience of the habit reveals indifference. In such cases, the post-mortem can produce better design and still fail, because design cannot manufacture value. The reconciliation is to treat that outcome as information too. A habit that repeatedly fails even after friction is reduced and fit is improved may be pointing to a deeper mismatch: the goal may belong to someone else's idea of success.

A second limitation is that post-mortems can become a refuge from action. Some people love analysis. They keep notebooks full of reflections and still avoid the rep. The sign is subtle: the post-mortem grows longer while behaviour remains unchanged. The black box becomes a theatre prop. The reconciliation is to keep the post-mortem short and tether it to a single revision that will be tested quickly. Analysis should buy experiments, not replace them.

The most humane part of this method is also the most demanding: it insists that you stop telling flattering stories about your future self and start respecting your current constraints. This does not mean lowering standards forever. It means building standards that can survive your life as it is. It means treating "season" as real. It means refusing to confuse a failed design with a failed person. That refusal is not softness. It is accuracy.

The quiet motif returns because it clarifies the final tension. If a habit fails, you can either file it under regret or open the black box. Regret is emotionally expensive and practically sterile. The black box is emotionally calmer and practically fertile. The forward test is simple and uncomfortable: when the next habit fails—and some will—will you turn it into a story about who you are, or will you treat it as evidence about friction, fit, and season, then revise the design and run the experiment again?

Rebuilding Confidence Gently

On 9 July 2001, at the All England Club in Wimbledon, London, Goran Ivanišević walked on to Centre Court as a wildcard and, six days later, left as the champion. The story is verifiable, the scorelines are public, and so is the strangeness of the moment: rain delays, damp grass underfoot, the nervous scrape of trainers on the baseline, an athlete whose career had frayed suddenly holding it together. This was not the triumph of permanent belief. It was the triumph of borrowed steadiness—of routines and manageable tasks executed under pressure long enough for belief to catch up.

Confidence is evidence, not vapour.

After repeated relapses, confidence becomes brittle in a particular way. It is not merely that you doubt whether you can succeed; you doubt whether you can even begin. The mind starts treating commitments as liabilities. Promises acquire a faint taste of humiliation, because you remember the last time you promised and did not follow through. You can feel the distrust as a physical hesitation: the hand hovering over the calendar invite, the cursor blinking in a blank document, the gym bag left where it can be ignored. People talk about "finding motivation" at this point, as if the right feeling could restore the old self. But the more useful question is how trust is rebuilt when trust has been damaged by experience.

Trust is built in small transactions. That is the quiet fact nobody glamorous wants to admit. Your confidence in yourself functions like a ledger: every kept commitment is a credit, every broken one a debit, and the balance changes slowly because the brain is cautious about updating beliefs that affect survival. When you have relapsed repeatedly, you are overdrawn—not morally, but psychologically. In that state, ambitious promises feel intoxicating for an hour and dangerous for a month. A gentle rebuild begins by acknowledging the ledger without melodrama. It stops trying to win the year in a day.

The first move is shrinking commitments until they are both honest and repeatable. This is not about lowering standards forever; it is about re-establishing reliability. Show it in a familiar scene. Someone decides to return to writing after months of inconsistency and commits to ninety minutes every morning. Day one happens in a burst of determination, day two is compromised by a meeting, day three collapses under fatigue, and by day five the plan has become an accusation. The pattern is not mysterious. The commitment was sized for a confident version of the person, and the person is currently operating with fragile confidence. The name for this is *commitment–capacity mismatch*. Explain why it matters: when capacity is low, large commitments create repeated failure, and repeated failure teaches the brain that commitments are unsafe. The implication is blunt. If you want confidence back, stop making promises you cannot reliably keep.

A smaller commitment has a second advantage: it restores the habit of starting. Starting is a skill. It degrades when unused. In a relapse period, the capacity to start begins to feel like a personality trait you have lost, rather than a behaviour you can practise. A small commitment makes starting cheap enough to repeat. That repetition matters because the brain's confidence system is essentially empirical. It asks: what do you do when you don't feel like it? If the answer becomes "I do something small anyway", the ledger begins to move.

Small is sane.

The second move is stacking easy wins, not as self-congratulation, but as evidence accumulation. Easy wins have a bad reputation because they are sometimes used as theatre: people tick trivial boxes to feel productive while avoiding the work that matters. That is not what is meant here. An easy win, properly chosen, is both doable and aligned. It is the smallest action that still points in the direction you care about. You are not chasing comfort. You are chasing credibility.

Consider how this works in practice with observable metrics. A sales professional has relapsed on outreach. Their intention is to rebuild pipeline. The temptation is to vow a heroic surge of calls, a day of relentless prospecting, a week of late-night follow-up. The cost of that vow is obvious: if it fails, the ledger takes another hit, and the person learns again that they cannot trust their own plans. A gentle rebuild would instead choose a unit of work that can be completed even on a messy day: one message to a live contact, one follow-up to a warm lead, one review of a list and a single send. The win is "I did the rep". The rep is countable. The mind can register it. The ledger updates.

This is where limiting promises becomes crucial. Promises are social technology; even when made privately, they carry the weight of your own witnessing. After relapse, people often over-promise because over-promising is a way to argue with reality. "I'm back now," the mind insists, as if volume could erase the record of the last month. Limiting promises is not pessimism; it is precision. You promise only what you are willing to complete in low energy, under pressure, in imperfect conditions. If you cannot imagine doing the commitment on a bad Tuesday, you do not promise it on a hopeful Sunday. The implication is subtle but powerful: you stop using promises as emotional medicine and start using them as behavioural contracts.

The through-line here is that confidence is not rebuilt by *belief* but by *prediction*. The brain becomes confident when it can predict that you will do what you say. Prediction is strengthened by consistency, not by speeches. A fragile confidence state is essentially a prediction failure: the mind predicts you will follow through, then observes you do not, and lowers its expectation. That lowering is painful, but it is not malicious. It is the brain doing risk management. The way out is to improve the prediction by improving the behaviour, not by arguing with your feelings.

A second named example grounds this. In 1842, Charles Darwin moved to Down House in Kent and developed the habit of walking the Sandwalk—a looping path on his property that became a daily rhythm of thinking and restoration. The detail is checkable in the historical record of his life at Down House. What matters here is not the romance of genius but the banality of routine: a repeatable, low-friction action that supported sustained work across years. Darwin did not rebuild intellectual confidence through declarations. He built it through a reliable cadence that allowed thought to happen even when he did not feel heroic. The implication for anyone emerging from a slump is not to imitate a nineteenth-century naturalist's lifestyle. It is to respect the mechanism: small repeatable actions create a stable platform from which larger work becomes possible again.

A credible counter-example needs to be admitted, because the ledger metaphor can be misused. Some losses of confidence are not primarily behavioural; they are rooted in circumstances that cannot be "repped" away quickly—bereavement, serious illness, severe burnout, major social disruption, or clinical mental health conditions that impair concentration and energy. In such cases, the demand for steady output may be inappropriate, and the obsession with optimisation can become another form of self-violence. The reconciliation is to keep the framework honest. A gentle rebuild is not a moral command to perform; it is a method for restoring trust where trust is realistically rebuildable through small actions. When circumstances radically constrain action, the gentlest rebuild may be a different kind of reliability: keeping commitments small enough to be humane, and measuring success by return rather than by intensity.

Now make this concrete through a person rebuilding step by step, without pretending this person is a celebrity or a statistic. Imagine a researcher—call her Nadia—who has had a long slump after a demanding project. For months, her work has been reactive: email, meetings, small tasks, late-night anxiety. The habit she valued most—deep reading and synthesis—has quietly disappeared. Each week she tells herself she will "get back to proper work", and each week ends with the same tired bargain: next Monday. Over time, her confidence in her own seriousness erodes. Not her intelligence. Her seriousness. She begins to doubt whether she can ever do focused work again.

Nadia's first mistake is the classic one: she tries to restore dignity by restoring scale. She blocks three hours on a morning, sets ambitious targets, and treats the session as a referendum on her identity. The morning arrives, she opens the document, and within twenty minutes she is checking messages. She lasts forty minutes, feels disgusted, and abandons the plan. The ledger takes a debit. That evening she rewrites the plan with more severity, as if severity could create steadiness.

A gentle rebuild changes only the design, but it changes it radically. The commitment shrinks to something she can complete even in a low state: ten minutes of reading a single paper, with one sentence written at the end capturing the core claim. That is the rep. It is clear. It is measurable. It is difficult to dramatise. It is also doable. She attaches it to a stable cue—the first time she sits down with coffee, before she opens email. Some days the ten minutes turns into twenty, but she does not count that as the standard; she treats it as a bonus. The standard is the minimum. She is not trying to feel inspired. She is trying to restore the habit of showing up.

Within a week, something shifts—not because she has become more gifted, but because she has become more predictable to herself. She begins to trust that she will at least do the ten minutes. That trust produces a secondary effect: she becomes less afraid of the work, because the work is no longer associated with failure. The dread loosens. She adds a second easy win that supports the first: she prepares the next day's paper in advance, open and ready, so the start does not require decisions. The ledger gains credits. The credits are small. They matter.

Notice what she does not do. She does not announce a dramatic comeback. She does not expand commitments in response to a good day. She does not promise anyone that she is "back". She limits her promises to the rep she can reliably deliver. That limitation feels almost insulting at first—surely a serious researcher should do more than ten minutes. But seriousness is not measured by the size of a promise. It is measured by the consistency of the follow-through.

This is where stacking easy wins becomes strategic rather than sentimental. Nadia's next win is not more work; it is a reduction of friction. She creates a single folder for reading, a single document for notes, a single place where the thread of her thinking lives. That organisation is not aesthetic. It is a behavioural intervention. It reduces the cognitive cost of re-entry. Each time she returns, she can see the thread. Seeing the thread restores continuity, and continuity restores confidence. The ledger metaphor returns: she is building a history of return that her brain can trust.

There is a philosophical point hiding in this practical sequence. Much of what people call confidence is actually a belief about reliability under uncertainty. When you relapse, uncertainty increases: you do not know whether you will do the thing, and that not-knowing is painful. The temptation is to chase certainty through big plans. But big plans increase uncertainty because they increase the chance of failure. Gentle rebuilding accepts uncertainty and reduces it by making the next action so small that it becomes predictable. Predictability becomes trust. Trust becomes room.

The final tension is that gentle rebuilding can feel slow, and impatience is a real threat. People want to be the person they were before the slump, and the gap between current capacity and past identity can create a kind of grief. That grief often pushes people into premature scaling: they add more habits, extend sessions, make bigger promises, and then relapse again. The question that matters is not "How quickly can I become impressive?" but "What level of commitment can I *verify* this week?" The ledger does not care about your aspirations. It cares about your receipts.

Chapter 11
Scaling Discipline Across Domains

On 22 July 2012, the Champs-Élysées in Paris carried the peculiar sound of a victory that had been engineered long before it was celebrated: carbon wheels ticking over seams in the road, helicopters chopping the air above the Arc de Triomphe, spectators pressed against barriers with the warm smell of tarmac and suncream rising in waves. Bradley Wiggins rolled towards yellow, and Team Sky's triumph was reported as a sporting headline, but it was also something more quietly instructive—a demonstration of how a method can travel. The public saw a rider in control. Behind him sat a system: routines, measurement, logistics, repetition, and a kind of unglamorous stubbornness that made excellence feel inevitable.

It is tempting to read moments like that as stories of exceptional people. It is usually a safer bet to read them as stories of repeatable structures.

The puzzle at the heart of discipline is not how to do one hard thing once. Most intelligent people can summon themselves for a sprint. The harder question is how to keep turning up when the work stops flattering the ego—when the novelty wears off, when life gets noisy, when the feedback is slow or humiliating, when the result is delayed beyond the horizon of enthusiasm. Even harder is the question that follows: once a person learns how to show up reliably in one domain, why does that reliability so often fail to transfer? Why can someone be meticulous in research and chaotic in health, or fearless in sales and inconsistent in study, or diligent in training and evasive in craft?

Part of the answer is that each domain flatters a different self-image. Craft invites the romance of inspiration. Sales invites the theatre of charisma. Study invites the fantasy of being naturally bright. Health invites the moralism of purity. Each domain carries its own myths, and myths have a way of making simple behaviours feel dramatic. A person who would never miss a meeting will miss sleep; a person who would never skip training will skip outreach; a person who will happily take a difficult exam will avoid the dull, daily work that makes the exam easy. The inconsistency is not stupidity. It is context. It is also design.

What makes this chapter necessary is the recognition that discipline has a grammar. Its vocabulary changes across domains—steps instead of sentences, calls instead of pages, code instead of canvases—but the underlying parts of speech remain stubbornly similar. There are cues and loops. There is friction and ease. There are tiny commitments that keep identity intact under stress. There are calendars that make repetition more probable than intention. There are feedback signals that reward reality rather than vanity. When those elements are built well, they do not merely produce outcomes; they produce a person who can be relied upon by their own future self.

A system that travels matters now because modern work and modern life are increasingly fragmented. Many professions reward deep specialism while demanding constant switching. The phone pings; the inbox fills; the day is sliced into thin, anxious strips. In that environment, talent can become a kind of liability: the gifted mind, accustomed to quick wins, becomes restless when results are slow. Meanwhile, the person with a small, repeatable method—someone who can generate progress in twenty minutes, not just in an ideal weekend—begins to look almost unfair. The method does not grant more time. It reduces waste. It makes consistency portable.

Portability is the thread running through this chapter. The tools already introduced are not meant to live in one neat corner of life like a hobby. They are meant to scale sideways. The same way a good checklist works in aviation, surgery, and software releases, the same way a good experimental habit works in a laboratory and a kitchen, the discipline architecture that produces reliable action can be carried from health to craft, from craft to sales, from sales to study. The surface changes; the structure holds. That is the promise, and also the test.

Begin with health, because health has a way of exposing the difference between aspirational identity and operational reality. People speak of movement, food, and sleep as if they were expressions of virtue, then behave as if they were optional luxuries.

A busy life tends to treat the body as an inconvenient device that must be kept running between meetings. Yet health is also one of the purest laboratories for discipline, precisely because the feedback is often delayed and unflattering. A single good day means very little. A week matters more. A month becomes noticeable. A year rewrites what feels normal. The challenge is not knowing what is "good" in the abstract; the challenge is designing actions that survive real schedules, travel, low mood, and the ordinary chaos of being human.

The distinctive difficulty of health is that it is everywhere. There is no single desk where health happens. There is no tidy boundary around it. Movement can be designed into a commute or erased by it. Meals can be made simple or made into a daily negotiation with time and fatigue. Sleep can be protected with rituals or sacrificed to late-night scrolling that feels harmless until it becomes a pattern. Health therefore becomes a question of defaults: what happens automatically, without argument, when the day goes sideways? People who manage health well rarely "try harder" every day. They set up their environment and commitments so that the easiest path still points roughly in the right direction. Their discipline is often quiet. It does not look like heroism. It looks like design.

Craft is a different beast. Where health is continuous, craft is often solitary and ambiguous. The feedback can be delayed, subjective, or cruelly absent. A day of writing can feel like failure even when it was necessary; a week of coding can be invisible to anyone who does not read the repository; a month of design work can be reduced to a single comment in a review meeting. This is why craft attracts both perfectionism and avoidance: if the outcome is judged, it becomes safer not to start. The person stays "full of potential" rather than risk making something imperfect and real.

Reliable craft, in contrast, is built on sessions, not moods. It is built on showing up to a place—literal or metaphorical—where the work becomes easier to begin. It is built on boredom tolerance and small variations that keep the mind engaged without losing the thread. It is built on measurement that respects the process: minutes spent, iterations produced, sketches drafted, tests written, pages revised. Not because numbers are noble, but because numbers are harder to argue with than feelings. A designer who quietly stacks a short review of yesterday's work on to the first opening of a laptop, who tracks outputs rather than applause, who protects a small daily session the way others protect meetings, is not relying on inspiration. They are relying on a system that generates inspiration as a side effect of contact with the work.

Sales and outreach add a further complication: rejection. In sales, inconsistency is not merely a scheduling problem; it is an emotional one. People avoid the actions that generate discomfort, then rationalise the avoidance as strategy. They polish presentations, reorganise notes, tweak messaging endlessly—useful tasks in moderation, evasions in excess—while the true leading indicator, contact attempts, remains stubbornly low. Talent can make this worse. A charismatic person might win big on days they feel confident and disappear when they do not, which produces a career shaped like a series of spikes rather than a line. The line wins.

What makes sales a powerful domain for discipline is that it rewards a certain kind of honesty. The outcome is partly outside anyone's control; the activity is not. When someone treats outreach as a daily rep rather than a dramatic performance, two things happen. The first is statistical: more attempts create more opportunities. The second is psychological: the self becomes less entangled with each individual outcome. A person who can say, with evidence, "the rep was completed," is less likely to spiral after rejection or overinflate after a win. The work becomes a process, not a referendum. In that shift lies the possibility of consistency that does not depend on mood.

Study completes the set because it exposes another common trap: the seduction of understanding as identity. Many bright students and thoughtful professionals love the feeling of grasping a new idea; fewer love the labour of revisiting it until recall is reliable. Study is where intelligence often tries to substitute for repetition. It works—until it does not. Formal exams, professional qualifications, language learning, technical mastery: these do not reward occasional brilliance; they reward retrieval, review, and endurance. The key behaviours are small and often invisible. A short session that includes recall rather than re-reading. A practice set rather than another explanatory video. A spaced return to material rather than the illusion of familiarity. Study is also where life gets in the way most brutally: jobs, families, fatigue, and the subtle exhaustion of decision-making. The question becomes whether learning can be designed into the seams of a day rather than postponed to the mythical "free time" that never arrives.

Across these domains, a single motif keeps reappearing: *transfer*. Not the transfer of motivation, which is fickle, but the transfer of method. The method is not one trick. It is a stance towards behaviour: measure what matters, reduce the cost of starting, build commitments small enough to keep under stress, protect continuity with sensible adaptations, and use calendars and feedback to stop negotiating with the self every day. The striking thing is how often people refuse to apply a method they already trust in one domain to the next. They will systematise meetings, budgets, and projects, then approach sleep as a moral struggle. They will track experiments meticulously, then treat study as inspiration. They will run outreach like a lottery and wonder why income swings. The refusal is not logical; it is cultural. Different domains have different stories about what "counts" as real effort. This chapter aims to puncture those stories with a more useful question: what produces reliable behaviour when life is not cooperating?

And yet there is a limitation worth respecting. Not everything scales neatly. Bodies vary, schedules vary, responsibilities vary, and seasons of life impose constraints that no amount of cleverness can erase. A system that works brilliantly for someone with control over their mornings may fail for someone whose mornings belong to children or shift work. A study cadence that suits one temperament may aggravate another. The point is not to force uniformity. The point is to build a discipline architecture that can be adapted without breaking—the way a good bridge design accounts for wind, weight, and movement rather than pretending the world is still.

The emotional payoff of scaling is subtle. It is not merely efficiency, though efficiency matters. It is coherence. When a person can bring the same steadiness to their health that they bring to their work, and the same steadiness to their study that they bring to their training, life begins to feel less like a series of moral battles and more like a set of decisions made in advance. The self becomes less dramatic. It becomes dependable. That dependability is not boring; it is liberating. It reduces the background noise of self-negotiation. It makes ambition less fragile.

The forward tension, then, is not whether discipline "works". It does. The tension is where to place it, and what it costs to make it transferable. A person can build a beautiful system in one domain and still keep a messy corner of life protected by excuses. The chapter's underlying challenge is diagnostic rather than motivational: which domain is currently living off talent, charm, or last-minute surges, and which domain is ready to be rebuilt around reps? The answer is rarely the one that sounds most impressive. It is the one that, if made reliable, would change the shape of everything else.

Applying Framework to Health

In March 2018, the National Health Service in England began rolling out the "Active 10" campaign, urging adults to build brisk walking into daily life, ten minutes at a time. The phrase was deliberately modest, almost plain to the point of offence. No dramatic "transformation". No heroic before-and-after arc. Just the quiet insistence that a body can be nudged, reliably, through the smallest doorway that still counts. The whole thing rested on a premise that is both ordinary and radical: health does not require a new personality. It requires repeatable contact with a few behaviours that the body recognises and rewards over time.

That premise matters because health is the domain where cleverness most often loses. People can organise projects, negotiate contracts, memorise complex material, and still find themselves eating whatever is closest at 9.30 p.m., scrolling until midnight, and calling it "a busy season". The problem is not ignorance. The problem is friction: the thousand invisible costs that sit between intention and action. Health, more than most arenas, is governed by what happens when the day is already ruined, when energy is thin, when decisions feel expensive. The body is not moved by lofty plans. The body is moved by reps.

The framework travels well here precisely because it refuses drama. It starts by treating movement, meals, and sleep as systems rather than moral projects. Systems can be measured. Systems can be simplified. Systems can be protected against disruption. This is not a promise of perfect health, whatever that might mean, and it is not instruction in medicine, nutrition, or treatment. It is an attempt to show how disciplined repetition—small enough to survive—can become a stabilising force in the midst of modern life's chaos.

The first step is to make health legible. Most people try to improve health by choosing a grand target, then trusting a future version of themselves to deliver it. That future person is always well-rested, rarely interrupted, and strangely immune to emails. A better approach begins with visible behaviours and simple counts. Steps are one such count, not because they are holy, but because they are concrete. A day can be measured without a laboratory. A week can be compared without a diary full of feelings. A person can look at a number and ask, without melodrama, whether it is rising, stable, or falling.

This is where minimum viable habits earn their keep. A minimum viable habit is not a compromise with mediocrity; it is a refusal to negotiate with collapse. In health, the most useful minimum is the one that preserves contact. Not the ideal routine. Not the session that would impress someone else. Contact. A ten-minute brisk walk. A short set of mobility movements. A "wind-down" ritual that takes five minutes. The habit is designed to be almost embarrassingly doable, because the enemy is not effort; it is discontinuity. A person who keeps contact can expand later. A person who loses contact begins again from scratch, and the repeated starting-over is where confidence quietly dies.

A friction audit makes this design practical rather than aspirational. Start with one behaviour, and map the obstacles between the moment it should happen and the moment it actually does. If the behaviour is "walk after lunch", the obstacles might include a calendar that turns lunch into meetings, shoes that are inconvenient, a building exit that feels like a commitment, weather, social awkwardness, or the simple fatigue of decision-making. Each obstacle is a design problem. A solution might be as dull as keeping comfortable shoes at work, scheduling a recurring ten-minute block, choosing a route that does not require changing clothes, or pairing the walk with a phone call that would otherwise be taken sitting down. The point is not to become virtuous. The point is to reduce the cost of starting until starting becomes the default.

The same logic applies to meals, where people often swing between restrictive ambition and resigned chaos. Many intelligent professionals do not lack nutritional information; they lack a stable pattern that survives the hard days. A meal routine becomes resilient when it reduces choices. Choice is expensive when a person is tired. The simplest systems are often built around repeats: a small number of reliable meals, ingredients that are easy to obtain, and defaults that prevent the end-of-day scramble. The visible behaviour is not "eat perfectly"; it is "eat the planned thing often enough". The metric might be as basic as how many evenings in a week a person eats the meal they expected to eat, rather than whatever happened to be available.

Here, the minimum viable habit might be a single meal anchor: one predictable breakfast on weekdays, or one repeatable lunch that requires minimal assembly, or one "fallback" dinner that is dull but dependable. It is easy to dismiss such repetition as boring. Boring is a feature. Boring reduces the friction of decision. A person does not need to become obsessed with food to build a stable meal system; they need to become consistent with a few defaults. When a day is busy, defaults do the work that willpower cannot.

A friction audit for meals looks different from a friction audit for walking, but it is governed by the same principles. If the plan is "eat a simple lunch", the obstacles may be shopping frequency, kitchen tools, time to prepare, social context, or workplace access to food storage. Some obstacles are structural: no fridge, no reliable lunch break, constant travel. The audit does not scold. It measures. It asks what the environment permits, then designs within that reality. The outcome is not a perfect diet; it is an operational routine that can be repeated in the real world. That is the only routine that matters.

Sleep, meanwhile, is the realm where high-functioning people most often treat themselves as machines. They cut sleep to create more time, then spend that time making worse decisions, tolerating lower mood, and burning more willpower than the saved hours could ever repay. Sleep is also the most fragile system: it cannot be "caught up" cleanly, and it does not respond well to last-minute intensity. The visible behaviours that shape sleep tend to be small and upstream: what time devices are put away, what the last hour looks like, whether the bedroom is treated as a place for rest or a place for everything.

Minimum viable habits for sleep are not glamorous. They are often rituals that mark a boundary between day and night. A five-minute wind-down can be as modest as laying out clothes for the next day, dimming lights, washing one's face, or writing a short note that closes mental loops. The value lies in repetition: the body begins to recognise the sequence as a cue. This is not mysticism. It is behavioural conditioning. A consistent sequence reduces the reliance on the mind's ability to "decide" to sleep in the midst of stimulation.

A friction audit for sleep tends to reveal unpleasant truths. The obstacle is rarely a lack of desire. The obstacle is often a device in the bedroom, an unstructured evening, work that spills into night, social media that steals time without noticing, or the habit of treating late-night hours as the only private time available. Naming the obstacle matters because it shifts the problem from "I have no discipline" to "my environment makes the wrong thing easy". When the wrong thing is easy, people do it. That is not weakness. That is design.

This is where default pathways become powerful in health. A default is not a rule written in the air; it is a path that requires less effort than the alternatives. If the default after dinner is tea in the same chair with the same scrolling, the body learns that default. If the default becomes a short walk, a quick tidy that makes mornings easier, or a simple wind-down ritual that begins at a fixed time, the body learns that instead. The system is not built on heroic restraint; it is built on predictable sequences.

Streak shields protect those sequences from the real world. Health habits fail most often not on ordinary days, but on unusual ones: travel, illness, deadlines, family emergencies, social events, the weeks where everything is out of rhythm. People who rely on an "all or nothing" version of health tend to interpret disruption as failure.

They skip once, then stop. A streak shield is the rule that prevents a slip from becoming a break. In movement, a shield might be a travel version of the habit: ten minutes of walking in an airport terminal, a set of simple bodyweight movements in a hotel room, or a single lap around the block after a late meeting. The key is that the shield is defined in advance. It removes negotiation. It preserves identity: the person remains someone who shows up, even when circumstances are imperfect.

In meals, a streak shield might be a "minimum meal structure" for chaotic days: eat something with protein and something plant-based, or return to a known fallback meal rather than grazing until bedtime. Again, this is educational, not prescriptive. The point is the form, not the content: a pre-decided minimum that can be executed without thought when time is short. In sleep, a streak shield might be a shortened wind-down ritual that still marks the boundary—five minutes becomes two, lights still dim, devices still out of bed. The shield does not claim to erase the cost of disruption. It claims to keep contact with the system so that tomorrow is a continuation rather than a restart.

A good health system also respects the counter-example that haunts all discipline talk: constraints that are genuinely outside an individual's control. Chronic illness, caregiving responsibilities, unstable work schedules, socioeconomic limits, and mental health challenges can make certain routines unrealistic. The framework does not deny this. It becomes more necessary under constraint, not less, because constraint increases the cost of failure. The honest reconciliation is simple: when life reduces options, the minimum viable habit becomes more important, and the definition of "counts" must be adapted to what is possible. The goal shifts from ideal optimisation to reliable contact. There is dignity in that shift, and practicality too. A person with a narrow margin cannot afford dramatic swings.

There is also a quieter limitation: some people use health systems as a socially acceptable form of avoidance. They perfect their step count while neglecting relationships. They refine meal routines while procrastinating on work that scares them. They chase sleep optimisation while refusing to address the stressors that keep them awake. The framework cannot solve that alone. It can, however, make the trade-offs visible. Health discipline should stabilise a life, not become its new obsession. The metric that matters is not how impressive the routine looks, but whether it is sustainable and whether it supports the rest of what the person values.

The distinctive strength of applying this framework to health is that it turns vague intentions into measurable, repeatable actions that survive stress. Steps become a visible signal of movement rather than a moral judgement. Meal routines become defaults rather than daily debates. Sleep becomes a protected system rather than the leftover of a busy day. The body, being stubbornly physical, responds to what is repeated, not what is imagined.

The forward test is not whether the reader "cares about health". Most people do, abstractly. The test is sharper: when the next busy week arrives, what will remain true without needing a heroic mood? Which minimum viable habit, which friction fix, and which streak shield will still operate when the calendar is hostile and the mind is tired? The answer to that question is the real design of a health system, and it is the difference between a plan that lives on paper and a practice that actually continues.

Applying Framework to Craft

On 9 December 1968, in San Francisco's Civic Auditorium, Douglas Engelbart stood in front of an audience of engineers and demonstrated a way of working that would later feel inevitable: a cursor that could be moved, text that could be edited, ideas that could be organised on a screen. The event became known as "the Mother of All Demos", and the name is deserved not because it predicted the future, but because it revealed something older than technology. It revealed a craftsperson's relationship to a bench: a place where small actions can be repeated until they become capability. The room smelled of dust. The projector whirred. What looked like genius from the back row was, from close up, a sequence of rehearsed moves—inputs, checks, corrections—performed with calm familiarity.

Craft is full of these moments: a performance that seems like inspiration, a deliverable that looks like effortless taste, a piece of software that feels clean and inevitable. Modern work encourages the myth that such outcomes arrive in bursts, delivered by rare minds in rare moods. The myth flatters, and it also paralyses. When craft is framed as temperament, the ordinary day becomes unimportant. When craft is framed as practice, the ordinary day becomes decisive.

The practical question, then, is not whether a person has ideas. Most people do. The question is whether those ideas repeatedly reach the bench. That bench might be literal—a desk, a studio table, a set of tools—or it might be a digital workspace: a repository, a design file, a draft document with its cursor blinking like a quiet dare. The difference between "I should create more" and actual output is rarely a lack of ambition. It is the absence of a cadence that survives fatigue, distraction, and boredom.

Cadence calendars make craft visible. Not visible in the sentimental sense—"I feel like an artist"—but visible in the measurable sense: hours booked, sessions completed, drafts produced, iterations made. A cadence calendar turns creative work from a vague aspiration into a recurring appointment with reality. The calendar does not guarantee excellence; it guarantees contact. Contact is where competence is built. In professional contexts, contact is also where trust accumulates: colleagues and clients do not need to admire one's talent if they can rely on one's output.

The point is not to romanticise routine. Routine can be sterile. Yet the alternative is worse: a life in which craft is performed only when conditions are perfect, which is to say, rarely. Cal Newport's *Deep Work* (2016) became popular for a reason: it named a modern problem plainly—the erosion of sustained attention—and it suggested that depth is not a personality trait so much as a practice defended. Whether one agrees with every prescription, the diagnosis matters. Craft requires uninterrupted stretches in which the mind can go past the obvious solution and into the interesting one. Without a cadence, those stretches become accidental. Accidents do not compound.

A cadence calendar also reframes risk. Creative work feels risky because it exposes judgement: a draft can be rejected, a design can be criticised, a piece of code can break. When sessions are rare, each session becomes precious, and the fear of wasting it grows. Scarcity makes perfectionism rational. Regular cadence does the opposite. It reduces the emotional stakes of any single session by increasing the number of sessions. The work becomes a stream rather than a gamble. A person can afford to test, compare, discard, and try again because there is another appointment with the bench tomorrow or next week. That shift—away from scarcity—is one of the most underappreciated gifts of consistency.

This is where boredom management stops being a gimmick and becomes a professional skill. Boredom is not merely a feeling to endure; it is a signal that the mind is seeking novelty. The trouble is that novelty is easily purchased now. A phone offers infinite stimulation at a thumb's distance, and the brain, being opportunistic, will often take it. Craft asks for a different kind of novelty: the novelty of refinement, of better choices, of cleaner structure. That novelty is slower to reveal itself. It requires staying at the bench long enough to notice what is wrong, and then long enough again to fix it.

Mihaly Csikszentmihalyi's work on flow (*Flow*, 1990) is often simplified into motivational wallpaper, but the underlying observation is useful: deep engagement tends to occur when challenge and skill are matched, not when work is either trivial or impossibly hard. Craft sessions that are too vague—"work on the project"—invite drifting and distraction. Craft sessions that are too ambitious—"finish the entire feature today"—invite dread and avoidance. The better design is specific enough to start and bounded enough to be attempted. The experience of boredom often sits at the boundary where the task is defined, but not yet interesting. Staying through that boundary is a learned capability.

Habit stacking helps because it reduces the cost of beginning. Beginning is the expensive part of craft. A person can spend an hour circling the work without touching it: reorganising files, checking messages, reading one more article, sharpening pencils that do not need sharpening. Stacking takes an existing anchor and attaches a short craft action to it, turning "sometime today" into "after this, then that". In a studio, that might mean that after morning coffee is poured, the design file is opened and one small element is adjusted. In programming, it might mean that after the first email check, a test suite is run and one failing test is addressed. In writing, it might mean that after the laptop opens, the last paragraph is reread and one sentence is revised. The action can be small, even faintly ridiculous. Small actions are not the final form of craft; they are the gateway to it.

A product designer in a London agency once described an uncomfortable truth: she did her best work in the first twenty minutes, provided she actually began. If she delayed, she lost the day to anxious preparation. Her solution was not to "try harder". She designed a stack. After arriving at her desk, she opened the same project file first, before messages, and made one change she could measure: one alignment corrected, one component renamed, one user flow annotated with a question that could later be tested. The metric was deliberately unglamorous—count of micro-iterations—because it could not be faked by mood. She reviewed the count each Friday, not to congratulate herself, but to diagnose whether the system was holding. The result was not constant brilliance. It was regular output, and output created the raw material from which brilliance occasionally emerged.

Feedback metrics keep craft honest. In creative work, vanity metrics are seductive: how inspired one felt, how many hours one sat at the desk, how aesthetically pleasing the workspace became. Useful metrics are visible and behavioural. In writing, words drafted can mislead, but time spent drafting is more reliable when paired with a simple output marker: "one completed scene", "one revised section", "one argument tightened". In design, iterations made, prototypes tested, or critiques completed are more informative than "hours in Figma". In coding, commits, tests written, bugs closed, or review cycles completed are more meaningful than the vague pride of having "worked on it".

Teresa Amabile and Steven Kramer's "progress principle" (*The Progress Principle*, 2011) is relevant here: in knowledge work, small wins and visible progress are strongly linked to positive inner work life. The point is not that happiness produces good work in a neat loop, but that progress—real, observable progress—changes the emotional climate in which work is done. A feedback metric that captures progress can therefore serve two masters. It informs adjustment, and it makes the work feel less like an endless fog.

Still, metrics can become their own trap. A person can optimise what is easy to count and neglect what is hard to measure: taste, judgement, originality, care. This is the credible counter-example that haunts every system. Some of the most important qualities of craft—style in writing, elegance in design, conceptual clarity in code—are not reducible to simple counts. The reconciliation is not to abandon metrics, but to treat them as guardrails rather than gods. A count of sessions completed protects cadence; it does not certify quality. A count of prototypes built protects experimentation; it does not guarantee insight. The craftsperson remains responsible for periodic qualitative review: stepping back, comparing outputs, noticing whether the work is merely prolific or actually improving.

This is where the earlier tools—friction audits and default pathways—quietly decide careers. Craft is vulnerable to friction because it often lacks external enforcement. A meeting will happen whether one feels ready or not. A deadline may force delivery. But the long arc of skill—becoming better, not just finishing—rarely has a supervisor. The obstacles are therefore intimate: a cluttered workspace, unclear next steps, a file system that induces dread, a toolchain that takes ten minutes to boot, a social feed that steals attention in micro-sips. When these obstacles are left unexamined, the mind starts associating craft with discomfort. The avoidance becomes "mysterious", as if motivation has evaporated. It has not evaporated. It has been outcompeted.

The most effective craft systems make the start easy and the continuation attractive. A writer who keeps the draft open to the next sentence reduces the threshold to resume. A programmer who keeps a list of tiny, concrete tasks—rename function, add test, refactor module—reduces the cognitive cost of choosing. A designer who maintains a small library of reusable components reduces the friction of building. These are not hacks. They are respect for the fact that human attention is finite and easily diverted. The craftsperson who survives is often the one who has designed their environment so that the bench is reachable.

Boredom, in such systems, is not eliminated. It is managed. The mind will still protest. It will still offer alternatives: a cleaner inbox, a better playlist, a new tool, a different project. The difference is that boredom is no longer treated as evidence that the work is wrong. It is treated as weather. The bench remains. The session begins. Often, the boredom dissolves once the hands are moving and the problem becomes specific.

The deeper promise of this framework in craft is not productivity in the narrow sense. It is integrity. Craft without cadence tends to become performance: a person talks about what they want to make, buys equipment, collects ideas, and waits for a mood that will justify starting. Craft with cadence becomes practice: a person produces imperfect work, reviews it, corrects it, and produces again. Over time, this practice changes identity in a way that no amount of aspiration can. The person becomes someone who makes things. That identity is not a slogan. It is an accumulated fact.

The forward test is simple and uncomfortable. When the next week arrives with its interruptions, will the bench still be visited—on the calendar, in the environment, in the default sequence of the day—or will craft return to the realm of "someday" and "when things calm down"? There is no universally correct answer, only a revealing one: whatever survives that week is the real system, and whatever does not survive was a wish dressed up as a plan.

Applying Framework to Sales

In 1988, in London, Neil Rackham published *SPIN Selling* after work at Huthwaite that drew on analysis of tens of thousands of sales calls—research built from transcripts, observation, and the slow grind of comparing what people said they did with what they actually did (Rackham, 1988). The glamour of selling, in the popular imagination, lives in the closing moment: the handshake, the signature, the relieved laugh. Rackham's material sits elsewhere, where the air is flatter. Paper shuffles. Voices repeat. The same objections return with different faces. The work looks less like charisma and more like pattern recognition earned through exposure.

Rejection is part of work.

That sentence is easy to nod at, and harder to inhabit. Sales is one of the few domains where an adult can be told "no" repeatedly and still be expected to sound calm, useful, and specific on the next call. The psychological toll is obvious, yet the professional stakes are often hidden: inconsistent outreach does not merely reduce pipeline; it makes forecasting unreliable, learning slow, and trust in the salesperson's judgement brittle. When activity arrives in anxious bursts—an intense week followed by a silent fortnight—the numbers might still add up in a good month, but the system does not. Sales becomes a mood. Moods do not scale.

A useful way to understand consistency in sales is to treat it as a metronome. A metronome does not create music. It creates timing. It provides a steady reference point against which practice becomes measurable: the same passage at the same tempo, again and again, until the fingers stop guessing. Sales has its own tempo, and when that tempo is stable, the work becomes diagnosable. The question is no longer "Why am I not closing?" but "What is happening at each beat: contacts, conversations, qualified meetings, proposals, decisions?" The metronome is not romantic. It is clinical. It is also kind, because it shifts attention from self-judgement to observable behaviour.

Consider the common scene of the erratic high-performer. A charismatic business development manager arrives at a conference, collects business cards in a flourish, makes promises with confident laughter, then disappears into "follow-up" that never quite happens. The energy is real. The results are inconsistent. In contrast, the quieter colleague returns to the office, opens a list, and completes a small number of contacts each working day, logging outcomes, tightening language, testing subject lines, noticing which industries respond and which do not. The second person may never dominate a room. Over time, they tend to dominate a pipeline. The advantage is not personality. It is repeatability.

The first major claim in sales is therefore simple: steady inputs create interpretable outcomes. The scene is familiar to anyone who has carried a number. A quarter is going poorly. A manager asks what is happening. The charismatic salesperson offers stories: "The market's cautious," "Decision-makers are distracted," "It's taking longer than usual." These explanations may be partially true, but they are often unfalsifiable. The methodical salesperson can answer differently: "I made this many first contacts, this many follow-ups, booked this many meetings, progressed this many opportunities to a defined next step." The concept has a name: a controllable leading indicator. The explanation is practical: leading indicators sit earlier in the chain than revenue, so they respond faster to change. The implication is organisational as well as personal. A team that measures behaviour can improve behaviour. A team that measures only outcomes tends to argue about luck.

This is where accountability loops matter, and why they are not the same as surveillance. The most effective accountability in sales is not a grand promise delivered to a manager on Monday and forgotten by Tuesday; it is a recurring review of observable actions and their immediate outputs. The loop does not ask whether someone "felt motivated". It asks what was done, what happened next, and what will be tested in the next cycle. That structure reduces the temptation to perform confidence while avoiding the work. It also protects the salesperson from their own story-making. Humans narrate; that is what minds do. Sales pressure turns narration into excuse. A loop interrupts that drift by insisting on evidence.

A second claim follows: consistency reduces emotional variance, and emotional variance is expensive in sales. The show is in the physiology of the work. After a run of rejections, the body tightens: the hand delays over the dial button, the email draft becomes cautious, the voice rises slightly at the end of sentences as if seeking permission. None of this is a moral failing. It is a predictable response to social threat. The concept is avoidance learning: when an action is paired repeatedly with discomfort, the mind learns to steer away from the cue that begins the action. The explanation is straightforward. If outreach is sporadic, each session carries the weight of proving one's competence. Each "no" lands harder because there are fewer "yes" events to dilute it. The implication is quietly radical: the most humane sales system is often the most consistent one, because it spreads rejection across time, making it survivable.

This is the logic behind minimum viable outreach. The aim is not to reduce ambition; it is to preserve contact with the work on days when resistance is high. Outreach has a steep start-up cost: finding the right person, choosing language, anticipating objections, deciding what to offer, deciding what not to offer. When someone waits until they have a perfect hour, outreach competes with everything else that also demands a perfect hour. The result is predictable: the day fills, and outreach becomes the thing postponed. A minimum viable version of outreach keeps the chain intact. It can be as small as one high-quality contact made deliberately—one email properly written, one follow-up completed with a clear next step, one call placed with notes ready. The key is that the action is real and observable, not a vague intention. The action touches the market. That contact matters.

Salesforce's early growth story is often told as a tale of vision and timing, but the mechanics are more revealing. When Salesforce launched in 1999 in San Francisco with its "No Software" message, the company was entering a crowded enterprise landscape that already had entrenched competitors and sceptical buyers. The visible behaviour that mattered was not merely branding; it was the daily repetition of outreach, demos, follow-up, and the patient conversion of curiosity into commitment, deal by deal. The concept here is pipeline physics: a pipeline is a system with inputs, friction, and throughput. The explanation is not mystical. When inputs are irregular, throughput becomes unpredictable. When inputs are steady, the organisation can learn which stages leak and can tighten those stages. The implication reaches beyond individual performance. Consistency creates organisational learning, and organisational learning is a compounding asset.

Metrics must be chosen with care. The temptation in sales is to measure what flatters rather than what informs. "Pipeline value" can become an emotional comfort blanket if it is not connected to stage definitions and real buyer actions. "Meetings booked" can be gamed by low-quality conversations that waste everyone's time. A useful metric is one that is hard to manipulate without actually doing the work. Counts of first contacts, follow-ups completed, meetings held with defined next steps, proposals submitted with a decision date, and opportunities moved because a buyer took a concrete action—these are less glamorous, and more honest. They also teach faster. When a salesperson can see, week by week, that follow-ups are not happening, or that meetings are happening without next steps, the problem is no longer mysterious. It is procedural.

The metronome returns here. A metronome makes tempo explicit, and explicit tempo allows variation that is purposeful rather than chaotic. When a salesperson keeps a steady beat of outreach, they can run controlled experiments: changing one variable at a time and comparing results over a meaningful window. They can test whether a new opening line produces more replies, whether a different industry responds better, whether a different call time improves connection rates. The system becomes scientific rather than superstitious. The emotional benefit is quiet but real. A person who is experimenting is less likely to interpret rejection as personal failure, because rejection becomes data about a hypothesis that did not hold.

A limitation must be admitted, because sales is not uniform. In some contexts—complex enterprise deals, public sector procurement, or industries with long buying cycles the fantasy of daily activity translating neatly into near-term revenue is just that: fantasy. A single deal can take months or years. Influence can be indirect. A procurement process can freeze for reasons unrelated to salesperson behaviour. This is not a reason to abandon consistency; it is a reason to define it properly. In long-cycle environments, the consistent behaviours may be different: maintaining stakeholder maps, documenting decision criteria, preparing tailored materials, and sustaining contact without becoming noise. The loop still exists. The metronome still exists. What changes is the unit of work. Consistency becomes the reliable maintenance of momentum inside a slow system, rather than the expectation of rapid visible wins.

The reconciliation is therefore conceptual: consistency does not mean "more volume at any cost". It means "repeatable, learnable actions that keep the system alive." In high-volume outbound roles, that may resemble daily contact rhythms and short feedback cycles.

In relationship-heavy roles, it may resemble planned check-ins, thoughtful follow-ups, and disciplined pipeline hygiene. In both cases, the same structure holds. The salesperson is not hoping their future self will become braver. The salesperson is designing behaviour so that bravery is less required.

Social accountability can strengthen this without turning it sour. Sales cultures can drift towards shame: public leaderboards, mockery of low numbers, the assumption that pressure automatically improves performance. Shame is a crude tool. It often produces short-term spikes and long-term avoidance. A more functional social structure is one where commitments are specific and observable, and where review is factual rather than theatrical. Two colleagues who agree to compare the week's activity—contacts made, follow-ups completed, meetings held—can create a loop that is both rigorous and humane. The point is not confession. The point is feedback. Sales already contains enough judgement from the market; internal systems do not need to add cruelty to achieve clarity.

The deeper stake in sales is trust. Buyers do not experience trust as an abstract virtue; they experience it as a sequence of behaviours: showing up prepared, following through on what was promised, responding within a predictable timeframe, being precise about next steps, and not disappearing when the buyer hesitates. These behaviours are, in a strong sense, consistency made visible. A salesperson can have excellent product knowledge and still lose trust through unreliable follow-up. A salesperson can be charming and still be quietly discounted because the buyer cannot predict what happens next. Trust, in sales, is often a calendar phenomenon: what gets done when it was said it would be done.

That returns the focus to system design. If the calendar cannot hold the rhythm, the rhythm cannot hold the pipeline. If the pipeline cannot be trusted, planning becomes guesswork. If planning becomes guesswork, leaders compensate with pressure. Pressure creates more emotional variance. The spiral is common. Breaking it rarely requires a new script or a new personality. It requires a repeatable cadence that can survive bad days, a feedback loop that measures behaviour rather than hope, and a form of accountability that turns performance into learning rather than theatre.

The unresolved tension that matters is not whether selling feels comfortable. It often will not. The tension is whether the discomfort is allowed to dictate tempo. When rejection arrives—as it will—does the metronome slow, stop, and wait for confidence to return, or does the system keep time long enough for confidence to be rebuilt through contact and evidence? The answer is not a slogan. It is observable in the next seven days of activity.

Applying Framework to Study

In September 1885, in Paris, Hermann Ebbinghaus began a private experiment that would quietly reshape how serious people think about memory. Working alone, he learned and re-learned lists of invented syllables, timing himself with the cold patience of a laboratory inside one mind, and he plotted what he called savings—how much faster a second learning became after a delay (Ebbinghaus, 1885/1913). The scene is almost comically unglamorous: paper, repetition, and the faint scratch of a pencil. Yet from that monotony came a blunt fact that every student eventually discovers the hard way. Forgetting is not a personal flaw. It is a feature of the system.

Learning hurts without a structure.

Study is the most widely attempted craft on earth. It is also the one most people practise with the least engineering. Professionals read a report once and assume it has "gone in". Students cram, perform, and then watch the knowledge drain away with unsettling speed. Researchers can spend years becoming precise in their domain while still being strangely casual about how their own memory works. The cost is not merely grades or promotions. The cost is a life spent repeatedly re-learning what could have been retained, and repeatedly abandoning subjects that might have become part of one's mind.

The core claim of disciplined study is simple: consistency beats intensity because memory rewards timing, not heroics. The show is in any exam hall. Two students sit in the same building and take the same paper. One has pulled late nights for a fortnight, living in a brittle state of urgency. The other has studied in shorter sessions for months, returning to material after delays, testing recall, keeping notes tidy enough to revisit, and treating revision as a routine rather than a rescue. The concept is spacing: distributing learning across time rather than packing it into a single block. The explanation is grounded in evidence. A large body of research has found that spaced practice tends to produce better long-term retention than massed practice, across materials and ages (Cepeda et al., 2006). The implication is quietly liberating. The student who studies in small, repeated bouts is not being quaint. They are working with the grain of memory.

This is where the framework matters, because study fails for predictable reasons. It fails because people overestimate what motivation can do, underestimate how quickly forgetting happens, and confuse familiarity with mastery. The practical tools—minimum viable habits, friction audits, streak shields, feedback loops—sound almost too ordinary for something as prestigious as learning. They are ordinary. Learning is ordinary too. The myth is that it should feel exceptional.

Start with micro-sessions, because study has a start-up cost. Anyone who has tried to "do two hours" after a full working day knows the feeling: the chair is wrong, the mind is loud, the material looks heavier than it did in the morning. The first ten minutes are often spent negotiating with oneself, not learning. A micro-session treats this honestly. It does not pretend the mind will arrive ready. It creates a doorway that is small enough to step through without drama. The behaviour might be ten minutes of retrieval practice, or one set of flashcards, or one worked example. The important part is not the clock; it is the re-contact. The concept is minimum viable study. The explanation is mechanical. When the threshold is low, the brain is less likely to trigger avoidance. The implication is profound over months. A person who repeatedly returns to the material becomes someone for whom learning is normal, not an event.

This is not a claim that micro-sessions are sufficient for mastery in every domain. They are not. Complex problem-solving, writing, and deep comprehension often require sustained attention. The point is that micro-sessions are often sufficient to maintain momentum, and momentum is the rare commodity. Once momentum exists, longer sessions can be scheduled deliberately rather than begged for emotionally.

Spacing is the second pillar, and it reshapes what "hard work" looks like. Many people equate effort with duration. Memory does not. Memory responds strongly to retrieval: pulling information out of the mind rather than pushing it in again. A learner who re-reads notes can spend hours feeling productive while building little durable recall. A learner who tests themselves for ten minutes can feel slow and exposed while building something that survives the week. The show is in the small humiliation of a blank page. The concept is retrieval practice. The explanation is backed by research. Testing oneself, even without feedback, can improve later retention compared with additional study time, and feedback strengthens this further (Roediger & Karpicke, 2006). The implication is a shift in what is measured. The question becomes not "How long did I study?" but "What could I recall without looking?"

This suggests a humane metric for study that resists vanity. Minutes are easy to inflate. Completed outputs are harder to fake. A set of flashcards reviewed to completion, a page of problems attempted with answers checked, a paragraph summarised from memory, a short explanation spoken aloud without notes—these are visible. They reveal where knowledge is brittle. They also protect against the common lie of familiarity, where the eyes glide over a page and the mind mistakes recognition for possession.

The third pillar is designing a study environment that reduces friction. The show is in a kitchen table that is also a desk, also a dumping ground for post, also a place where family life collapses at 6 p.m. The concept is cue design: making the right behaviour easier to start. The explanation is practical. If study requires clearing clutter, finding the right resources, locating headphones, remembering what to do next, and fighting for silence, the mind learns a simple equation: study equals hassle. The implication is not moral. It is logistical. Study becomes less frequent.

A friction audit in study is blunt and surprisingly revealing. The obstacles are often boring: the textbook is on a different device; the login has expired; the lecture notes are scattered across platforms;

the flashcard app is buried in a folder; the "plan" is a vague intention. None of these obstacles are intellectually interesting. They are exactly what kills learning for time-conscious people. A friction audit treats this as a design problem. The point is to make the first step obvious and available. If the next action is "open the folder, open the document titled Week 6, do questions 1–3", the mind can comply. If the next action is "revise", the mind stalls.

Habit stacking fits study unusually well because education already has stable anchors. Tea is an anchor. The commute can be an anchor. Opening a laptop is an anchor. The end of lunch can be an anchor. The question is not whether a person has time in the abstract; it is where learning can attach without having to compete with a full narrative of one's day. "After I make my morning coffee, I complete one retrieval set" is a small sentence that, repeated, becomes a system. The behaviour is visible. The identity shift is quiet: someone who studies every day, even briefly, does not have to repeatedly restart their relationship with a subject.

Streaks, used carefully, become a psychological scaffold rather than a cage. Study is vulnerable to disruption because it is easy to skip once and then skip again. A streak counter makes the cost of skipping visible. Yet streaks can become brittle if they are designed as all-or-nothing. A study streak shield prevents this by defining a travel version, a tired version, and an impossible-day version. The shield is not an excuse. It is a pre-commitment to continuity. It says: on a normal day, study looks like a full session; on a disrupted day, study looks like five minutes of recall or one page of reading with a short summary. The result is that the streak represents showing up, not performing perfectly.

A named, checkable example helps make this concrete. In 2012, the open online course boom—popularised by organisations such as Coursera, founded in April 2012 in the United States—made it easy for professionals to enrol in high-quality classes with a click, and just as easy to drift away once the initial excitement faded. Completion rates vary by course and definition, and they are often low for open-enrolment MOOCs; the pattern is consistent enough to be widely discussed in research and institutional reports. The point is not to scold anyone for dropping out. The point is to notice what happens when learning is treated as a mood. The implication is that access is not the same as progress. The bottleneck moves from availability to adherence.

Now bring the framework down to an individual scale. Imagine a full-time employee—call her Aisha—working in Manchester in 2024, aiming to gain a professional qualification while balancing deadlines and family obligations. She does not lack intelligence. She lacks predictable study contact. She begins with a noble plan: evenings of two hours, four times a week. The first week looks fine. The second week becomes patchy. By the third week, a missed session carries shame, and shame makes restarting harder. The system is brittle.

Aisha's turning point is not a surge of willpower. It is a redesign. She reduces the minimum viable habit to a daily micro-session that can occur even on a hard day: ten minutes of retrieval practice after lunch, with materials pre-loaded. She runs a friction audit and removes small obstacles: a single notebook, one folder, one set of flashcards, and a clear "next action" written at the end of each session. She sets a streak shield: if she is travelling or exhausted, the rule becomes "review five cards and write one sentence from memory". She tracks simple feedback metrics: number of retrieval sets completed per week, and a weekly self-test score on a fixed set of questions. The system begins to teach her. When her score stalls, she does not panic; she adjusts. When she misses a day, she uses the shield and maintains contact. Over time, her confidence stops being a pep talk and becomes evidence.

The value of this approach is not confined to formal exams. Self-directed learning—languages, statistics, history, coding—suffers from the same failure mode: enthusiasm spikes, and then life resumes. People tell themselves they are "too busy" and then scroll through their phones with the hollow fatigue of a day that contained no deliberate practice. The framework does not moralise this. It treats attention as a scarce resource that must be scheduled and protected. A cadence calendar for study—deciding which days contain longer sessions, which contain reviews, and which contain rest—turns "learning" into a rhythm rather than a vague aspiration.

Rest matters here, and not as a sentimental reward. Cognitive fatigue is real. Long sessions without recovery can reduce attention, increase errors, and build aversion. A sustainable study system includes lighter days: review instead of new material, short recall instead of heavy problem sets. The concept is load management. The explanation is practical. If the mind associates study with depletion, it will avoid it. The implication is that rest becomes part of consistency rather than the collapse after inconsistency.

A credible counter-example deserves space. There are moments where cramming works—at least superficially. If the aim is short-term performance on a narrow assessment, massed practice can boost immediate recall. People do pass exams this way. The limitation is the decay. The material often disappears quickly, and the learner is left with a brittle competence that does not transfer. The reconciliation is not moral, but strategic. If the aim is long-term capability—being able to use the knowledge months later, explain it, build on it—then spacing and retrieval are not optional extras. They are the method.

Study also confronts a special psychological friction: the ego. In many professional environments, adults are praised for competence and speed. Learning reintroduces clumsiness. Early sessions are full of errors. Retrieval practice exposes gaps. A person can feel stupid while doing exactly the right thing. The framework protects against this by shifting the locus of judgement from self-image to process. The metric is not "Did I feel clever?" The metric is "Did I do the reps?" Progress becomes something measured and compared rather than something felt. That is not cold. It is stabilising.

A quiet motif helps unify the work: the tide. Memory is tidal. It comes in and goes out. A person who studies once and expects the sea to remain at high tide forever is setting themselves up for disappointment. A person who returns to shore at regular intervals learns what the tide does, and learns to work with it. Spaced repetition is, in effect, timing one's visits to the shoreline so that the waterline moves less dramatically. The work looks repetitive because the mind is repetitive. The tide does not apologise. It simply moves.

The forward test at the end is not whether learning is important. That is obvious. The test is whether a person is willing to trade a small daily inconvenience for a long-term change in what their mind can hold. When the next burst of enthusiasm arrives—as it will—does it become a fragile promise about a future version of oneself, or does it become a calendar rhythm with a minimum viable floor, a shield for disruption, and a feedback loop that teaches? The answer shows up in an ordinary place: the next ten minutes.

Chapter 12
Living the Reps Over Brains Way

On 2 July 1776, in Philadelphia, the room was hot and the stakes were not theoretical. John Adams wrote to his wife that the heat was "very hot", the debates exhausting, and the work relentless; history later made the moment ceremonial, but the day itself was closer to committee fatigue than myth. Paper moved from hand to hand. Words were revised. Arguments were tested. The republic, if it was to exist at all, would be built in increments that looked painfully ordinary at the time. A notebook can change everything.

That is the quiet scandal of discipline: it is not a thunderclap. It is an accumulation. People want transformation to announce itself with a mood, a crisis, a vow, a clean calendar and a better personality. Reality is meaner and kinder than that. Reality offers repetition. Reality offers a small set of rules written down, revisited, amended, and used on the days when the mind feels uncooperative. The aim is not to become a different species of human. The aim is to become the sort who can be trusted by their own future.

Somewhere along the way, "discipline" acquired the flavour of punishment, as though reliability were a penitential practice and rest a moral failing. That misunderstanding has consequences. It turns ordinary lapses into identity crises. It makes planning feel like a prison rather than a kindness. It keeps people forever searching for the one perfect routine that will finally fit, as if life were a static puzzle with a single correct solution. The truth is more practical: discipline works when it is treated as design, and design works when it is documented. What is not written down gets reinvented under stress, and reinvention under stress usually looks like self-blame.

The move from theory to lived practice begins with a personal playbook—something compact enough to consult, sturdy enough to survive a bad week, and specific enough to settle arguments with oneself. The show is in the moment someone sits down on a Sunday evening with a pen, a calendar, and a mild sense of dread, trying to remember what they promised themselves last month. The concept is external memory. The explanation is blunt: the mind is a poor filing system when it is tired, distracted, or emotionally activated. A written playbook relocates decision-making from the heat of the moment to a calmer hour. The implication is not romance; it is reduced friction. When the next day arrives with its emails, delays, and sudden demands, the person is not negotiating from scratch. They are consulting a document they prepared when they were thinking clearly.

A useful playbook does not read like a manifesto. It reads like a field note. It contains the few habits that matter, the smallest version that counts, the triggers that start them, the shields that protect them, and the reset plan that prevents a slip becoming a season. It also contains what not to do: the tempting behaviours that reliably derail the week, the stacks that looked elegant on paper but collapsed in practice, the times of day when willpower pretends to exist and then vanishes. The show is the difference between a person who says, "I'll try to be better", and a person who can say, "When I travel, I use the travel version; when I miss a day, I run the reset; when I feel bored, I switch to the planned variation." The concept is pre-commitment. The explanation is that the playbook decides in advance what the future self will do when the future self is less noble. The implication is a gentler kind of strength: fewer dramatic promises, more consistent follow-through.

The modern relevance is not hard to find, because modern life is a factory for fragmentation. Work arrives in pings. News arrives in shocks. Social life arrives through screens in a constant drizzle of other people's urgency. Even leisure has become oddly performative, as if rest must justify itself. In such an atmosphere, it is easy to confuse movement with progress and busyness with meaning. A playbook pushes back by narrowing the number of decisions that require daily debate. It says: the point is not to do everything; the point is to do the right things reliably, even when the surrounding world is loud. This is not a denial of complexity. It is a refusal to be ruled by it.

And yet systems do not stay useful simply because they are written down. A playbook that cannot evolve becomes a relic: impressive, sincere, and quietly irrelevant. The show is the person who built a beautiful morning routine in one season of life and then clings to it through a new job, a new commute, a newborn, or a caring responsibility, insisting the routine must be "maintained" as proof of virtue. The concept is seasonal fit. The explanation is that routines are not character traits; they are tools, and tools are judged by whether they still work. The implication is permission to iterate without drama. A change in life does not require abandoning discipline. It requires redesigning it—shrinking where the load has increased, shifting anchors to more stable moments, updating shields to match new constraints, and removing a habit that no longer earns its place.

This is where many people become oddly superstitious. They treat their past consistency as a fragile artefact, as though altering a routine will break the spell. They cling to a specific behaviour instead of clinging to the deeper commitment that behaviour represented. A runner who becomes a parent may not have the same training windows. A researcher taking on management may not have the same uninterrupted hours. A student entering full-time work may lose the open afternoons that made study easy. The discipline response is not nostalgia. It is adaptation. A resilient system expects change and has a method for absorbing it, the way a well-made bridge expects wind and traffic rather than hoping for calm days forever.

Sharing these ideas with others adds another layer of temptation: preaching. Nobody enjoys being recruited into someone else's self-improvement project, and discipline talk can become a kind of social harassment dressed as care. The humane approach is different. The show is a manager who is tired of watching a team stumble through the same meeting chaos every week—late starts, vague actions, forgotten decisions—and quietly redesigns the routine. The concept is structural leadership. The explanation is that people copy what is made easy, not what is merely demanded. The manager does not lecture about productivity. The manager introduces a short, consistent check-in rhythm, a visible list of commitments, and a brief review of what happened last week, then sticks to it. The implication is that discipline can be taught without sermons. It can be taught by modelling clarity, asking good questions, and offering tools only when they are wanted.

This matters beyond work. Families develop patterns. Friendships develop rhythms. Study groups either become dependable or dissolve into polite chaos. The discipline-minded person learns to offer structure as an invitation, not a judgement. They learn to ask, "What would make this easier to keep doing?" rather than, "Why can't you just be consistent?" They learn to separate accountability from shame, and to treat feedback as information rather than a verdict. When discipline becomes contagious, it is usually because it looks calm and useful, not because it sounds impressive.

At some point, though, the question becomes sharper. What counts as success here? Without a definition, people default to what is loud: visible outcomes, short-term numbers, applause, the feeling of being "on track". Those are not meaningless, but they are unreliable as a compass. The show is the person who hits a target and still feels unsettled, because the path there was frantic and the win did not change their relationship with their own promises. The concept is success markers. The explanation is that a system needs feedback that is not purely external. If success is defined only as results, then disruption becomes catastrophic and progress becomes brittle. The implication is a more durable set of markers: reliability under stress, fast recovery after slips, the ability to keep going when work becomes dull, and the quiet confidence that comes from being the sort of person who shows up.

These markers are not mystical. They are observable. A person can measure whether they return to the habit after travel. They can notice whether a missed day becomes a missed week. They can test whether the minimum viable version is truly doable on their worst ordinary day, not their best heroic day. They can see whether their calendar supports their values or merely reflects their interruptions. They can record whether they are refining the system or repeatedly restarting it. These are not glamorous metrics. That is the point.

The deeper tension is this: discipline can be used to build a life, or it can be used to avoid one. People sometimes hide inside routines as a way of dodging harder questions—about purpose, relationships, courage, or what they actually want. A personal playbook should not become a substitute for reflection. It should become a support for it. The aim is not to be endlessly efficient. The aim is to be dependable enough that the meaningful work has a place to land.

The motif returns here, because the notebook is not merely paper. It is a contract with the future self, written in a language the future self can obey. It holds the decisions that otherwise evaporate. It also holds the revisions that prove a person is learning. A playbook with crossed-out lines is healthier than a pristine one, because it shows contact with reality. Perfection does not survive the month. Learning does.

The chapter's promise, if it has one, is not inspiration. It is a way of living that trades a little romance for a great deal of stability. The daily reps remain ordinary. The difference is that they are no longer accidental. They are chosen, recorded, protected, and adjusted with the calm seriousness of someone who understands that progress is usually quiet. The forward test is not whether discipline can work; it can. The test is whether a person will keep a record that is honest enough to guide them when life changes, kind enough to help them restart without shame, and strict enough to prevent the easy days from writing cheques the hard days cannot cash.

Building a Personal Playbook

In August 2018, at Microsoft's Build developer conference in Seattle, the company announced that GitHub—acquired earlier that year—had reached 100 million repositories. The figure was a neat headline, but the more revealing fact sat behind it: repositories are not ideas. They are artefacts. They are work made visible, structured, and revisitable. An engineer who returns to a codebase after six months does not rely on mood or memory; they rely on what was written, versioned, and tested. The same logic applies to discipline, even when the work is private and unglamorous. The proof is always in the artefact.

Memory is a glamorous liar. It recounts good intentions as if they were actions, and it edits the past to protect self-image. It forgets the small frictions that sabotaged last week and remembers only the grand plan. It also performs a quiet trick under stress: it makes the next decision feel bigger than it is, because there is no map. A personal playbook is the opposite of that trick. It is a map. It is not motivational; it is logistical. Five lines decide the day.

A playbook is simply a written system that survives a tired mind. The first show is mundane: a person comes home late, sits at the kitchen table, and tries to reconstruct the commitments that were so clear on Sunday. The concept is externalisation. The explanation is mechanical: when plans remain in the head, they must be rebuilt every time life bumps them, and rebuilding is expensive. Writing reduces rebuild costs. The implication is reliability. The system does not become perfect; it becomes easier to resume.

There is a reason pilots use checklists. In 1935, at Wright Field in Ohio, the Boeing Model 299—later the B-17—crashed during a demonstration flight because the crew forgot to release a control lock. The aircraft was not "too complex to fly"; it was too complex to fly from memory alone, and the response was not a moral lecture about attentiveness but a new tool: the checklist. The point is not that daily habits are aviation. The point is that human brains, even skilled ones, make predictable errors when they rely on recall under pressure. A personal playbook is a checklist for civilian life: not because the stakes are identical, but because the cognitive machinery is.

A good playbook begins by choosing what deserves permanence. Many people treat "discipline" as a personality, a general promise to be better at everything. A playbook refuses that vagueness. It records a small number of core habits that justify the space they take, along with the *minimum viable* form that still counts. The show is the person who writes "exercise" and feels virtuous, then misses three days because "exercise" contained ten hidden steps and a silent demand to be heroic. The concept is definitional sharpness. The explanation is that an undefined habit is a moving target; it can always be postponed because its start line is unclear. The implication is that definition is not pedantry. It is friction removal.

This is where the playbook becomes more than a list. A list says what should happen. A playbook says what will happen when it does not. It documents streak rules and, crucially, streak shields: the travel version, the illness version, the time-crunch version. Without shields, a streak becomes brittle, and brittle systems breed guilt. With shields, a system bends without breaking. The show is the day of disruption: a delayed train, a sick child, an unexpected meeting, the evening collapsing into triage. The concept is continuity protection. The explanation is that identity is built less by intensity than by repeat appearance: "I am someone who shows up" survives when the system allows a smaller showing up. The implication is that a playbook protects identity from circumstance, not by denial, but by design.

The playbook also captures habit stacks: sequences that reduce the number of starts required. Starts are costly; mid-flight is cheap. A stack does not multiply effort; it reduces initiation overhead. The show is the difference between someone who must "decide to work out" and someone who simply does what comes after a stable anchor, like making tea or opening a laptop. The concept is sequencing. The explanation is straightforward: when the cue is reliable, the routine borrows reliability. The implication is that the playbook becomes a choreography, not a wish. It turns isolated effort into a repeatable chain.

At this point, the sceptical reader raises a fair objection: writing things down is not the same as doing them. Plenty of people own pristine notebooks and still drift. The limitation is real. A playbook can become a decorative object, a form of procrastination dressed as seriousness. And yet the answer is not to abandon documentation; it is to document the right level of detail and to treat the playbook as a working instrument. The show is not a beautifully designed template. The show is an ugly page with crossed-out lines, dates in the margins, and revisions that admit error. The concept is operational writing. The explanation is that an instrument is judged by use, not aesthetics. The implication is that the playbook must be built to be handled, not admired.

What, then, belongs inside a simple playbook template? It must be brief enough to consult and specific enough to settle disputes with oneself. A competent template records four things: the habits, the triggers, the protections, and the resets. It starts with core habits expressed as behaviours with an obvious first action and a countable minimum. “Write” becomes “open the document and add one sentence”. “Study” becomes “open the notes and review one card”. “Outreach” becomes “send one message to a prospect list”. The abstraction is replaced by a visible action. That replacement is not a motivational trick; it is an engineering move. The brain executes what it can see.

Triggers are next. A habit without a trigger is a habit that requires constant remembering, and constant remembering is a tax. The playbook records the cue in concrete terms: time of day, location, object, social context. The show is a person who “plans” to study and then finds the evening consumed by low-grade decisions. The concept is cue specificity. The explanation is that the environment is always cueing something; the question is whether it cues what is wanted. The implication is that the playbook should describe where the habit begins, not merely what the habit is.

Then come protections: friction audits and default pathways. The playbook records the obstacles that repeatedly appear between intention and action—missing equipment, a cluttered desk, an ambiguous next step—and the fixes that remove them. This is where “discipline” stops being moral and becomes practical. A crowded hallway to the habit is widened, lit, and signposted. The show is a writer who stops at the edge of dread because the “next step” is not visible. The concept is first-step clarity. The explanation is that vague work invites avoidance; concrete work invites motion. The implication is that a playbook should include the first visible action for each habit, written in language so plain it feels almost embarrassing.

Finally, the playbook needs reset plans. Everyone relapses; the difference is whether relapse becomes data or doom. The playbook records what happens the day after a miss: a minimum viable restart step, a short reflection, and a small win that re-establishes agency. The show is a person who misses three days and then cannot bear to look at the habit because it now carries shame. The concept is recovery design. The explanation is that shame narrows attention and reduces problem-solving; curiosity widens attention and improves it. The implication is that the playbook’s reset plan is not a punishment. It is a route back.

Two examples make this concrete without turning it into a sermon. In October 2019, the British National Health Service began piloting the NHS App more widely across England, giving many patients a new default for appointments, prescriptions, and records. It did not "motivate" people into managing health; it reduced friction by changing the default pathway. The playbook lesson is structural: when a system makes the desired action simpler than the undesired one, behaviour shifts without requiring heroic will. The second example sits in sport. In 2003, England won the Rugby World Cup in Sydney, and post-match analysis repeatedly returned to Jonny Wilkinson's relentless practice habits—the repetitions that made performance under pressure less dependent on mood. The playbook lesson is again structural: reliable performance is built in rehearsal and stored in routines. Neither example proves that discipline is easy; they show that good systems behave like good infrastructure.

A playbook also needs feedback, because systems without feedback become faith. The reader is not asked to worship metrics; they are asked to record a few that are hard to manipulate and easy to observe. Reps, minutes, outputs, and leading indicators belong here because they guide behaviour without pretending to control outcomes. A researcher can record hours of deep work rather than publication acceptance. A salesperson can record outreach attempts rather than closed deals. A student can record review sessions rather than grades. The abstraction of "progress" is attached to visible behaviour, and visible behaviour can be adjusted.

The motif returns because the playbook is not a metaphor; it is literally a document. A notebook, a folder, a single page pinned to a wall—any format that can be consulted quickly. The key is that it exists outside the head. When life gets noisy, the playbook becomes a quiet authority. It says: this is what matters; this is what counts; this is how to restart. It turns the internal argument into a reference check.

There is also a moral dimension, though it is not the pious kind. A playbook is a promise not to gaslight oneself. It prevents the weekly cycle of overpromising and underdelivering, then rewriting the story to preserve dignity. It replaces the drama of self-judgement with the steadier discipline of revision. The show is a person who can admit, without theatrics, that a habit design did not fit the current season. The concept is honest iteration. The explanation is that systems fail for reasons—timing, friction, scope, unclear triggers—and reasons can be addressed. The implication is that self-trust is rebuilt through accuracy, not affirmations.

The playbook should also state boundaries. Not every desirable behaviour belongs in it. Some ambitions are projects, not habits; some are too vague; some are better served by a short sprint than a lifelong streak. A playbook that tries to hold an entire life becomes unreadable, and unreadable systems are abandoned. The show is the person who designs a grand plan, then avoids it because opening it induces overwhelm. The concept is selective inclusion. The explanation is that a small system that is used beats a large system that is admired. The implication is restraint: fewer commitments, better kept.

The final test is uncomfortable in the right way. When the next disruption arrives—and it will, because life is a machine for interruptions—will the person rely on memory and mood, or will they consult the artefact they built? The trade-off is clear. A playbook demands a little upfront precision and the humility to write down what is true rather than what sounds impressive. The reward is not a surge of motivation. The reward is a quieter kind of freedom: the ability to keep moving when feelings become unhelpful. The diagnostic question is simple enough to fit on the first page of the notebook and sharp enough to matter: when the week collapses, what will still count?

Evolving Systems Over Time

In April 1993, IBM appointed Louis V. Gerstner Jr. as chief executive and installed him at Armonk, New York, at a moment when the company's old operating assumptions were failing in public. Mainframes still existed, talent still existed, effort still existed, yet the system that had once turned effort into outcomes had started to leak. Meetings multiplied. Product lines sprawled. Promises drifted. A person could work very hard inside a decaying structure and still feel as if they were pushing a piano through sand. The interesting detail is not the corporate drama; it is the mechanical lesson. Organisations do not collapse from laziness alone. They collapse from systems that no longer fit their conditions.

That mismatch is not reserved for boardrooms. It happens in kitchens and on trains. It happens in the weeks after a new role begins, or when a household gains a child, or when the body stops tolerating the same sleep pattern without protest. A habit design that once felt like a sturdy bridge can become a narrow plank: still technically crossable, but now requiring constant balancing, constant self-talk, constant strain. That strain is information. It is not a verdict.

Change arrives; systems must follow.

The first misunderstanding to retire is the idea that a good system is one that never changes. The show is familiar: someone finds a routine that works, repeats it for months, and then feels betrayed when it suddenly stops working. The concept is drift. The explanation is plain biology and plain economics: energy, time, responsibilities, and social context do not remain constant, and routines are built from those ingredients. When the ingredients change, the recipe behaves differently. The implication is relief mixed with responsibility. A stalled habit is often not a character flaw; it is an outdated design.

Consider how the most admired systems in industry evolved precisely because their creators treated them as living artefacts. In 1950, at Toyota Motor Company in Toyota City, Japan, Taiichi Ohno began shaping what became the Toyota Production System under conditions that forced ingenuity: limited capital, intense competition, and an urgent need to reduce waste. The early system was not a polished doctrine delivered from a mountaintop. It was an accumulation of experiments, adjustments, and learning loops—written down, tested on the floor, revised, tested again. The show is not inspirational; it is concrete. A worker signals a defect. A line stops. A cause is examined. The concept is continuous improvement. The explanation is that a system survives by learning faster than its environment changes. The implication is that stability is not sameness. Stability is the ability to keep producing desired outcomes amid change.

Personal discipline works the same way, with one extra complication: the person and the environment are entangled. A new job does not merely steal hours; it alters attention. A new commute does not merely move a calendar block; it shifts fatigue to a different part of the day. A new relationship does not merely add joy; it adds social rhythms and obligations. When a habit design fails after such shifts, the failure often looks like a motivation problem because the person experiences it as emotion. Underneath, it is usually logistics. The difference matters. Emotions are weather. Logistics are architecture.

A system becomes outdated in recognisable ways, even when the mind prefers moral interpretations. One sign is repeated renegotiation. The habit becomes a daily courtroom drama, with arguments for and against, and the verdict keeps changing. The show is a person standing in front of the wardrobe, weighing whether gym clothes are worth the trouble, as if each day were a referendum on fitness. The concept is decision tax. The explanation is that a good system reduces deliberation; an outdated one increases it. The implication is measurable: when a habit requires frequent debate, it is likely under-specified, under-protected, or anchored to a cue that no longer holds.

Another sign is "friction creep". What once took five minutes to start now takes fifteen, because the steps around it have quietly expanded. The desk that used to be clear is now a dumping ground. The software that used to open instantly now demands updates and logins. The equipment that used to live by the door now migrates, item by item, into cupboards. The show is a person losing the first ten minutes of a planned work session to scavenging. The concept is start-up cost. The explanation is that behaviour is shaped more by the cost of starting than by the cost of continuing. The implication is that discipline begins before the action: it begins at the threshold.

A third sign is resentment. Not dramatic hatred, just a low hum of "this is too much", even when the activity itself is still valued. Resentment is often the psyche's way of reporting that the system is extracting more than it returns. The show is the runner who still likes running but dreads the elaborate pre-run routine that has grown around it. The concept is misaligned intensity. The explanation is that intensity is not only physical; it is organisational. A system can be too heavy even when the task is light. The implication is again design-oriented. If resentment clusters around preparation, the preparation is part of the habit and must be redesigned, not ignored.

The deeper question is what replaces an outdated system without turning life into a perpetual refit. The replacement mechanism is not heroism. It is versioning: small, deliberate changes tracked over time, like edits in the margin of a working document. The motif matters because it keeps the process grounded. A personal playbook with margin notes is different from a grand plan rewritten from scratch each Monday. Margin notes acknowledge continuity. They also acknowledge reality: the same person is still here, but the conditions have shifted.

A practical way to think about replacement is to separate the value from the implementation. The value might be "maintain health", but the implementation may have been "forty-five minutes at the gym at 6 a.m." When the implementation breaks under new conditions—say, a baby's sleep pattern or a new shift schedule—there is a temptation to treat the value as broken too. The show is the person who abandons movement entirely because the old routine no longer fits. The concept is conflation. The explanation is that minds often bind identity to a single method: "If I cannot do it my way, I cannot do it." The implication is harsh: that binding creates unnecessary all-or-nothing collapse. Systems evolve when values stay steady and implementations adapt.

This is where minimum viable habits stop being a cute idea and become a serious tool. When conditions change, the minimum viable version of a behaviour functions as a continuity bridge. It preserves the identity of showing up while the larger structure is rebuilt. The show is the new parent whose previous reading practice was an hour of deep study and whose present reality offers fragments. The concept is continuity threshold. The explanation is that habits survive disruption when the threshold for "counting" is low enough to be met during chaos. The implication is that the minimum is not a forever size; it is a stabiliser during transition.

Two named examples help here because they show the same logic at scale. IBM in the early 1990s faced conditions that made its existing system unreliable: sprawling complexity and competitive pressure. The company could not simply "try harder" inside the same structure; the structure had to change to make effort meaningful again. Toyota in 1950 faced constraints that punished waste and rewarded learning; the system evolved because it had to. In both cases, the real achievement was not a heroic burst of willpower. It was a shift in operational design: decisions moved closer to evidence, feedback loops tightened, and the organisation treated its processes as revisable.

Personal systems can fail for a different reason: not that the world changed, but that the person changed their understanding of themselves. A system built during a season of ambition can become unfit during a season of recovery. A system designed for solitary work can become unfit when collaboration becomes central. The show is the researcher whose old discipline relied on long, silent blocks and who now manages a team with constant interruptions. The concept is role transition. The explanation is that roles reallocate attention and autonomy; a system that ignores those constraints becomes brittle. The implication is that a person's playbook must match their actual authority over time and space, not the authority they wish they had.

Still, evolution has a shadow side. Constant tinkering can become a sophisticated form of avoidance, a way to stay busy with planning while postponing the discomfort of repetition. This is the credible counter-example that deserves respect. Some systems do not need refinement; they need endurance. The show is the person who changes their routine every week because novelty feels like progress. The concept is churn. The explanation is that churn produces motion without accumulation; it keeps the mind entertained while leaving the underlying skill undeveloped. The implication is a caution: evolution must be triggered by evidence—missed reps, rising friction, persistent renegotiation—not by boredom alone.

There is also a second limitation, and it is worth stating plainly because intelligent readers notice it. In safety-critical domains—aviation, medicine, nuclear power—systems are evolved slowly and tested rigorously because the cost of failure is high. That reality does not make personal habit design dangerous, but it does highlight a useful principle: where the consequences are high, changes should be deliberate and traceable. The personal analogue is simple. If a habit supports something fragile—mental health, recovery from illness, a family relationship—reckless experimentation can be destabilising. The playbook should record changes, not merely imagine them, and the changes should be sized to the stakes. A pencil mark, not an explosion.

How does iteration happen without becoming chaos? The answer lies in feedback metrics and review rhythm, because systems evolve best when they are observed. The show is a person who "feels" that their routine is failing but cannot say why. The concept is measurement as diagnosis. The explanation is that feelings are useful signals but poor logs; they compress weeks into a single mood. A simple record of reps completed, minutes spent, or sessions started turns vague frustration into a pattern. The implication is that redesign becomes targeted: one bottleneck at a time, one change at a time, recorded like a small amendment in the margin.

A common evolution is anchor substitution. When one stable cue disappears, another can take its place. A habit once anchored to "arrive at the office" may need to move to "finish breakfast" when work becomes remote. A habit once anchored to "return from the commute" may need to move to "close the laptop" when the commute vanishes. The show is the remote worker whose days blur because the old boundaries were physical and the new boundaries are not. The concept is cue migration. The explanation is that cues are not mystical; they are regularities. When a regularity changes, the cue must be relocated. The implication is practical: many habit failures after life transitions are cue failures in disguise.

Another evolution is scope reduction followed by controlled expansion. During stable seasons, a system can afford more volume; during unstable seasons, volume can be the first thing that breaks. The show is the person who tries to keep an old cadence calendar intact while starting a demanding role, then watches it collapse and interprets that collapse as weakness. The concept is load matching. The explanation is that time and attention are finite, and a system that assumes infinite capacity will fail regardless of character. The implication is that a system can be made honest by shrinking the most fragile commitments first and keeping the rest intact, preserving continuity rather than staging a dramatic restart.

A third evolution is context consolidation. When life becomes crowded, switching contexts becomes expensive. A system that was once fine-grained—many small habits scattered across the day—may need to become chunked, with fewer transitions and clearer boundaries. The show is the busy professional who used to do a brief study session at lunch, a workout mid-afternoon, and creative work at night, and who now finds the day fractured by meetings and responsibilities. The concept is transition cost. The explanation is that each switch demands set-up, orientation, and a fresh start; too many starts drain the day. The implication is that a revised system often looks less ambitious on paper but performs better in reality because it respects the cost of changing gears.

The motif returns again because this is where the playbook earns its keep. A system that evolves only in the head evolves through forgetfulness and self-justification. A system that evolves on paper evolves through recorded decisions. The margins show what changed and when, and that traceability builds trust: the person can see that they did not simply "give up"; they adjusted with intent. The record also prevents a subtle form of self-deception: returning to a failed design and pretending it is new, repeating the same mismatch because the lessons were never captured.

The emotional payoff of evolving systems is not perpetual comfort. It is dignity under change. Life will alter the terms without asking permission. The question is whether the person clings to outdated structures out of pride—because abandoning an old routine feels like admitting defeat—or whether they treat the routine as a tool, and tools are allowed to be replaced. The forward tension sits here. A system can be faithful to a value or faithful to a method, but rarely both forever. When the next season arrives, which loyalty wins: loyalty to the identity of showing up, or loyalty to the exact shape of yesterday's plan?

Teaching Discipline to Others

In 1981, at the US Army's National Training Center at Fort Irwin, California, commanders began formalising a ritual that looked almost too plain to matter: a structured debrief after training, later widely known as the After Action Review. Soldiers and officers gathered, compared what was meant to happen with what actually happened, and named the gap without theatrics. The outcome was not a motivational high. It was improvement you could see in the next iteration: clearer roles, cleaner handovers, fewer repeated errors. The striking part is how little charisma the method requires. The system does the heavy lifting.

Make the next step visible.

Most attempts to "teach discipline" fail for a predictable reason: they treat discipline as a personality trait that can be delivered through a lecture. People do not resist discipline because they dislike effort in the abstract. They resist being managed like a project, shamed like a delinquent, or recruited into somebody else's fantasy version of their life. When teaching becomes a disguised power move, it provokes a disguised defence: polite nods, delayed compliance, quiet sabotage. The results are familiar. The mentor feels ignored. The learner feels judged. Nothing sticks.

The alternative is to treat discipline as a design problem that can be shared, not a virtue that must be imposed. The show is a manager who stops giving pep talks and starts adjusting routines, cues, and feedback. The name for this shift is *behavioural modelling* coupled with *structural support*. The explanation is that people learn behaviours most reliably when they can observe them, practise them in small slices, and receive non-punitive feedback. The implication is both ethical and practical: the best way to help others is to reduce friction and increase clarity, not to increase pressure.

Modelling is the first lever, and it is more potent than most people want to admit because it removes the comforting belief that we can teach what we do not live. In 1961, psychologist Albert Bandura ran the Bobo doll experiment at Stanford University in Palo Alto,

California, showing that children who watched an adult model aggressive behaviour were more likely to reproduce it (Bandura, Ross & Ross, 1961). Strip the lab away and the lesson becomes uncomfortably personal: humans copy what they see rewarded, repeated, and made normal. When a leader consistently shows up for the dull parts—preparing, reviewing, resetting after slips—others absorb that pattern as a default. The concept is social learning. The explanation is that observation reduces uncertainty about what "counts" and what happens after mistakes. The implication is simple: your behaviour is the handrail people reach for when the stairs feel steep.

This is why preaching is such a weak instrument. Preaching asks the listener to do emotional work first: to accept the speaker's framing, to trust their motives, to tolerate the implied hierarchy. Design asks less. Design makes the behaviour easier to perform than to avoid. That is why the After Action Review matters as an opening case. It is a teaching mechanism that does not need charisma. It teaches through a repeatable loop: do the work, review the work, adjust the work. The teacher is the structure.

The next lever is the question—not the clever question that signals intelligence, but the question that creates autonomy. Autonomy is not indulgence; it is a functional requirement for sustained behaviour. Self-determination theory, developed by Edward Deci and Richard Ryan, argues that motivation strengthens when autonomy, competence, and relatedness are supported rather than undermined (Deci & Ryan, 1985; Ryan & Deci, 2000). In plain terms: people persist when they feel the choice is theirs, the task is doable, and they are not being humiliated. When you offer discipline tools as options rather than commands, you preserve autonomy. When you shrink the task to a minimum viable version, you build competence. When you review without contempt, you preserve relatedness. The implication is that the "soft" approach is not soft at all. It is mechanically aligned with how motivation holds together under stress.

This is where gentle questions outperform persuasive speeches. A well-placed question makes the person author the plan. It also forces the plan into the open, where it can be improved. The show is a colleague saying, "I'm going to write every morning," and a friend responding, "Where will you sit, and what will the first two minutes look like?" The name is concreteness. The explanation is that vague intentions cannot be executed; they can only be hoped for. The implication is a discipline-friendly form of respect: you assume the person is serious enough to benefit from specifics, rather than dramatic encouragement.

There is a mature art to offering tools "on request" without waiting passively for a request that will never come. The trick is to make the tool visible in your own life first. Use it in conversation without turning it into a sermon. "I noticed I kept skipping, so I changed the trigger." "I missed three days, so I ran my reset." "I'm trialling a smaller version this week." This is not humblebragging. It is normalising the mechanics: mistakes are expected, and adjustments are allowed. When the other person eventually asks, they are not asking for your approval; they are asking for the method.

Yet modelling has limits. People can admire your routine and still be unable to copy it, because their constraints are different. This is the first credible limitation worth naming: imitation without fit becomes failure dressed as inspiration. The show is the junior colleague who tries to replicate a senior leader's 5 a.m. routine while managing childcare or shift work, then collapses and blames themselves. The concept is constraint blindness. The explanation is that advice often smuggles in hidden prerequisites: time, privacy, money, health, control of schedule. The implication is moral as well as practical: teaching discipline must start with the learner's constraints, not the teacher's preferences.

This is where the manager example becomes concrete rather than sentimental. Imagine a team lead in Manchester in September 2024 inheriting a project that is technically competent yet chronically late. The team is not lazy; it is noisy. Tasks are half-started, priorities shift midweek, and "urgent" requests arrive like weather. The lead's first instinct might be to demand more focus. Instead, she runs a small friction audit on the team's workflow: where do tasks stall, where do decisions wait, what triggers rework, what gets missed in handover. She changes one thing first: a fifteen-minute weekly review in which the team lists completed outputs, identifies one bottleneck, and agrees on one adjustment for the next week. No grand transformation. Just a loop.

The show, in week one, is awkwardness: people want to defend themselves. The name for what she is building is psychological safety—the shared belief that it is acceptable to speak up, name errors, and learn without punishment. Amy Edmondson's work on psychological safety in teams emphasises that learning behaviour depends on the interpersonal climate (Edmondson, 1999). The explanation is that when shame is present, information goes missing; people hide problems until they become crises. The implication is measurable: the team with safety surfaces issues earlier, when they are cheap to fix. Discipline in groups is not primarily about willpower. It is about the quality of truth-telling.

In month two, the manager adds a feedback metric that is hard to game. Not "be more productive," but "ship two reviewable increments each week," with increments defined in advance. The behaviour becomes visible: either the increments exist or they do not. She pairs the metric with a streak shield: during weeks with heavy client demands, the minimum becomes one increment, not zero. The team learns that consistency is valued over heroics. The handrail is sturdy. People stop waiting for the perfect week to do the work that matters.

Notice what she does not do. She does not demand that people care more. She does not insult their professionalism. She does not frame failure as a moral lapse. She redesigns the path so that the desired behaviour is the easiest behaviour to perform. Teaching discipline, in this sense, is simply good management: create clarity, reduce friction, build feedback, protect continuity.

Social accountability can amplify this, but it must be handled with care because social pressure is a volatile fuel. Used well, it supports follow-through; used badly, it produces avoidance and resentment. The show is the workplace "challenge" that turns into public shaming when someone misses a day. The name is coercion masquerading as motivation. The explanation is that public exposure raises the cost of failure, and when the cost is too high, people protect themselves by quitting or lying. The implication is that teaching discipline to others requires a bias towards humane accountability: private check-ins, permission-based sharing, and metrics that describe behaviour rather than worth.

Research on incentives offers a caution here. Deci, Koestner and Ryan's meta-analytic work discussed how certain forms of extrinsic reward can undermine intrinsic motivation, particularly when rewards are experienced as controlling (Deci, Koestner & Ryan, 1999). The show is the manager who offers prizes for "perfect streaks," then watches people stop engaging once the prize disappears—or worse, watches them chase the prize and lose interest in the underlying craft. The implication is not that rewards are evil. It is that control is expensive. If teaching discipline depends on controlling others, it will fail the moment your control weakens.

A better approach is to turn accountability into a shared design practice. Instead of "Did you do it, yes or no?", the check-in becomes "What made it easy, what made it hard, what will we adjust?" The show is a colleague who missed a session and is met with curiosity rather than contempt. The name is diagnostic accountability. The explanation is that diagnosis invites truth; judgement invites concealment. The implication is that your teaching creates not merely compliance but learning capacity.

There is also a quieter, more personal reason to teach discipline to others: it sharpens your own understanding. When you explain a method, you discover whether you actually understand it. When you watch someone else use it, you see edges you missed. This is not mystical. It is cognition with feedback. Education researchers have long observed that teaching can improve the teacher's mastery because it forces retrieval, organisation, and error correction—mechanisms widely discussed in learning science (see, for example, Roediger & Karpicke, 2006, on retrieval practice). The implication is that sharing tools is not purely altruistic; it is a disciplined way to deepen your own craft, provided you do it without ego.

A practical ethic emerges from all of this: teach discipline as you would lend a tool. You do not throw a spanner at someone's head and call it help. You place it within reach, explain what it does, and let them decide whether to pick it up. When they do pick it up, you stay near enough to answer questions, but not so near that your presence becomes surveillance. The handrail is offered, not enforced.

So the forward test is not "How can I motivate them?" That question tempts you into manipulation. A better diagnostic question is sharper and slightly uncomfortable: when this person is tired, stressed, or embarrassed, does my influence make the behaviour easier to do, or harder to admit?

Defining Your Success Markers

In 2009, at University College London, a health psychologist named Phillippa Lally began tracking something most people swear they do not have time to measure: the slow, unglamorous formation of everyday habits. Her team followed volunteers as they repeated small behaviours—drinking water, eating fruit, taking a short run—until those behaviours began to feel automatic. The work was later published in 2010, and it contained a detail that lands like a quiet rebuke to the modern attention span: habit formation is not a weekend project (Lally et al., 2010). The popular headline number—about sixty-six days on average—matters less than what it implies. If change takes that long to settle into the nervous system, then judging yourself on day six is not "high standards". It is a faulty measuring instrument.

Progress is not public applause.

That single sentence is worth keeping near your desk, not because it sounds noble, but because it tells the truth about how discipline is built. The world hands out trophies for spikes—viral moments, sudden promotions, heroic sprints—and then wonders why so many capable people burn out, drift, or quietly stop trusting themselves. If you let the world choose your success markers, you inherit the world's biases: loud outcomes, short windows, visible wins. Your discipline will become performative. Your motivation will become rented. Eventually, your effort will become fragile.

The final task, then, is not to add another habit, stack, calendar, shield, or accountability loop. It is to decide what *counts* as success in a way that supports the life you are actually living. This is not semantics. It is engineering. Without clear markers, your system cannot self-correct. With the wrong markers, it will correct itself in the wrong direction—towards vanity, exhaustion, or a brittle identity that collapses the first time you miss a day.

The first success marker worth reclaiming is identity, but not in the sugary sense of repeating affirmations into the mirror. Identity is what your behaviour makes believable. When you act, you create evidence, and evidence changes the story you can honestly tell about yourself. Psychologist Daryl Bem described this logic in self-perception theory: we infer who we are by observing what we do, especially when the internal signals are ambiguous (Bem, 1972). The show is a person who does one small rep even when they would rather not, then notices—almost with surprise—that they are the kind of person who shows up. The name is identity shift. The explanation is that repeated actions are a form of testimony; they persuade you more effectively than slogans do. The implication is sharp: a good success marker is not "I feel disciplined". It is "I behaved like a disciplined person."

This is where professionals often mis-measure. They set success markers that require a mood. "I'll feel confident." "I'll be inspired." "I'll want to do it." Moods are weather. Useful, real, unreliable. A better success marker names an observable behaviour that can happen in foul weather. You can measure whether you opened the document, walked to the meeting room, wrote the first line, sent the first message, reviewed the notes, laid out the equipment. You can count reps. You can track minutes. You can record outputs. You can compare weeks. The moment you anchor success to something visible, discipline becomes less emotional. It becomes more mechanical. That is not coldness. It is relief.

A second marker is reliability under stress, because stress is the true habitat of discipline. Anyone can be consistent during a calm week; that is merely comfort dressed as virtue. What you want to know is whether your system survives contact with reality: travel, deadlines, illness, family demands, sudden disappointment, a body that feels heavy, a brain that feels loud. Here, the show is not flawless performance. The show is continuity. The name is resilience. The explanation is that resilience is not the absence of disruption; it is the ability to resume quickly and cleanly after disruption. The implication is practical: one of your success markers should describe your *recovery time*—how rapidly you return to your minimum after a slip.

Notice how different this is from perfection. Perfection has no reset button. Perfection treats every break as a verdict. A resilience marker treats a break as data. "How many days did it take me to restart?" is a ruthless question in the best way. It is hard to game. It forces design improvements. It also protects your dignity. You can fail and still succeed, provided you recover faster next time.

A third marker is long-horizon progress, because discipline is built on compounding, and compounding is invisible at first. The early phase feels dull precisely because the outcomes are not yet loud enough to impress you. This is where many people sabotage themselves by using daily emotion as the scoreboard. The instrument panel must sit further away. It must show trend, not drama. If you measure your progress only by how you feel after each rep, you will overreact to noise. If you measure by a weekly or monthly pattern, you can see signal.

This is not theory. It shows up in elite practice. Consider British Cycling under performance director Dave Brailsford, appointed in 2003 in Manchester. The popular story is that Brailsford championed the "aggregation of marginal gains": small improvements across many controllable factors. Whatever you think of the slogan, the measurable outcome is difficult to dispute. At the London 2012 Olympics, Great Britain topped the cycling medal table, with a haul that signalled a programme operating on repeatable systems rather than occasional genius. The show is not a single heroic ride. The name is cumulative advantage. The explanation is that long-horizon markers—training quality, process adherence, review loops—create outcomes that short-horizon markers cannot reliably produce. The implication for a reader building discipline is clear: if your success markers only reward spectacular days, your system will prefer spectacle over continuity.

Yet metrics can rot. This is the counter-example that intelligent people, in particular, need to take seriously because they are skilled at gaming their own systems. When a measure becomes a target, it can stop being a good measure—an observation widely associated with economist Charles Goodhart, writing in the mid-1970s about policy targets (Goodhart, 1975). The show is a salesperson who hits "calls made" by dialling low-quality leads, or a student who hits "hours studied" by reading the same page with a wandering mind. The name is metric corruption. The explanation is that measurement changes behaviour, and if the metric is easy to manipulate, behaviour will drift towards manipulation. The implication is sobering: success markers must be chosen not only for what they track, but for what they *invite.*

This is why "hard to manipulate" matters more than "easy to track". Easy metrics often seduce because they look clean. Clean does not mean true. A good success marker sits close to the behaviour you care about and contains its own integrity check. If you track "pages written", you can also track "pages revised", because revision resists pure quantity. If you track "problems attempted", you can track "problems corrected", because correction reveals whether learning occurred. If you track "outreach sent", you can track "replies received" on a longer horizon, because replies expose whether the outreach was thoughtful. The reconciliation here is not to abandon metrics in fear of Goodhart's law, but to choose markers that pull you towards the kind of discipline you actually value: honest reps, not theatrical numbers.

A useful success marker also respects autonomy, because discipline that feels like captivity rarely lasts. Deci and Ryan's work on self-determination theory argues that motivation is strengthened when autonomy, competence, and relatedness are supported (Ryan & Deci, 2000). The show is the person who chooses a marker they can own—one that fits their season, their constraints, their values. The name is self-authorship. The explanation is that you protect your motivation by ensuring the system serves you rather than performing for an imaginary judge. The implication is direct: a success marker that makes you feel trapped will slowly teach you to hate your own goals.

This is where many bright professionals trip: they outsource their markers to competitive environments and then wonder why discipline turns sour. Academia rewards publication counts and citations; business rewards revenue and promotions; social media rewards visibility; sport rewards podiums. None of these are inherently evil. They are simply narrow. If your inner system uses only external markers, you will live in a permanent audition. Auditions create tension. Tension can power a sprint. It cannot power a life.

So define success markers that include, but are not limited to, outcomes. Outcomes matter. They are the reason you do the reps at all. But outcomes are often delayed, noisy, and partly outside your control. If you require outcome proof before you allow yourself to feel successful, you will be training discouragement. The discipline you are building depends on showing up before the applause arrives. That requires a marker that can reward you while the world is still indifferent.

This is where a quiet motif helps: build an instrument panel, not a mirror. A mirror tells you what you look like in one instant, under one light. An instrument panel tells you whether the system is functioning across time. A mirror breeds obsession. An instrument panel invites adjustment. When you choose success markers, you are choosing dials. Choose dials that help you steer.

One dial measures identity evidence: "How often did I behave like the person I claim to be?" Another measures recovery: "How quickly did I return after disruption?" Another measures trend: "Is my output, capability, or skill improving over months, not hours?" Another measures honesty: "Did I do real reps, or merely record them?" These are not slogans. They are design choices.

You can see the difference immediately in how the system feels. A mirror marker asks, "Am I impressive?" An instrument-marker asks, "Am I consistent?" A mirror-marker asks, "Did I win?" An instrument-marker asks, "Did I do the work that makes winning more likely later?" A mirror-marker asks, "What will people think?" An instrument-marker asks, "What did I practise, and what did I learn?" This is not spiritual. It is operational.

The deepest success marker, though, is not a number. It is a capability: the ability to keep promises to yourself in small units. This is the foundation of self-trust, and self-trust is the substrate of ambition. Without it, you will crave grand plans because grand plans feel like control, but you will avoid small reps because small reps require contact with reality. With self-trust, you can choose modest actions without feeling diminished, because you understand the arithmetic of compounding. You stop needing to be dramatic. You become dependable.

If that sounds too gentle, test it against a hard week. When work squeezes you, when sleep is thin, when your mind is sharp but your spirit is weary, what do you want your definition of success to do? Do you want it to accuse you? Or do you want it to guide you back to the smallest rep that keeps the system alive?

This is the closing tension you must sit with, because there is no neutral choice. If your success markers reward intensity, you will eventually break. If they reward continuity, you will sometimes feel ordinary. Ordinary is the point. Ordinary is where the reps live. The unresolved diagnostic question is therefore simple, and it belongs on your instrument panel: when life becomes inconvenient, do your success markers pull you towards a smaller, truer version of the work—or do they push you towards quitting because only the perfect version "counts"?

About the Author

Victor Serrano writes for people who are tired of waiting to feel ready and would rather get on with the work. Over years of trying, failing and trying again in his own projects, he became obsessed with a simple question: why do some ordinary people quietly outpace brighter, louder peers?

His experience spans sales targets hit one call at a time, creative work built draft by draft, and qualifications earned late at night after long days. Along the way he has sat at kitchen tables, in break rooms and on video calls listening to others describe the same battles with inconsistency, distraction and relapse.

Victor draws inspiration from long traditions of craft apprentices and labourers whose lives were defined less by flashes of genius and more by turning up every day. He believes that in an age of constant novelty, rediscovering that older, steadier rhythm is quietly revolutionary.

His work is guided by a practical conviction: you do not need to become a different person to change your life. You need a better way to design your days. Reps Over Brains is his most focused attempt to hand that design over to you, in plain, honest language.

www.ingramcontent.com/pod-product-compliance
Lightning Source LLC
Chambersburg PA
CBHW031336230926
51848CB00002B/267
9789376551804